PRESERVING
POST-WAR
HERITAGE

THE CARE AND
CONSERVATION
OF
MID-TWENTIETH
CENTURY
ARCHITECTURE

PRESERVING

POST-WAR

HERITAGE

THE CARE AND

CONSERVATION

OF

MID-TWENTIETH

CENTURY

ARCHITECTURE

Edited by
Susan Macdonald

DONHEAD

Editor: Susan Macdonald
Consultant Editor: Kit Wedd

First published in the United Kingdom 2001 by
Donhead Publishing
Lower Coombe
Donhead St Mary
Shaftesbury
Dorset SP7 9LY
Tel: 01747 828422

ISBN 1 873394 35 7

A CIP catalogue record is available for this book from the British Library

Production: Sara Clay
Printed in Great Britain by The Bath Press, Bath

CONTENTS

LIST OF FIGURES

ACKNOWLEDGEMENTS

The papers reproduced in this book have been edited for publication from those originally given at English Heritage's Preserving Post-war Heritage conference of 3–4 June 1998. By its very nature, this book is a collaborative effort and thanks are owed to a large number of people. Firstly, to the staff of the Royal Institute of British Architects conference centre, who were involved in organizing the event alongside Suzie Zumpe from English Heritage. Special thanks are also due to Peter Ross and Michael Bussell for assisting in the organisation of the visit to The Royal College of Physicians and for providing such an informative background to the conservation works. The Royal College was generous in allowing the delegates free access to the building during the visit.

The contributors have been as generous with their knowledge, time and patience in helping to prepare this book as they were in presenting their papers or chairing sessions at the conference. I am particularly grateful to the international speakers who travelled to London for the conference. I thank Allen Cunningham for stepping in to chair the final session and for leading the debate at such late notice. The staff of English Heritage also deserve special thanks for their drive and determination to ensure that the importance of the architecture of the recent past is recognized and the best examples protected. I am indebted to Kit Wedd, English Heritage's consultant editor, for preparing the book for publication and to Lori Aument, English Heritage's intern from the University of Pennsylvania, for co-ordinating its final delivery to the publisher.

As ever the enthusiasm of Christopher Dean infused much of the conference debate, and his dedication to the issues is much missed since he passed away shortly after the event in 1999. Sadly another key contributor, Dr Michael Stratton, also died after illness in the spring of the same year. Part of the delay in publishing the proceedings involved finishing his important part-completed text and bibliography. The book is therefore a lasting testament to these two gentlemen and their passion for post-war heritage.

Photographs are reproduced by agreement. The copyright holders are acknowledged in the captions.

Susan Macdonald
Principal Heritage Officer, Local Government Heritage Management,
New South Wales Heritage Office, Sydney, Australia
formerly Senior Architectural Conservator, Building Conservation & Research Team,
Department of Conservation Management, English Heritage, London, UK

AUTHOR BIOGRAPHIES

John Allan, Avanti Architects Ltd

John Allan's work at Avanti Architects, where he has been a director since 1983, has included community and medical projects, and the restoration of Modern Movement buildings such as the Penguin Pool, Highpoint, the Gorilla House and Finsbury Health Centre by Lubetkin, The White House by Amyas Connell, Willow Road by Goldfinger and The Homewood by Patrick Gwynne. Recent and current work includes the new Ambulatory Care and Diagnostic Centre for Central Middlesex Hospital and the restoration of Wynford House, Priory Green, by Lubetkin and Tecton. John Allan was the first chairman (1989–91) of DOCOMOMO UK, and is the author of *Berthold Lubetkin: Architecture and the Tradition of Progress* (RIBA Publications 1992) and 'The Conservation of Modern Buildings' in *Building Maintenance and Preservation* (Butterworth-Heinemann, 1994). He has contributed to *Ove Arup, 1895–1988* (ICE 1995), *Modern Matters* (English Heritage, 1996), *Park Hill – What Next?* (Architectural Association, 1996) and *Modern Movement Heritage* (DOCOMOMO/Routledge, 1998).

Andrew Beard, Sheffield City Council

Andrew Beard worked as a planner in the London Borough of Lambeth and in Stockholm, as a conservation officer for Sheffield City Council and as an architect for a housing association and in private practice before joining the Architects Division at Sheffield City Council in 1983. Here, he worked initially on housing and was responsible for developing regeneration proposals for a number of estates, including Hyde Park/Park Hill. He has been Chief Architect since 1990, heading a multi-disciplinary division that has won numerous awards, including a RIBA/DoE Housing Design Award for the refurbishment of Hyde Park, Sheffield. He is currently involved in the £120 million *Heart of the City* Millennium project and two Historic Parks restoration schemes funded through the Heritage Lottery Fund.

Michael Bussell

Michael Bussell worked as a structural engineer with Ove Arup & Partners for 30 years and is now an independent consultant. His experience includes both the design of numerous concrete structures and, more recently, the investigation and repair of concrete structures where distress or deterioration has occurred. He has a long-standing interest in the history of buildings, and in their appraisal for adaptive reuse. He is the author of *A Guide to the Appraisal of Existing Iron and Steel Structures*, published in 1997 by the Steel Construction Institute, and has contributed papers on the use and development of reinforced concrete construction in Britain, published as part of a Thomas Telford collection of essays on concrete history.

Bridget Cherry

Bridget Cherry is editor of *The Buildings of England, Ireland, Scotland and Wales*, the series of architectural guides founded by Sir Nikolaus Pevsner. She is a Commissioner for English Heritage, a member of its committees concerned with London and with Historic Buildings and Areas, and chair of the Post-war Listing Steering Group.

Kevin Davies

Kevin Davies has been involved with concrete durability, degradation and repair in a consulting engineering capacity for over 20 years. He specializes in electrochemical repair technology for reinforced concrete structures, including cathodic protection, re-alkalization, desalination and advanced *in situ* corrosion rate monitoring techniques.

Jimi Fadayomi, Sika Ltd

Jimi Fadayomi is a chemistry graduate from the University of Reading and has an MBA from Henley Management College. Since 1986 he has worked at Sika, where he is the market manager for buildings, specializing in technologies for the repair and protection of reinforced concrete. He is a member of the executive committee of the Concrete Repair Association.

Elain Harwood

Elain Harwood is responsible for English Heritage's post-war research and listing programme. She has written extensively on London and on twentieth-century issues, most recently *Tayler and Green, Architects 1938–1973* with Alan Powers, and an extended essay on 1960s liturgy for *The Twentieth Century Church*, published by the Twentieth Century Society. Her book on English post-war architecture for English Heritage and Yale University Press has just been published.

Stephen J. Kelley, Wiss, Janney, Elstner Associates Inc

Stephen J. Kelley is an architect and structural engineer at Wiss, Janney, Elstner Associates Inc, based in Chicago, USA. He has extensive experience in building preservation and in the treatment of windows and curtain walls. The significant landmark projects he has worked on include the Reliance Building, the Rookery, Tribune Tower, Auditorium Building, and Elks Lodge Memorial in Chicago, the Railway Exchange Building in St Louis, Blanchard Hall at Wheaton College in Wheaton, Illinois, the Kentucky and Nebraska State Capitols, and the MidContinent Tower in Tulsa, Oklahoma.

Stephen Kelley serves on the Board of Directors of the US National Committee of ICOMOS. He chairs the ASTM technology committee and participates in ASTM committees which set standards for curtain wall testing and evaluation. He has lectured and published extensively on the topics of curtain walls, windows, and preservation technology, and edited the recently published book, *Standards for Preservation and Rehabilitation* (ASTM STP 1258).

Paul Lambert, Mott MacDonald

Paul Lambert is an associate with Mott MacDonald and leads their materials and corrosion group, based in Altrincham. Following a degree in materials and a PhD in the corrosion and passivation of reinforced concrete, he has spent over fifteen years working in the field of material degradation, investigation and repair. He is a regular speaker on materials, corrosion and repair and has written more than 60 publications on these subjects. He is a Chartered Materials Engineer, a Fellow of the Institute of Corrosion and a past chairman of the Society for Cathodic Protection of Reinforced Concrete (now the Corrosion Prevention Association).

Susan Macdonald, English Heritage

Susan Macdonald recently returned to her native Australia, where she works for the NSW Heritage Office in Sydney. She studied architecture in Sydney and completed her MA in Conservation at ICCROM in Rome and at the Institute of Advanced Architectural Studies in York. She worked in a number of practices in London before joining the building conservation and research team at English Heritage. She is a past secretary of DOCOMOMO UK and a member of the DOCOMOMO International Specialist Committee on Technology.

Martin O'Rourke, English Heritage

After working for the Greater London Council's Historic Buildings Division, Martin O'Rourke became a conservation officer with Hertfordshire County Council and then worked in private practice for twelve years. He has been a Historic Buildings Inspector in the North-east London team at English Heritage for four years.

Jeff Parkes, Rain One

Jeff Parkes was a director of Buro Happold for many years before becoming an independent consultant. He is particularly interested in designing services to enable post-war buildings to meet modern environmental standards without undue intervention, thereby prolonging their useful life. He has worked on a wide range of building types and projects, and on the refurbishment of pre- and post-war and new buildings, including the former Playboy Club on Park Lane, the Portman Hotel, Sanderson House, 7 St Martin's Place, Highpoint and 45–50 Mayfair Place. He is also the creative director of Graphical Maintenance Interface Ltd (GMI), a company developing software and internet solutions for the production of building operating and maintenance documentation and the long-term maintenance of buildings. In addition, he develops multimedia solutions to explain the design of services, particularly for existing buildings.

Alan Powers, Twentieth Century Society/ Prince of Wales's Institute of Architecture

Alan Powers is an architectural historian. He is vice-chairman of the Twentieth Century Society and is both librarian and course tutor at the Prince of Wales's Institute of Architecture. He is a member of the English Heritage Post-war Listing Steering Group and a contributor to many magazines and journals on architecture and other aspects of visual culture. Together with Elain Harwood, he was curator of the exhibitions *Tayler & Green, Architects 1938–1973* and *The Spirit of Modern Housing* (1998).

Peter Ross, Ove Arup and Partners

Peter Ross is an Associate Director of Ove Arup and Partners, working within Arup Research and Development with special responsibility for work to existing and historic buildings. He has been responsible for many surveys and remedial work to a wide variety of structures, from the Synagogue of 1902 in Hong Kong to the frigate *Unicorn* in Dundee, but his best-known project is probably the new roof to the south transept of York Minster, following the fire in 1984.

Robert Silman, Robert Silman Associates

Robert Silman is a structural engineer with specialist expertise in historic buildings. Following graduation from Cornell and New York Universities, he worked for various structural engineers in the USA and for Ove Arup in London before founding Robert Silman Associates in 1966. He has worked on many important historic structures, including Carnegie Hall, the Museum of Immigration at Ellis Island, and Frank Lloyd Wright's Wingspan house and Fallingwater. His work has been recognized by a number of awards and he is a fellow of the American Society of Civil Engineers. He teaches and lectures on building technology and is presently adjunct professor of Architecture at Columbia University. He has also published a number of articles on a range of subjects from structural systems to sustainability.

Michael Stratton

Michael Stratton was Lecturer in Conservation Studies and Director of Heritage Management in the Archaeology Department of the University of York. He was a member of English Heritage's Industrial Archaeology Panel. He edited *Structure and Style: Conserving Twentieth-century Buildings* (1997), and his other books include *Industrial England* (Batsford 1997) and studies of architectural terracotta, the design of historic car factories and power stations, and the conservation of the railway heritage. Preparing notes for the bibliography of the present volume was one of the last tasks he undertook before his untimely death in 1999.

Anthony Walker, Damond Lock Grabowski and Partners

Anthony Walker studied architecture at the London Polytechnic, now Westminster University, and qualified with distinction in thesis in 1964. He developed a particular interest in the role of commercial development in urban regeneration and, after working in several practices, joined Damond Lock and Stanislaw Grabowski in 1972 to establish Damond Lock Grabowski & Partners, where he is now senior partner. He studied building conservation at the Architectural Association, where he became interested in the conservation of plastics. He served on the British Standards Institute Committee: Principles of Building Conservation and is a committee member of the Plastics Historical Society, where he has a particular role in extending the awareness of plastics conservation in building.

FOREWORD

This book presents papers given at the conference held by English Heritage on 3–4 June 1998, which explored issues relevant to the conservation of listed buildings of the second half of the twentieth century, developing themes tackled in the 'Modern Matters' conference of 1995.[1] 'Post-war listing' has now been in operation for over ten years and, as we move into the twenty-first century, it appears natural rather than eccentric to reflect on the architecture of the recent past, and to consider which buildings should be preserved and how they can be given a future. Recent government response to the proposals emerging from English Heritage's post-war research programme and the public consultations that followed have been encouraging. The result is that an intriguingly broad range of post-war building types expressing the character and achievements of the twentieth century are now represented in the official lists, from prefabs to new universities, from bus garages to Jodrell Bank, including long-established building types as well – churches, houses and schools. Some may offer examples of excellent craftsmanship, and some may challenge conventions by employing innovative materials, unconventional aesthetics or novel concepts of design. For those involved in the research, discovering the diverse character of the twentieth century through its built heritage has been a rewarding and inspiring journey of discovery, the excitement of which is well conveyed in Elain Harwood's essay.

At present, listed post-war buildings are still relatively rare (less than 1% of the total of nearly 350,000 buildings listed in England), although as the years pass more will become eligible. They are scattered thinly over the country, with only a handful in most cities, and with very few indeed in more rural areas. When confronted with an isolated example – perhaps the only one in the neighbourhood – the conservation officer, the owner or the passer-by may at first feel baffled as to how they should react. Ridicule was a not uncommon initial response, dismay another (particularly where listing was conferred on buildings on valuable urban sites). Such negative reactions are not surprising (and echo much of the public response when Victorian architecture began to be listed in the 1960s). To qualify for listing, buildings have to be over thirty years old (except for threatened buildings, which may be listed when ten years old if they are judged outstanding). So buildings of this age are no longer in the height of fashion, and even well-respected examples may lack topical allure. The virtues of others may have been obscured by changed patterns of use, poor maintenance, neglected surroundings or unsympathetic alterations. And the use of modern, sometimes experimental, materials and construction may mean that professionals involved in repair, alteration or adaptation face technical and philosophical problems that cannot always be solved by recourse to tried-and-tested approaches to older listed buildings.

These problems offer challenges. It is the obligation of those responsible for listing to explain clearly why the building is special; and to reconcile the presumption in favour of preservation, which listing demands, with the need to make changes to ensure that the building has a secure future. It is important to dispel the widely held misconception that listing does not allow any alterations at all. Repairs pose other questions. How should the conservationist's concern for authenticity of fabric be applied to modern buildings where new materials appear to have failed? Does listing's emphasis on material 'substance', as defined in Alan Powers' essay, lead to inadequate appreciation of the 'essence' of the design intention or of the handling of space, for example, which is often so crucial in defining the character of modern architecture?

The common theme that runs through all the contributions to this book is the vital need to understand both the historical and technical character of a building before decisions are reached about repair or alterations. Both historians and those concerned with the practicalities of repair will find much of interest in the fascinating story of the development and use of plastics, and in the essays on cladding, curtain walling and concrete, which also provide guidelines for recognizing the nature of the material and for diagnosing the problems. Part Three offers thought-provoking case studies of some particularly significant but problematic iconic examples, from Frank Lloyd Wright's Fallingwater to the monumental housing complex at Park Hill, Sheffield.

Conservation issues do not stand still. Martin O'Rourke's contribution on the housing of London's East End emphasizes how listed buildings can be a positive force in the regeneration of urban areas, a theme that has been receiving increasing attention since the conference. It is now widely recognized that sensitive treatment of individual buildings needs to be combined with holistic appraisal of the context of urban landscape, street or garden, even though current statutory protection does not make such a unified approach easy. Indeed, John Allan argues in the challenging final essay that there is a need to consider the post-war inheritance of 'ordinary' buildings as well as those that are special, an approach that ties in with growing concern with principles of sustainability. His conclusion, that conservationists must learn to work together with others who have different priorities, offers an agenda for the future.

Bridget Cherry

References

1   Macdonald, S. (ed) (1996), *Modern Matters: Principles and Practice in Conserving Recent Architecture*, Shaftesbury: Donhead.

PART ONE

THE HISTORICAL
CONTEXT
AND THE
FRAMEWORK
FOR
PROTECTION

CHAPTER 1
STYLE OR SUBSTANCE? WHAT ARE WE TRYING TO CONSERVE?

Alan Powers

I wish to take the opportunity in this paper to take a step or two back from the subject of conserving post-war buildings and see how it looks in a wider frame. My expertise, if I have any, is partly as a historian, but in the world of action, as someone involved over the course of seventeen years or so with politics and ideology of the conservation of twentieth-century architecture. I do not think this subject is given enough discussion. When we speak of the philosophy of conservation, we generally imagine that there is a building already present as the subject, and that the discussion concerns what should be done with it physically. I am stepping back to the point where the presence of this building as an object for conservation cannot be assumed, which is the case for all but a handful of post-1914 buildings in Britain, and quite right too.

The knowledge that these buildings are not listed, and not likely to be listed, does not, to my mind, enable us to wash our hands of them. It only exposes the limited alternative means that exist for engaging with such buildings, and the lack of realistic understanding and assessment of what is carried out in the almost invisible interstices of the built environment.

Since I wrote the abstract for this paper, I have been given a helpful starting point in the form of Martin Pawley's recent book, *Terminal Architecture*. Pawley is well known as a critic of the whole idea of conservation, and in this book he devotes the fifth chapter, 'Over the Top with Art History', to the contribution made by conservation to the dissolution of what he sees as a potentially valid pre-existing programme for architecture in the post-war years. I quote at length:

> *Looking back from the close of the twentieth century one can only wonder at the way in which art history has skilfully outflanked and eventually absorbed every philistine attack and every redistributive political measure. Every movement in modern art, from Dadaism to the International Style in modern architecture, no matter how aggressively directed against the art-historical establishment, has eventually succumbed to its 'treasure house' accounting system. The fate of modern architecture, perhaps the greatest and most sustained mutiny against the tyranny of the treasure house to have taken place since the coming of connoisseurship in*

the eighteenth century, serves as an example of what happens to those over-weening ambition leads them to dream of dragging the whole ramshackle structure of 'pricelessness' crashing down.

We have seen in Chapter 3 how the means by which the Modern Movement attempted to end the housing scarcity inherited from the nineteenth century came to be subverted. By the end of the 1980s, the last surviving Modernists, like a tribe of Native Americans surrounded by soldiers, sued for peace. Through the formation of a quisling organisation DOCOMOMO, they agreed to surrender their modern heritage and endorse its absorption into the art-historical classification system as a style, which it never was. In return, they received museum status for many modern buildings, converting their once-proud revolutionary instruments back into monuments for the delectation of the masses alongside the palaces of the ancien régime. Thus was the great artistic mutiny of Modernism finally brought to heel. As the great modern architect confessed near the end of his life, 'I abandoned architecture because it had lost its line. It was the harbinger of a better world and it ended up in miniskirts.'[1]

I think this passage summarizes much of the rest of the material. I would like to pick apart some of what I see as its fallacies, and set them alongside the conclusions we might draw from its truths.

The role of the historian (including the art historian) is to discover truth, not to manipulate information. I think that many historians are guilty in some ways of the sins that Pawley accuses them of, but this does not mean that they cannot do some good through the proper exercise of their task, or that Pawley can strengthen his arguments by making things up. Pawley assumes a complete unity of intention between modern art and modern architecture which is just historically wrong, even though many statements piously wished it. Much modern art was not destructive; it was highly idealistic – although not many artists excluded themselves voluntarily from the market system if it offered them a place. Cézanne said he wanted to make something solid like the art of the museums. In its self-definition against the background of nineteenth-century eclecticism, some lines within Modernism can just as well be seen as an alternative form of classicism, with, in the case of architecture, the help of machines and with a dedication to social improvement. Architecture is not the same as the non-contingent arts of painting and sculpture. modern architecture must go to extremes to become so very unlike traditional architecture as to be totally distinct, extremes that tend to become so self-serving in respect of trying to escape from convention as to negate all other aims.

Modernism's social mission seems to interest Pawley very little, although he does share in making the false syllogism that has been current in England since the early 1930s, namely that if modern architecture is self-declared social architecture, then what is not modern cannot be social architecture. It depends what evidence you want to look at. I remember once asking Sir James Richards whether the London City Council's brick flats with sash windows of the 1920s or the neo-Georgian health centres of the 1930s were not social architecture too. He could not agree that they were, but had absolutely no reasons to give. This was the effect that Modernist propaganda in the 1930s had, and I believe still has, on our received ideas. The point I would like to make here is that to acknowledge the social content of non-modern architecture does not diminish the strength or importance of the same quality in Modernism; rather it goes to confirm that this was the existing spirit of the time, which Modernism found a more articulate way of expressing.

I am thus unable to accept modern architecture as 'the greatest and most sustained mutiny against the tyranny of the treasure house to have taken place since the coming of connoisseurship in the eighteenth century', not because the idea shocks me, but because there never was any 'tyranny of the treasure house'. Industrial production of buildings from the mid-nineteenth century onwards put all architecture under the same constraints, whether they went with this flow or against it. Pawley's description of the way that Modernism became absorbed into conservation is equally removed from what happened, in this country or, I believe, in any other. Modern Movement buildings have actually tended to be the Trojan horses that have opened the gates to the conservation of other twentieth-century buildings, even in England. The period of reaction against Modernism in the 1980s will, I think, be seen in future not as a norm but as a temporary, if significant, inversion of the norm. I don't think DOCOMOMO was involved in any such transaction as he describes, although I do remember a shiver of *schadenfreude* when it became evident that many of those who had spoken against conservation in general found themselves having to argue that their own buildings were exceptions to the rule.

Is the purpose of conserving modern buildings to 'convert their once-proud revolutionary instruments back into monuments for the delectation of the masses alongside the palaces of the *ancien régime*'? I do not acknowledge the existence of this mutually exclusive duality. If these buildings are rightly described as revolutionary instruments, something I am quite willing to accept, then their function as such does not cease if they become absorbed in some process of conservation. Rather the reverse. If they were altered, mutilated or demolished, their potential for continuing revolutionary activity would certainly be lost. Look at the restoration and repair of the Finsbury Health Centre as a working building serving its original purpose. It was once proud, became rather messed up, and is now proud again, at least in parts. I believe that the visitors to 2 Willow Road stand to benefit from the experience of being inside a modern house, which is convincing in a way that no amount of reading or photographs could be. As Ernö Goldfinger designed the house as a sort of lesson in life values for his wife Ursula, so these values are transmitted today without any corruption, to those willing to be receptive to them. 'Goodness, love, art; they are in our heart and in us, and they will not be satisfied by little shows of propaganda', as Goldfinger wrote in an early letter to his future wife.

The problem with Martin Pawley's diagnosis of the 'heritage problem' is that it sets up two false paradigms in opposition to each other. One is his paradigm of Modernism, which is simplified to the point of falsity. The other is his paradigm of conservation, which is presented as an entirely self-serving process, without even the potential for any social context. I will return to this later. I will only observe in passing that Martin Pawley is not the only person promoting this two-dimensional caricature of conservation. Paul Finch writes in the *Architects' Journal*:

The heritage brigade, broadly speaking, want to save things at any cost (except to themselves). They represent, politically, that stream of authoritarian government which goes around telling people what is good for them.[2]

If this version ever had any truth, it was in the high noon of heritage in the late 1970s and early 1980s. The brigade has been disbanded and is no longer on active service. The discussion is now a little wider, due in many ways to the need to adjust to the issues of conserving post-war buildings. The example of Cedric Price's Interaction Centre shows that the heritage brigade does not have a common line, and does not believe in doing things at any cost. We simply could not operate in such a detached world. Things have changed since then, but the changes have not been observed, reported or incorporated into the architectural journalists' lexicon of clichés and truisms. I hope that they will change still further, for while I cannot accept the Finch or Pawley caricatures as true, I deplore the self-defensive lack of questioning in the conservation community concerning our wider aims and our potential for collateral damage. We have generally deserved nothing better than these assaults and I think we shall die, not from the dagger thrusts of our ranting enemies, but of entropy and boredom amongst ourselves, unless we find a better rationale for our activity.

The title of this paper is 'Style or Substance?' To separate *substance* from something implies the philosophical distinction of *essence* and *substance*, which for us stems from ancient Greek philosophy, although it is found in varying forms in all the world traditions. It was of considerable importance in the philosophy of the Middle Ages, when the empirical philosophy of Aristotle began to prevail over the idealist philosophy of Plato.

I quote from St Thomas Aquinas's *Summa Theologica*, and before you ask yourselves what this has to do with modern architecture, I will tell you that I have taken this extract from page 172 of Frank Schulze's biography of Mies van der Rohe. As Schulze says, 'For Mies ... Aquinas posited a spiritual realm – of which fact was an earthly manifestation – through which a higher truth might be reached and, by the artist, conveyed'.[3]

Now we do not judge of a thing by what is in it accidentally, but by what is in it essentially. Hence, everything is said to be true absolutely in so far as it is related to the intellect from which it depends; and thus it is that artificial things are said to be true as being related to our intellect. For a house is said to be true that expresses the likeness of the form in the architect's mind, and words are said to be true in so far as they are signs of truth in the intellect. In the same way natural things are said to be true in so far as they express the likeness of the species that are in the divine mind. For a stone is called true, because it expresses the nature proper to a stone, according to the preconception of the divine intellect. Thus, then, truth is principally in the intellect, and secondarily in things according as they are related to the intellect as their principle ...

Now since everything is true according as it has the form proper to its nature, the intellect, in so far as it is knowing must be true so far as it has the likeness of the thing known, which is in the form in so far as it is knowing. For this reason, truth is defined by the conformity of the intellect and thing, and hence to know this conformity is to know truth.[4]

This to me is a paradigm for modern architecture every bit as true as the one of technological and social evolutionism described by Martin Pawley. In fact, it must be more true, for he talks only of substance and leaves out entirely the question of essence, which we might paraphrase as the aesthetic content of design. Mies's devotion to Aquinas comes partly, I suspect, from a desire to redress the over-materialism of the foregoing period of architecture. It accounts for the apparently exaggerated attention that Mies gave to small, even invisible, details. When he said 'God is in the details', it was not just a figure of speech; he really meant it.

We may therefore conclude that one of the characteristics of modern architecture, across its whole field, is an unstable balance of *essence* and *substance*. Neither exists in isolation and, although they may be oppositional categories, their opposition can never be a case of 'either/or'. This is one of its great fascinations, and one of the ways in which it embodies the ideological conflicts of the century. Sometimes *essence* is over-dominant, which leads to leaking roofs and freezing cold rooms, as in the very Platonic white concrete architecture of the 1920s and 1930s. At other times, *substance* is over-dominant, which leads to buildings lacking in any inspiration. You could paraphrase *essence* and *substance* as *quality* and *quantity*, which in traditional systems have to be held in balance. The American writer on comparative religion, Whittall Perry explains:

> ... the subjective and qualitative pole will be very much in predominance at the beginning of a cosmic cycle, just as, by the law of inverse analogy, the objective and quantitative pole will – in appearance at least – have the ascendancy as the cycle approaches its end. The inference to be drawn from this is that a cycle will be characterized in its early stages by luminosity and transparency, making it propitious for the play of 'angelic' influences, and in its later stages by increasing opacity and tenebrousness, making it propitious for the action of disordered and eventually subversive forces.

He goes on to explain that:

> ... the cyclical succession must not be thought of as uniformly linear and uninterrupted; rather it is like a series of varying waves united only in the larger current that propels them onwards.[5]

Is this perhaps a rather elaborate way of thinking about post-war conservation? To many people, the way that many post-war buildings do not conform to conventional construction is a serious problem, virtually eliminating them from the domain of conservation. We are assembled here to learn about the potential technical solutions to such problems, but in devoting ourselves entirely in this way to the subjective or quantitative study of substance, we may lose sight of the quality, the *essence* and the *style*, which Aquinas tells us is logically prior to *substance*.

As I have proposed, there is a necessary balance of the two poles and it is patent to common sense that *essence* without *substance* cannot be experienced in a material realm. A follower of Aquinas would insist that *substance* alone cannot contain *essence*, although the Nominalists of the Middle Ages came to believe that there was nothing in the world apart from *substance*.

If we allow Mies to guide us, then, in treating of *substance*, we must not lose sight of *essence*. Architects when designing have to be guided by *essence*. Conservationists tend professionally to be nominalists, on the other hand, because they must operate politically in a field that depends on *quantity*. I do not believe that the word 'beautiful' would be allowed to appear in a list description, any more than the word 'useful' appears, but I would like to explore the parallel universe in which these two terms were present alongside existing values of 'important', 'historic' or 'well-documented'.

I refer to the political arena of conservation advisedly, because this brings us to one of the potential points of reconciliation with the ideals of Modernism, which so many people on different sides of the argument find make a bad fit with ideas of conservation. Political idealism is manifested in some of the *substance* of post-war buildings, but that is perhaps chiefly apparent only to the eye of the informed observer. This does not mean that it is not apparent in other ways to other people. There are many attributes of a building that are not strictly substantial. These include its internal spaces, the quality of light within them, the sequence of plan and circulation and its spatial realization, and – a most important attribute for many post-war buildings – the external spaces and landscaping. If these are protected by listing, it is only in a secondary manner. Listing is primarily about *substance*. *Essence* is found only in the interpretation and the subliminal discourses around conservation issues. You can list structure but not space, yet space is the *essence* of modern architecture.

If *essence* came first in our discussion of post-war conservation, what would be the consequences? We might mind less, in many cases, about the retention of original fabric, and indeed this non-SPAB approach has already become acknowledged. The questionable value of replicating obsolete technology for very small production runs at high cost, implied by the need to repair certain modern buildings, demands a greater flexibility of approach. In these cases, to be guided by *essence* would imply a willingness to consider complete alternative systems, and to judge their appropriateness not by strictly art historical terms, but more subjectively. We might mind just as much as we now do about the replacement of windows, because these seem, in philosophical as well as general terms, often to be essential to the character of the building. Yet these substantial aspects might recede in the face of a consideration of the wider values embodied in the building and its site. The Twentieth Century Society opposed the covering-over of the South Bank Arts Centre with a glass roof, not necessarily because it affected the *substance* of the buildings on the site, but because it so drastically changed their *essence*, which we could also describe as their meaning.

Bankside Power Station, being neither listed nor in a conservation area, was not within the ambit of legal conservation. It was interesting to discuss the scheme for the Tate Modern Gallery with architects from Herzog and de Meuron, who were not used to the English system of confrontation over historic buildings. An English architect in these circumstances would probably set up an elaborate strategy in order to achieve a specific aim, introducing deliberately sacrificial elements into the scheme so that the core might get through in a process of give and take. Herzog and de Meuron did nothing of the kind. They expected their work to be taken seriously, and were very patient in discussing the reasoning behind certain design decisions. Seen in total, it was clear that their scheme was in the spirit or *essence* of the building, even though some of the *substance* was going to be lost. Had it been a listed building, the Twentieth Century Society might have felt constrained by the fear that to approve these changes would set a dangerous precedent, giving adversaries in future cases grounds for arguing what might be less virtous cases. I think this fear should not be underestimated. It is a constraint on the relaxation of conservation and it requires a shift in the discussion away from legalistic, precedent-based evidence towards a more qualitative basis. At the same time, the highly confrontational politics of conservation that were typical of the 1970s (and were to my mind absolutely necessary to redress the balance of that time) are now largely a thing of the past. Parties on both sides have shifted, and the official arbitrators are themselves more openly involved in the process of discussion.

The current discussion about Pimlico School is an interesting case in this respect, and was indeed the subject of Paul Finch's editorial in the *Architects' Journal*, which I quoted earlier. This, as Finch acknowledges, is as much as anything a political case. It is about ownership of space and its benefits. The school owns a lot of open space, and, if the Private Finance Initiative scheme goes through, this space will be lost to the school and to the local community and passers-by who may at present get some benefit from it. Similar cases have occurred in respect of other post-war buildings whose dowry of circumambient space is too rich to resist pillage from the forces of commerce. Conservation is one of the few ways in which citizens can act to influence market forces. The building at the centre of the argument may be secondary in its importance to the main issue, which might be the erection of a new supermarket with all that it implies in terms of the disruption of existing patterns of economic and social life. The protesters will be lucky to get the building listed, although they may halt the juggernaut only temporarily, or dress the wolf in sheep's (conservation) clothing. Who, meanwhile, occupies themselves with the real issue at stake, of shopping and its social consequences? What interest group has any mechanism half so valuable as the conservation of historic buildings to give them effective leverage?

A call for an approach to conservation based on *essence* as much as *substance* would require the historian (as presently described) to become something he or she probably is already, but only unofficially: that is, an aesthete. This would be a heavy responsibility, and would require a certain kind of training and professional expertise different from that currently demanded in the field. Aesthetes have never been popular in England, but this does not remove the fact that somebody somewhere has to make aesthetic choices, and it does not help to try to disguise these as objective. Saul Ostrow writes in the foreword to the recent book *England and its Aesthetes*, by David Carrier:

> ... *my generation, educated in the 1960s, were taught to avoid developing a refined taste and being concerned with aesthetics. Aestheticism was equated with elegance, taste and beauty, everything that we were being taught not to aspire to. These effects had earned bad names for themselves, and had become too easy to affect.*[6]

Conservation has enormous potential to contribute to the enhancement of the environment as a whole, not just in the little patches it can call its own, but in adapting its discourses to serve as one way of articulating the need for visual order in the public realm – a subject in which architects or planners on their own cannot, it seems, get a sufficient foothold to make an effective difference.

It is perhaps not completely fanciful to replace Martin Pawley's twin paradigms of Modernism and conservation in conflict with another paradigm, in which we see the social idealism of Modernism acting through the agency of conservation, but perhaps not conservation as we know it, more a general building culture which balances *essence* and *substance*.

The Modernist critique of conservation is not to be dismissed, but its logical outcome is transhistorical rather than anti-historical. The *essence* of Modernism would be to recognize the beautiful of any age, and value it accordingly. Only the *quantitative* side of Modernism attaches itself to the doctrine of historicism, in which each period has its style, and everything can be graded and assessed objectively, Modernism as much as anything else. This status quo has seen us through times of great difficulty, but we need not, perhaps, always live with our backs to the wall. As Saul Ostrow writes later in the same piece:

> The inability to objectify Modernism's criteria and standards has resulted in the return of subjectivity as well as other issues long thought resolved. These have re-emerged – from the margins – significantly changed.[7]

I would like to quote in this respect from Tim Bennett, an architectural student in the 1930s, who was acknowledged by all who knew him as a something of a visionary (he was killed in action in 1942). In 1939, in a letter to the painter Ben Nicholson, he wrote:

> I look forward to the time when we have something less rarefied and more robust, a vernacular, in fact, which will not stand in need of preservation. And I doubt very much whether this will ever be imposed from the top down – valid signs of it now are nearly all the other way.[8]

Judged on this basis, modern architecture is not a historical phase that is now over, or the subject of a revival. It has hardly even begun and, if it comes, could look something like what we can now begin, from projects such as Bankside, to recognize as conservation. In the light of that new day, conservation and Modernism will both wither away like the insubstantial spectres we know them to be.

References

1   Pawley, M. (1998), *Terminal Architecture*, London: Reaktion Books, 98. The quote is from Berthold Lubetkin.

2   Finch, P. (1998), *Architects' Journal*, **207**, (28 May), 23.

3   Schulze, F. (1985), *Mies van der Rohe, A Critical Biography*, London and Chicago: Chicago University Press.

4   *Ibid.*, 172–3; Aquinas, St Thomas (1952), *Summa Theologica*, translation by the Fathers of the Dominican Province, rev. by Daniel J. Sullivan, Chicago.

5   Perry, Whittall N. (1995), *The Widening Breach, Evolutionism in the Mirror of Cosmology*, Cambridge: Quinta Essentia.

6   Carrier, D. (ed) (1997), *England and its Aesthetes*, Amsterdam: OPA.

7   *Ibid.*, xiv.

8   Tim Bennett to Ben Nicholson, 19 October 1939, Tate Archive BN 87/7/1.2–168.

CHAPTER 2
THIS IS TOMORROW: THE STORY OF POST-WAR ARCHITECTURE IN ENGLAND

Elain Harwood

'Just what is it that makes today's homes so different, so appealing?' was the title of Richard Hamilton's collage poster for the 1956 exhibition *This is Tomorrow*, for which twelve apocalyptic tableaux were assembled by teams of artists and architects. This is the question people are now asking of a wider range of architecture from the years between 1945 and 1975. There are many ways in which we might treat the coherent body of architecture that emerged. This book concentrates on the new ways found to use materials, but we should also be aware of the ideas the new architecture embodied. Of particular importance is the emergence of a distinctive client base; local authorities and publicly funded bodies such as universities were the overwhelmingly dominant clients of the period. The whole story could also be paraphrased by a study of a small number of representative architects, or expanded by placing the aesthetic concerns of architecture within the social and intellectual framework of the period.

Ways of looking at the 1950s and 1960s

An amendment to the listing legislation in 1987 means that English Heritage can now consider listing any building that is over thirty years old. Thus, an initial concentration on the period 1940–57 enabled us to re-evaluate an essentially humane architecture in isolation from the headier fireworks that followed in the early 1960s, which claimed our attention in the early 1990s. We are now turning to the even more eclectic range of buildings and ideas from around 1970. English Heritage's research has been by building type, judging buildings with their peers both aesthetically and by the way in which they met a similar brief. This has brought out the importance of some of the little-known but exciting buildings, such as railway stations. We have now to try to draw together the threads of this research, and to reintroduce some understanding of the personalities who created them.

We rapidly realized that, while there is a remarkable consistency in the choice of individual details, there was not a single overall style, movement or period. Changing values have made us more aware of the neoclassical architects who continued to work for the more traditional clients with considerable success: Raymond Erith and Donald McMorran were the most inventive younger architects working in the public domain, while Claud Phillimore, Francis Johnson and others based extensive practices on the building and remodelling of country houses. Throughout the period, many novel ideas were explored in the building of small private houses, some for the architects themselves, others little more than weekend homes for sympathetic friends and clients. These were scarcely, if ever, published, but provide an exciting undercurrent to the more complicated briefs and client committees that went with an architecture of public service.

Advances in construction and the confident use of materials were major factors in determining the form of buildings in the post-war period. There are timber, plastic, steel and concrete; the movement of reinforcement out of external walls and into internal crosswalls; shells and space frames. Britain emerges as the most innovative user of timber in Europe in the late 1950s, with the possible exception of the Soviet Union.

The history of post-war building to the 1970s can be written by a study of just two exemplary architects, or architectural firms. One is Sir Leslie Martin, who in the post-war period worked on prefabrication for the railways and organised the London County Council (LCC) Architect's Department – then the largest in the world – into creative working teams, before setting up a private practice centred on his teaching at Cambridge University and collaborative work with younger architects. The other is Powell and Moya, founded by Philip and Michael Powell and Hidalgo Moya in 1946 after they had won the first post-war competition for public housing, at Churchill Gardens, Westminster. The firm went on to win a Festival of Britain competition with their 'Skylon' vertical feature (1951), and to build schools, housing and hospitals in the 1950s before securing a series of prestigious commissions for extensions to Oxbridge colleges in the 1960s. Philip Powell and Hidalgo Moya were the first architects to win jointly the Royal Institute of British Architects Gold Medal, in 1974. While Martin occupied a series of key public positions from which he could overview ideas on prefabrication, planning and the organization of architectural practice, Powell and Moya epitomized the successful small firm working almost exclusively within the public sector.

We are only just beginning to recognize the international importance of English architecture, as critical reassessment of figures like James Stirling begins. With the Modern Movement came an unprecedented cross-fertilization of ideas through personal contacts, holiday travel and magazines, which culminated in the meetings of the Congrès Internationaux d'Architecture Moderne (CIAM), which was founded in 1928. In the 1950s CIAM broke down into a series of study groups and spin-offs, such as Team X, the international steering party set up to organise the tenth conference, where new British thinking came to the fore. England did not produce one architect as dominant as were Le Corbusier, Alvar Aalto, or perhaps even the firm of Gillespie, Kidd and Coia in their respective countries. Our more reticent, less visual culture gave us Basil Spence and Richard Seifert, coincidentally suggested by Robert Maxwell as the two 'top architects' of the 1960s. The first, at least, became a household name through the building of Coventry Cathedral, while the second was the name behind some of the most symbolic buildings of the 1960s, including Centre Point.[1]

Where does the work of Denys Lasdun fit into this picture? He has much closer links with the 1930s experience of English modern architecture, which the Stirling/Smithson generation sought to reject, yet his principal buildings share their respective concerns with form and the movement through space. Will history accord Lasdun an international reputation such as Stirling is beginning to enjoy? The gates of the Florey Building in Oxford are already bedecked with signs forbidding access to the intrepid architectural tourist. Are we fortunate or culturally unimaginative not to be driven by the adulation that causes Aalto's Finlandia Hall to be reclad with Carrara marble panels – the first having failed within 25 years – or that keeps Le Corbusier's principal buildings in an excellent state of repair?

In November 1968, the Italian journal *Zodiac* devoted its eighteenth issue entirely to British architecture. Its editor suggested that British architecture was interesting because of its complexity, while in the New Towns and new universities we were experimenting with building on an exceptional scale not found elsewhere. Elsewhere the issue argues that the mid-1950s saw a burst of creative thinking in Britain, based around the historical essays that continued to appear in the *Architectural Review* and the remodelled *Architectural Design*, which from 1954 became a focus for shorter, more technical articles and the first manifestos of the New Brutalists and the Archigram group.[2] The international impact of this dynamic British writing gives an added value to the architecture that grew out of these ideas.

The post-war period can be usefully divided into three sections, the first being the most clear cut and best known. It was followed by an exceptional period of building, in terms of the number of buildings constructed and the ambition and high quality of many of them. In the later 1960s, this optimism waned in the face of mounting inflation, though large schemes continued to be built and a great variety of styles and materials is apparent.

The years of austerity

A system of building licences was in force until the end of 1954, because building materials – notably steel but also at times bricks and timber – were in short supply. Priority for building was given to schools and housing, while private houses had to be of a stipulated size. Only foreign money could circumvent the system (witness the Time and Life Building by Michael Rosenauer in Westminster) and the takeover of city-centre accommodation as offices is a lasting testament to the freeze on office building. The biggest licence applications were for the Brabazon Hangar at Filton, Bristol, and for Coventry Cathedral, though the latter was not completed until 1962.

The British economy at the end of the war was in desperate shape. In London alone, the Blitz had destroyed half a million homes and left a further quarter of a million severely damaged; there was a thirty-month maintenance backlog on the railways, and some five hundred churches were beyond repair.[3] The war left another legacy, however, in the recognition that the collective economy of the war – in which all aspects of life in Britain had been brought under government control to a far greater extent than in Nazi Germany – had brought social benefits in terms of prosperity, diet and health for the more disadvantaged sections of the community, and that the *laissez-faire* capitalism of the 1930s had thus been shamed. Alan Powers and I are increasingly persuaded that the years immediately after 1945 saw no great shift in ideas, but attempted to fulfil long-cherished aspirations from the 1920s and 1930s. The emphasis was on self-improvement by the creation of greater opportunities through welfare and education provision. Thus the three-tier system of secondary education introduced with the Butler Act of

1944 had first been proposed by the Hadow Commission in 1926 and, by the 1940s, had been supplanted in advanced circles by the concept of comprehensive schools. The centralization of medical services during the war had ended the divide between voluntary provision depending upon flag days, and the larger but less prestigious local authority hospitals inherited from the Poor Law. Their unification within the National Health Service in 1948 confirmed an existing state of affairs.

The *Beveridge Report*, published in December 1942, was a five-pronged attack on 'Want, Disease, Ignorance, Squalor and Idleness':

> *The historian of social administration finds in the Beveridge Report the blueprint of the post-war welfare state in Britain. The political historian sees it also as a brilliant coup by one man, which at once synthesised the pressures for a more progressive capitalism, and jolted all three parties into accepting the resulting formula as the basis of a new post-war consensus.*[4]

The creative phase of post-war socialism is considered by political commentators to have ended as early as 1948, though the Festival of Britain may be seen as the last fling of this idealism, as well as of Attlee's Labour government.[5]

The biggest change for architecture in the post-war period was the passing of patronage to the public purse after some thirty years when local authority expenditure on buildings was frustrated and inadequate. In the years 1945–55 most building work was publicly funded, albeit sometimes indirectly through development grants for industry and the work of the War Damages Commission. The Commission, which was not abolished until 1964, made special provision for churches, and funded the most lavish restorations and rebuildings. Much of the best post-war housing, both socially and architecturally, was that built in the late 1940s before a series of cost controls was introduced, first by Stafford Cripps in 1948, more fiercely under the Conservatives in 1951 and 1953, and then by the abolition of 'general needs' subsidies in 1954–6.

Nevertheless, there is perhaps more continuity than upset, despite a change in government in 1951, and the years until the early 1960s see a relatively calm growth in the number of projects as shortages of money and materials eased. There is a greater continuity of urbane, Scandinavian-inspired design than radical theorists were prepared to admit, and we can only now appreciate that the first wave of New Towns, begun in 1946 with the foundation of Stevenage, included architecture of discipline that has worn well and made pleasant places to live. The first phases of Harlow, such as Mark Hall North, are ambitious in their use of contrasting masses of flats and houses to create a pioneering 'mixed development' of housing for all sectors of the community, in their use of art and in their intelligent landscaping by Frederick Gibberd and Sylvia Crowe – features that contribute to a total environment of quality. Frederick Gibberd is one example of the architect/planner working successfully with a stable development corporation over some thirty years.

This Scandinavian-style architecture has its sources in the proportions of neoclassicism, but its organic elements and subtlety of layout, the emphasis given to landscape and heraldic art, were appropriate to an English culture with a strong sense of place.[6] On a simplistic level, this is an architecture of social democracy, its asymmetrical picturesqueness and informality a contrast to the overt classicism and straight-line planning of dictatorships, whether of left or right. It is also the architecture of the new humanism, or the new empiricism, of the picturesque movement championed by the *Architectural Review* and a generation of architects who qualified just before the war and for whom the social aims of the Modern Movement went hand in hand with the political situation.

The finest flowering of the new humanism was the Festival of Britain, where a series of pavilions, intertwined with walks and gardens on several levels, provided a one-off opportunity for the generation of architects trained immediately before the war to have fun. The only building designed to be permanent was the Royal Festival Hall, where Peter Moro designed a uniquely svelte interior to Leslie Martin's plan of an 'egg in a box'. The Festival hall is the culmination of ideas from the late 1930s onwards, combining ideas honed from across northern Europe and Moro's experience with Tecton, yet the refacing of its more clearly Scandinavian modern facades only ten years later shows just how short-lived this influence was to be among the leaders in English taste.

The war was important, too, in providing a framework for the way a generation of young architects tackled problems and worked as a team. Whereas in the 1930s any architect of ambition would hope to set up in private practice, the 1940s saw them entering local authority service, either as consultants for a five-year housing programme, as Herbert Taylor and David Green did initially at Little Loddon Rural District Council, or directly into a growing team such as Hertfordshire or Middlesex.[7] In the early to mid-1950s the place to be was the London County Council Architect's Department, following its reorganization under first Robert Matthew and then Leslie Martin. Some LCC buildings of this period are known to have been designed by architects who went on to make names for themselves in private practice; the authorship of others, equally good, remains obscure. The rationalism of this architecture goes beyond style; careful thought and a methodical approach to problem-solving are evident in plan types and every other component of the design.

The first architectural office to call itself a Research and Development Department was that established by the London, Midland and Scottish Railways in 1935, which took on Leslie Martin and Richard Lewellyn Davies in 1939. It looked at the prefabrication of staff canteens, hostels and station buildings. Its prototype platform building erected at Queen's Park in 1945 (it was moved to West Hampstead around 1950) was given finishes that could withstand soot from steam engines and knocks from barrows, and was designed to be built quickly so as not to inconvenience train timetables. The result was a lightweight steel-framed building based on a tartan grid of 8'3" and 3'4" units, which anticipated the more famous Hertfordshire schools by a couple of years.[8]

The demand for new schools was such that the Ministry of Education began to issue directives in favour of prefabrication as early as 1944, when a Building Committee including Denis Clarke Hall and C.G. Stillman recommended 'standardized construction' as the only means of coping with the backlog of building. Its suggestion was adopted most pervasively by Hertfordshire County Council, which was faced with an exceptional need to build ten new schools a year to cope with a rising population. The Deputy County Architect, Stirrat Johnson-Marshall, and his assistants took a proprietary prefabrication system for wartime hutments and remodelled it into a flexible kit of parts that could be assembled to a range of plans. The genius of the Hertfordshire schools is that they also responded to the demand that education become more child centred, with windows small people could see out of, sinks and chairs to their size, bright colours and murals. They perfectly suited new ideas of primary education that Britain pioneered, and which were demonstrated by the building and complete fitting-out of a CLASP (Consortium of Local Authorities' Special Programme) primary school by Nottinghamshire County Council at the Milan Triennale of 1960 (Figure 2.1). It is this rationality of building, rather than individual examples, that has made them so significant historically. Now, however, their users are expressing the same enthusiasm for their school buildings as prefab dwellers for their houses. And after sixty years of successful use, who are we to deny that they are architecture?

The new brutalism

This was not the attitude of all post-war architects, however, particularly those just too young to have experienced work for the wartime shadow factories and camouflage units. Austerity in Britain lasted a lot longer than the war itself, some forms of rationing continuing until 1954. There was frustration that restrictions, on all aspects of consumer and cultural life, lasted far longer in Britain than in Western Europe, while America seemed to offer an abundance of opportunities:

Figure 2.1   Greenfields School, South Oxhey, Near Watford, by Hertfordshire County Council, 1951–2. This was the prototype for the second generation of Hertfordshire school, designed to a tighter plan than the earlier ones and with less corridor, to reduce costs. However, the lightness and delicacy of Oxhey is exceptional in the Herts canon and it is listed grade II. (English Heritage)

Mass communication, science fiction and Americana. Subjects of that kind which we had not touched upon till then and which were very much in the minds of the younger generation of art students and students of all sorts really.[9]

As the Smithsons recalled,

1954 was for us a key year ... American advertising equal to Dada in its impact of overlaid imagery ... that automotive masterpiece the Cadillac convertible – parallel with the ground, four elevations – classic box on wheels ... The start of a new way of thinking by CIAM.[10]

If social provision was the dominant focus of architecture in the 1940s, by the mid-1950s more artistic concerns were being reasserted. Yet, although there was a change in approach, in which standardization became but one of a wider range of options, the public sector continued to provide all the most prestigious commissions until the end of the 1960s.

But first the idea of architecture as art had to be re-established. The close association between avant-garde art and architecture that existed in the 1930s could be found again among the young architects of the mid-1950s. There was a reinvestment in elevational design, which became the subject of the same serious questioning as the plan and functional requirements of a building. This was, perhaps, the first generation for whom a crucial early influence was formal teaching in architectural history, by John Summerson at the Architectural Association, and most profoundly by Rudolf Wittkower there and at the Royal Academy.

Dr Wittkower's book The Architectural Principles of the Age of Humanism *[sic] sent a whole generation of young architects to the Palladian Villas, to Alberti, to a reexamination of the construction of the architect's mental framework and his role.*[11]

Colin Rowe developed the theory that such decisive modern icons as Le Corbusier's Villa Savoye were not determined by function alone, but had a formal Palladian basis to their design, and that this was seen still more clearly in the work of Mies van der Rohe. In such work, as in Auguste Perret's before it, the purity of materials had to be purely expressed. The influence of humanism is profound in work like Maguire and Murray's centrally planned churches, beginning with St Paul, Bow Common, of 1958–60. Elsewhere the direct influence of classical proportions declined, as it did in Le Corbusier's own work, so that by the early 1960s architects like James Stirling had developed their own language, which was both expressive and – in its vigorous way – also picturesque.[12]

Alison and Peter Smithson contributed to a series of exhibitions with Eduardo Paolozzi and Nigel Henderson, a photographer who had had a nervous breakdown after serving with the Air Force in the war. In Henderson's giant heads, images of bomb sites and social studies of life in Bethnal Green (where his wife worked as a sociologist) are assembled many 1950s issues, of fear – whether of nuclear attack or a new holocaust – and of the potential conflict between old communities and new, more scientific ways of living. The four's collaboration at *This is Tomorrow* was 'Patio and Pavilion', a vision of the house of the future as a high-tech customized bunker not unlike the backyard pigeon lofts of Bethnal Green. It was a very different use of collage and 'as found' techniques from the overtly science fantasy exhibit by John Voekler, Richard Hamilton and John McHale, which featured Robbie the Robot and Hamilton's *Just what is it … ?*, a surreal collage of the all-American couple and their ideal home. Paolozzi had become aware of Dubuffet's *Art Brut* while studying in Paris in the late 1940s, while the Smithsons themselves laid claim to the term '*béton brut*'; Reyner Banham claims the phrase was introduced from Sweden as early as 1950 to the LCC, where it served as a term of Communist abuse.[13] The Smithsons, however, adopted it as their own, to mean an architecture that respected 'the sensuous use of each material' and a 'formal use of proportion'. It first appeared in a review (December 1953) of an 'unbuilt house in Soho' for themselves; by January 1955 it had become a manifesto, by June 1955 a polemic. 'Each generation feels a new dissatisfaction, and conceives of a new idea of order … This is architecture.'[14] Yet by that date the Smithsons had already produced their most influential individual schemes, of which only that for Hunstanton School (1950-54) was built, while opportunities for architects in private practice remained bleak despite the lifting of building licences the previous year. When 'Brutalist' buildings began to be erected they were not by the Smithsons, who thus can best be seen as perhaps the voice of a wide circle of fellow-thinkers.

In Bethnal Green, social workers like Judith Henderson and Young and Wilmott charted the breakdown of working-class traditions, noting in particular the demise of the extended family in favour of the 'nuclear' family of two adults and their children, a change founded on wartime dislocation, smaller families, increased prosperity and middle-class models, not simply the transition from city slum to the characterless suburban estate that is usually blamed.[15] By the mid-1950s, the bleakness of these new estates was prompting architects to look for new alternatives, while the critic Ian Nairn prophesied that, unchecked, England could degenerate into 'isolated oases of preserved monuments in a desert of wire, concrete roads, cosy plots and bungalows' or what he termed 'Subtopia'.[16]

Architects and planners in Britain and the United States looked at the dynamics of cities and rejected the concept of flats in open landscape championed by Le Corbusier, Ludwig Hilberseimer, and other established members of CIAM, in favour or preserving the small-scale 'grain' of the street or the 'cluster' of a neighbourhood. Denys Lasdun recalls exploring the back yards and pigeon lofts of Bethnal Green when drawing up his 'cluster block' for a tiny site at Claredale Street, in which he sought to increase privacy and reduce noise by organizing the flats into small, separate towers grouped round an independent lift shaft.

Lack of land was the single greatest reason for building high in the late 1950s and 1960s, for the only way to counter the lure of the suburbs was to find a means of providing spacious accommodation with modern amenities at high density. Most authorities were anxious to hang on to their voters, the basis of political power in northern industrial cities such as Leeds, Sheffield and Glasgow, as well as in small London boroughs like Bethnal Green. The only authority committed to a dispersal policy was the LCC, whose philosophy went back to the Garden City ideals of the 1890s. With limited opportunity to build within its boundaries, save for its award-winning developments at Roehampton, it was already one of the few authorities permitted to build outside its boundaries. In 1952, it secured the Town Development Act to build substantial additions to existing market towns across the southeast, beginning with Bletchley in Buckinghamshire.

The City of London was another authority that initially favoured the dispersal of its minimal population. However, it recognized a need to provide limited accommodation for those working unsocial hours in the City, such as caretakers and nurses. In 1952, Geoffry Powell won a competition for a scheme housing 200 persons per acre at Golden Lane in a mixture of flats and maisonettes, with one sixteen-storey block that was briefly the tallest residential tower in Europe.

In two unplaced entries for the same competition, the Smithsons and Jack Lynn independently experimented with the idea of longer, lower slabs served by raised 'streets in the sky'; when Lynn was taken on by Sheffield a year or so later, he was given the perfect opportunity to put his ideas into practice.[17] A steep hillside site overlooking the city meant that the building could rise from four storeys to thirteen while keeping a constant roofline, and all but the uppermost 'street' could be entered from ground level. With shops and four pubs, Park Hill is unusual in being conceived as a complete community. It is also 'traditional' in construction, in having a concrete frame and crosswalls, which were then clad in brick (Figure 2.2). It is important to distinguish these one-off constructions from the rash of system-built tower blocks built in the early 1960s as part of a drive to meet housing targets of up to 400,000 new homes per year (1963). 'Urban renewal' through system building was seen as a vote winner by an incongruous alliance of Macmillan's last Conservative government with the most traditional, secure Labour authorities. These vast developments built with prefabricated systems, many imported from abroad, which repeated standard designs across the country, have failed to interest the conservation world, and there is no indication, in England, that this will change.

Figure 2.2   Park Hill, Sheffield, by Jack Lynn and Ivor Smith, Sheffield City Council Architect's Department, 1957–60. The first truly large-scale building of the post-war era and the one that came closest to achieving the high ambition of being the first step to a better Britain. (Elain Harwood)

The years of prosperity

Buildings like Park Hill mark the moment when England's years of austerity at last gave way to a consumer boom. John Summerson nominated 1957 as the crucial year, not just for the number of buildings erected then, but also for their size and style, as the effect of the LCC's easing of restrictions on the height of buildings began to be felt.[18] Then began an exceptional period in British architectural history, in terms of the number of buildings constructed and the ambition and high quality of many of them, which lasted until about 1965 or so. More churches were built in these few years than in any Victorian decade save the 1860s. Twenty-four new universities and a university college were founded between 1961 and 1968, if one includes those that were upgraded from technical college status, and the number of further education places was almost doubled.

Park Hill, the first major building by members of the *This is Tomorrow* generation, also demonstrates a belief in architecture as the expression of a total concept of life. Here at last the most profound ideals of the infant Modern Movement of the 1920s found fruition. The form of a building was inspired by how it was used; materials were expressed honestly; standardized industrial components were chosen not merely for economy, but actually in preference to special designs; steel and concrete spans, covering large areas, enabled the relationship between indoor and outdoor space to be redefined, as the external wall no longer had to be structural. These ideas were manifested far more robustly than had been possible with the fragile technology of the post-war era.

To us, now, there seems to be an unintended irony in the Smithson's proclamation of the 1920s as the 'heroic period of modern architecture' in their writings forty years later.[19] Oscar Niemeyer, working in Brazil during the war years, and Le Corbusier's work thereafter, suggested a rougher, more massive, sculptural quality of a thickness appropriate to warm climates. Alvar Aalto showed that buildings could be erected on a small scale, in brick, and still achieve monumentality. Le Corbusier's Maisons Jaoul, completed in 1954, brought these two ideals together, and had a forceful influence on British architecture as nowhere else, for the use of red brick was perfectly suited to the work of a young generation acutely aware of its nineteenth-century industrial heritage. This influence is best seen in the work of James Stirling, who was first to review the Maisons Jaoul, for the *Architectural Review*. Stirling and James Gowan achieved the ultimate synthesis of red brick, patent glazing and formal references at their Leicester University School of Engineering (1959–63) (Figure 2.3, *overleaf*).

> *The architects gloried in the ambiguities arising from having to pack too much accommodation on an awkward site, which made radical forms unavoidable, while being sophisticated enough to understand exactly what historical echoes each radical form could stir.*[20]

The same strength and formalism is present in a building superficially more akin to the white architecture of the 1930s, and designed to an unusually luxurious budget. Denys Lasdun conceived the Royal College of Physicians in Regent's Park, London, entirely around the senior fellows' processional route from a central Censor's office to the formal lecture hall and dining suite, at either side of the first floor.

Figure 2.3   Leicester University Engineering Building, by James Stirling and James Gowan, 1959–63. A post-war building of international importance, and one of the first buildings that marked the universities as the most distinguished clients of the 1960s. Listed grade II*. (English Heritage)

> *Of the architects who qualified before the war only Denys Lasdun seems to be moving in the same direction as the post-war generation: what this direction is, is difficult to define, but these architects have a seriousness which is quite foreign to [the International Movement] against which they are in revolt.*[21]

The new style was not attractive to everyone. Nikolaus Pevsner, grounded in early Modernism and the Picturesque, and with a belief that architecture had to respond to the scientific age by becoming a 'human science' responsive to need rather than artistic conceit, provoked a heated debate at the Architectural Association (AA). In his reaction there is, however, a clear recognition that the leading buildings of the 1960s had attained a new individuality:

> *The fact that my enthusiasms cannot be roused by Ronchamp, or Chandigarh, by Churchill College and the Physicians, does not blind me to the existence today of a new style, successor to my International Modern of the 1930s, a post-modern style, I would be tempted to call it, but the legitimate style of the 1950s and 1960s.*[22]

The focus for new architecture in the early 1960s was the universities, where the shortage of student places was at last recognized. The old universities expanded, in particular Oxford and Cambridge with their large budgets, while colleges founded in the twentieth century were upgraded to university status and new ones established. Across the country, universities expanded their science departments, and there was a rush to build modern facilities for the teaching of physics and engineering. Most provincial cities gained at least one sleek new university building of the finest quality: the Engineering Building at Leicester; the Arts Tower at Sheffield (Gollins Melvin Ward, 1960–5); a vast complex for maths and science, with lecture theatres and a library, at Leeds (Chamberlin, Powell and Bon, 1963–78).

University architecture in the 1960s in Britain has released, and is consuming, a long pent-up flood of interest and skill in the planning and shaping of total environments. It commands, and exploits, the whole gamut of architectural activities.[23]

Most English towns were also transformed in the 1960s, supposedly for the ease of the shopper, office worker and motorist, those who had 'never had it so good', as Harold Macmillan declared, in that key year of 1957. In practice, the chief beneficiaries were a handful of property developers who had set up business in the 1930s and had shrewdly bought up land in the war, and local authorities that nursed the rate income from city centre redevelopments.

Newcastle was exceptional in that it did not seek to redevelop its centre until 1959, when the first Labour council for many years was elected. Its leader, T. Dan Smith, rose to the challenge of confirming his city's pre-eminence in the North:

We live in a city which is a potential goldmine, and it astonishes those of us who are Socialists that you who talk about vested interests and private enterprise have been living on top of a goldmine for ten years and have failed to exploit it. You talk about the cost to the ratepayer. The cost of not developing Percy Street and Northumberland Street is measured in millions of pounds.[24]

Croydon had nurtured its dream of a major new road filled with offices (its so-called 'Manhattan skyline') since the war, and this was a more common scenario. Most commercial architecture is of a transitory nature, although in the 1960s it sparkled with much that was most vibrant about the period. Rodney Gordon, who left the LCC in 1960 to become the design architect of the Owen Luder Partnership, was exhilarated to find, after years of producing designs for committees to gestate and reject, that suddenly he could design as he liked – so long as he achieved the maximum plot ratio. Eros House, his first office development for Luder and the Alex Colman Group, won the Royal Institute of British Architects' Bronze Medal for 1963. The Building Design Partnership, in Preston, produced one of the few buildings that celebrates the threefold increase in car ownership in the years 1948–63 with architectural style. With these buildings, too, we are beginning to see the emergence of the megastructure.

The idea of placing the entire function of a city within a single building goes back to the futurist projects of Sant'Elia around 1914 and to Le Corbusier's housing concepts of the 1920s and 1930s. It can be argued, though, that the modern city complex has precedents in the vast railways, markets and industrial conglomerations of the nineteenth century, and in housing schemes of the inter-war period such as Henri Sauvage's flats and swimming pool in the Rue des Amiraux, Paris.[25]

But the idea of the megastructure really took shape with proposals to separate the pedestrian from traffic. In the first post-war plans this led to a simple pedestrian precinct at ground level, such as was proposed for Coventry as early as 1941, and which can also be found at the Lansbury Estate in Poplar (1950–1, Frederick Gibberd) and at Harlow and Stevenage (1959). In the early 1960s, increasing car ownership forced architects and planners to look for a new way of easing congestion in older city centres. Again, the starting point was Le Corbusier's more idealistic town planning schemes, such as his Ville Radieuse of 1930–5 and plan for Algiers (1932–42), as refined by modern commentators such as the Smithsons, whose scheme for a 'pedestrian platform net' intertwined with an urban motorway system was placed third in a competition for Haupstadt Berlin in 1959.[26] The City of London, Leeds, Manchester, Nottingham and other urban centres conceived schemes that used the slope of the land to give pedestrians a separate walkway, granting them a sterile safety in return for longer journeys and a denial of the street. Few of these schemes were ever completed. But as buildings were joined up at two levels, often with car parking in addition, the megastructure was made.

The megastructure was well suited to the demands of new university buildings on greenfield sites. Seven entirely new universities were approved in England between 1957 and 1963, and all found attractive parkland sites outside historic towns. They were the first foundations since London and Durham in the 1830s to be given full university status from the beginning, with the power to grant their own degrees, and they were encouraged to be innovative in the courses of study they set up. The design of these 'new towns' of learning offered better budgets and an opportunity for a greater homogeneity than did real towns, for added to the convenience of a populace limited in its age and social mix was the clarity brought about by a distinct client – the vice-chancellor acting alone or with a small group of department heads. The re-evaluation of teaching and course structures led, for example, to a demand for flexible teaching spaces, notably at the University of East Anglia, where Denys Lasdun devised a 'ten minute university' with parallel ranges of residential and teaching buildings (1964–8) linked by pedestrian walkways above the level of cars. The vice-chancellor at Essex, Albert Sloman, explained his very personal vision of university planning in a series of Reith Lectures (1963); he preferred a few, very large departments that created economies of scale for purchasing equipment and large-scale buildings. The final design for Essex, a series of raised courtyards with residential towers to the north and south, was devised by Kenneth Capon of the Architects' Co-Partnership working with Sloman alone – an example of how a single man could direct huge amounts of public spending in the 1960s.[27] Capon's heroically scaled plan is intriguing, too, because it is the nearest built example we have to the LCC's grand New Town project for Hook – widely published after its rejection by Hampshire authorities in 1961 – and to AA student projects of the 1950s like Zone for the megastructural city surrounded by its own agricultural hegemony. All these schemes took over an entire river valley, albeit at Essex a relatively small one.

Yet it was the unbuilt projects, unfettered by the difficulties of site construction and subsequent problems of funding that beset Essex, that were most widely considered. Whereas in the 1950s there was a limited interest in student projects and in unbuilt competition entries, in the

1960s the project took on a life of its own. This is seen most clearly in the work of Archigram, to one Viennese commentator the 'six Beatles of the architectural world', who, like the pop group, developed from a synthesis of British post-industrial urbanism with American culture and scientific exploration towards a more abstract hippiedom. *Archigram 1* was a magazine produced by Peter Cook, David Greens and Mike Webb, who subsequently met up with Warren Chalk, Ron Herron and Dennis Compton, then working at the LCC, and together worked on projects using drawing, collage, models and poetry to create a series of cultural icons. The early works share the comic book, sci-fi images of *This is Tomorrow*, with which there was a connection through friends like Eduardo Paolozzi and Theo Crosby. 'Walking City', 'Plug-in City', the 'Living Pod' and 'Instant City' are among the most significant architectural images of the decade, yet by dissolving ideas of habitation and transportation into purely theoretical concepts, they came to question the need for building at all. Archigram's development parallels that of the 1960s, from a sincere belief in modern science manifest in the city schemes of around 1963–4, to a growing interest in the individual, in smaller mobile schemes such as 'suits that are homes', and by 1970 into landscapes and 'Dreams come True'. By 1972 they were enclosing a free packet of seeds with each issue, as they harnessed real ecological needs to their concepts. Their writings and subsequent teaching careers have been profoundly influential internationally, particularly in the United States, Germany and Austria, where they inspired early deconstructivists like Coop Himmelblau. Since they built so little, those structures that manifest anything of their ideas have a special significance, such as Heron and Chalk's work at the South Bank Centre for the LCC.[28]

Refinement and realignment from the late 1960s

James Stirling was fond of a drawing by a Leicester student that showed the Engineering Building as a jaunty steamer in a rough sea.[29] The influence of early Modernism, especially the *De Stijl* movement, present as early as 1957 in Stirling and Gowan's housing at Preston, became more apparent in the work of James Gowan after his partnership with Stirling ended. It was most clearly seen at his Trafalgar Road Estate, Greenwich (1966), a small, sensitive scheme of maisonettes which has been ruthlessly compromised by the addition of pitched roofs and new windows. The 1930s theme, with its ocean liner connotations, is most noticeable in Bicknell and Hamilton's Paddington Maintenance Depot, built in 1966–8 at the interchange between the Greater London Council's (GLC) western motorway and the Harrow Road, adjoining the Regent's Canal. The transport motif seems particularly appropriate here. Younger architects, however, also began to reinterpret the sources of modern architecture, usually in concrete block. One was Richard Rogers, at Creek Vean, Cornwall (1964–7), another Georgie Woolton, whose Cliff Road Studios of 1968 and 1971 marry something of the formalism of early Lubetkin and Tecton with the use of angled patent glazing derived from her former tutor, James Stirling.

An increasing sophistication can be found in specially commissioned office buildings, which became increasingly distinct from speculations. A number of large companies turned to leading American firms for their UK headquarters. The Cummins Engine Company provided Roche and Dinkeloo, successor practice to Eero Saarinen, with their first independent commission, for a factory outside Darlington (1962–6). Constructed of Cor-ten steel, designed to weather over 800 years, with glazing fixed by mastic derived from the Detroit car industry, the building offered a simple sophistication not found in British architecture at that date. For its European headquarters at Hayes, Heinz turned to Gordon Bunshaft of Skidmore, Owings and Merrill's New York office, for a strictly precise design in white concrete (1962–5) (Figure 2.4).

Such transatlantic commissions might be expected of American companies who wished to assert an image of their global success. However, British companies seeking a similarly sophisticated image also turned to American firms, particularly to SOM's Chicago office. Boots' D90 office at Beeston, Nottinghamshire (1967–9) was a coolly detailed box, inspired by Mies van der Rohe, which explored the latest American ideas in open planning, then still a novelty, and was designed by Bruce Graham in conjunction with the British firm Yorke Rosenberg Mardall. The same combination went on to build a still larger headquarters for W. D. and H. O. Wills on a specially landscaped site at Hartcliffe, Bristol, won in competition in 1968 and built in 1970–5. Here they created a complete corporate environment in Cor-ten steel: offices spanning an artificial lake, with an adjoining factory, and shops, banking facilities and transport services all provided on site.

Figure 2.4   Heinz Headquarters, Hayes, London Borough of Hillingdon, by Gordon Bunshaft of Skidmore, Owings and Merrill, 1962–5. European headquarters and research laboratories, built with the attention to every detail one would expect of the product – such simplicity is the result of careful deliberation. Listed grade II*. (English Heritage)

Gradually, British firms became adept at the use of steel technology and attention to sophisticated detailing. Norman Foster and Richard Rogers, as Team 4, designed a clean, neatly welded factory and offices for the American company, Reliance Controls, as early as 1964–5. In the early 1970s they, Arup Associates, YRM and Ryder and Yates, could combine engineering know-how with an understanding of office planning to produce buildings as striking as their American counterparts'. A measure of Britain's success at what is now termed 'high tech' architecture can be seen as early as 1972, when the young British firm of Farrell and Grimshaw built near-identical factories for the American company Rock Controls at Bath, and in Cambridge, Maryland.[30] These buildings showed that new materials, fixings and technology had their place, where there was sufficient budget to do them well. However, with the exceptions of Farrell and Grimshaw's flats in Park Road, Westminster (1970), and a number of one-off private houses in steel and Cor-ten, the new decade saw a divergence between office design and housing: 'high tech' for one; a brick vernacular for the other.

Small is beautiful

Archigram's development from science fiction strip to mental 'trip' mirrors the dilemma of the later 1960s and the eventual reaction to over-optimistic technology that was not highly tuned and properly budgeted. The reaction can be seen in housing well before the collapse of Ronan Point in the London Borough of Newham, in May 1968, with analyses begun in 1963 into the real cost of public housing that led to the introduction of cost 'yardsticks'.[31] One unfortunate alternative was the long slab of 'streets in the sky', usually prefabricated and without the budget or breadth of vision that had informed Park Hill. However, where a long building of medium height might act as a barrier to a busy road or railway, or – in London – be more in accord with the surrounding terraces, there could be interesting results if a traditional means of construction (including *in situ* concrete) was chosen.

Back in the late 1950s, Sir Leslie Martin and a group of Cambridge graduates had researched low-rise, high-density housing as a means of renewing the urban fabric with a more humane grain than single towers or slabs could produce. A project for St Pancras was developed as a specific scheme for land owned by the Foundling Estate in Bloomsbury, in reaction to a forty-storey development proposed by Covell and Matthews. The end result was the Brunswick Centre (1968–72) by Patrick Hodgkinson, a complex of shops and housing, with small offices and a cinema, all set over a basement car park. As this scheme was being developed, in 1961, John Darbourne won a competition for housing at Lillington Gardens, Westminster, with a low-rise, high density scheme of remarkable complexity. Like Leslie Martin's work in Cambridge, Lillington Gardens is constructed of brick – here a dark red chosen to complement G.E. Street's church of St James the Less, which the development surrounds. Lillington Gardens began as another example of Victorian influence on the tough, industrial aesthetic of the early 1960s, but rapidly came to mark the start of a revival of brick as a sensitive neo-vernacular idiom that was much repeated in small and often complex layouts of housing across the country.

This kind of scheme was to be refined across London by several London boroughs, which following their reorganization in 1965 had larger budgets and greater powers to build their own housing schemes. Lambeth used the steep slope of Central Hill, Crystal Palace, to produce stepped terraces of maisonettes, entered from street level on either side. Southwark used seven-storey slabs for their larger redevelopment schemes and more sensitive courtyard schemes for their smaller infill sites. However, the most distinctive housing was produced under the auspices of the Camden Architect's Department, using a mixture of directly employed and contracted architects, who gave the Leslie Martin/Brunswick Centre model architectural finesse and greater practicality. Between 1965 and 1979, schemes like Alexandra Road, Maiden Lane and Branch Hill reinterpreted the terrace to serve as a barrier to railway and traffic noise, with pedestrian and vehicular segregation, or as a series of linked pairs dropping down a steep hill. They were also sophisticated in their planning, maximizing the size and sunny aspects of living rooms and giving all larger units their own gardens. The sources for these experiments can be seen in a terrace of private houses, also in Camden, developed by Neave Brown, architect of Alexandra Road, for himself and friends. Alexandra Road is among the few schemes built in the 1970s that continue the sense of the heroic from the previous decade, with its continued preoccupation with classical proportion and geometry, scale and breadth of vision.

The most ambitious project of the Greater London Council, which also came into being in 1965, was for a low-rise megastructure at Thamesmead, where by-laws controlling flooding forced the building of raised access decks.[32] Thamesmead is a typical story from the early 1970s. The GLC broke with its earlier tradition of not using a proprietary building system, as the long spine blocks and towers at Thamesmead were intended to be built using the Balency system, for which a special factory was built on site. The first – and architecturally most successful – units were too complex in design to be built in this way, and were erected *in situ*; subsequent delays and rising costs saw the abandonment of the project and the demolition of the factory, as fashion returned to favour the traditional house and garden, no matter how small.

The change in housing design has also been interpreted as a loss of confidence in 'thinking big'. Economics played a big part. The incoming Labour government in 1964 inherited a vast balance of payments deficit, while 1966 saw a sterling crisis, followed by devaluation in 1967. By the time that Labour left office in 1970, the balance of payments was respectable; and while the traditional heavy industries continued the quiet decline that had begun in the late 1950s, the opportunities in other industries seemingly remained good. What had changed was inflation, as compared with Europe and most particularly with the United States. Martin Goalen recounts how his father, Gerard Goalen, designed a series of Catholic churches in the 1960s for £100,000 each – and how each was of necessity smaller and simpler than the last. The *Architectural Review*, in its 'previews' each January, could by 1967 counterbalance 'an increasingly mature and versatile vocabulary of design on every scale' with a growing concern with greater government interventions that impeded building: the 'Office Ban, the Freeze, the National Plan, the Bank and Mortgage Rates, the Industrialised Package Deal'. The next year's preview is even more outspoken in its condemnation of 'the economic stop-go'.[33] By the 1970s, very large projects like Alexandra Road, and the City of London's Barbican development, were taking ever longer to complete. Financial uncertainty meant that there were fewer opportunities to build in Britain, although some architects reactivated their careers by securing prestigious commissions in Europe and the Middle East.

Low, brick housing schemes and 'high-tech' office buildings of mirror glass marked a 'retreat from the "big building image"'.[34] The retreat was also marked by an acceptance of the rehabilitation and conversion of old buildings in conjunction with new design. All these ideas come together at Milton Keynes, with low-rise housing schemes integrated with existing buildings and villages (the residential areas increasingly adopting a brick vernacular), while the central grid squares were conceived as a Chicago-like strip in Miesian glass and steel. Arup Associates' offices for Truman's Brewery (1971) and Foster Associates' headquarters for Willis Faber Dumas (1973–5) confirm the need for big business to appear clean-cut and sophisticated, their sleek forms derived from a decade of close study of American office practice, while their glass facades coyly reflect historic buildings across the street.

Smaller housing schemes, whether by local authorities, housing associations or individuals, took on a greater significance in the 1970s. They reflect the greater significance given to the individual. The result, as in the work of Peter Aldington and John Craig, is a gentle and very personal architecture, to a brief that would be determined after perhaps a year of close discussion. A series of houses in Buckinghamshire in the mid-1960s, and a health centre in Chinnor, Oxfordshire, saw them evolve a very personal working practice in which a brief carefully developed with the client became a significant part of the architectural process. Their buildings combined open planning with small areas given to very specific uses, and demonstrated an awareness of local materials and traditions. A strong sense of enclosure and the euse of Wychert walling distinguish Aldington's own house at Haddenham, Bucks (1963–5), while Goodleigh, Devon (1970–1) retains a sense of the longhouse plan. At Surrey University, faced with a high suicide rate, Maguire and Murray conducted an extensive survey of student requirements before producing a series of terraced houses with high attic rooms in 1970. The search was on for 'a new humane environment', in which ecological and sensory experiences have a place.[35]

During the war, the architect Walter Segal published a series of low-rise, high-density terraced house plans that offered models to architects of the New Towns and reflected the work being done by, for example, Tayler and Green. His own work, however, largely consisted of small blocks of flats or individual one-off houses, save for a group of eight houses round a communal green, built in Highgate for a group of fellow architects and himself. But in 1962 he designed himself a temporary home, also in Highgate, simply built to a timber system, which he subsequently refined. By the early 1970s, this methodology had been refined in further one-off houses, but Segal had begun to see it as having potential as a cheap way of building by groups of people on the housing lists prepared to construct their own homes. The 'Segal method', small, libertarian and attuned to Schumacher's ideas, was to 1970s ideology what the big local authority housing schemes were to the 1950s and 1960s, though it was not until 1976 that enterprising councillors at Lewisham offered a hillside gap site for the system's first full realization, at what became Segal Close (Figure 2.5, *overleaf*). Modernism had come full circle.[36]

*Figure 2.5   Segal Close, London Borough of Lewisham.
Built by its residents from a system devised by Walter
Segal, 1977–80. This was the house of Jon Broome,
Segal's assistant, who has carried on Segal's methodology
after his death. (Nigel Corrie)*

References

1   Maxwell, R. (1972), *New British
Architecture,* London: Thames and Hudson, 9.

2   Bottero, M. (1968), 'Questo Numero', *Zodiac*,
18, (November), 5 (translation, 256).

3   Addison, P. (1985), *Now the War is Over: A
Social History of Britain 1945–51*, London: BBC,
56.

4   Addison, P. (1975, 1977), *The Road to
1945, British Politics and the Second World War*,
London: Quartet Books, 211.

5   Garlake, M. (1998), *New Art New World:
British Art in Postwar Society*, London: Yale
University Press, 7.

6   Mikkola, K. (1985), 'The transition from clas-
sicism to functionalism in Scandinavia', *Classical
Tradition and the Modern Movement, The Second
International Alvar Aalto Symposium*, Helsinki:
Finnish Association of Architects.

7   Saint, A. (1987), *Towards a Social
Architecture*, London: Yale University Press.

8   Anon. (1942), 'LMS Railway Building',
Official Architecture and Planning, **5**, (4), (April),
175–83; *Architects' Journal* (1945), **102**, (2654),
(6 December), 415–19.

9   Morland, D., 'A memoir', unpublished manu-
script, quoted in D. Robbins (ed), (1990), *The
Independent Group: Postwar Britain and the
Aesthetics of Plenty*, Cambridge: MIT Press, 33.

10   Smithson, A., and Smithson, P. (1973),
*Without Rhetoric, An Architectural Aesthetic
1955–1972*, London: Latimer New Dimensions, 2.

11   Gill, M. (Alison Smithson) (1960), 'Libation on
a Hot Patio Floor', *Architects' Journal*, **131**, (3395),
(12 May), 707; Wittkower, R. (1949), *Architectural
Principles in the Age of Humanism*, London:
Warburg Institute; Academy Editions (1988).

12 Banham, R. (1966), *The New Brutalism*, London: The Architectural Press; Maguire, R. (1996), 'Continuity and Modernity in the Holy Place', *Architectural History*, **39**, 1–18; Banham, R. (1968), 'Revenge of the Picturesque', in John Summerson (ed), *Concerning Architecture*, London: Allen Lane, 265–73.

13 Garlake, M. (1998), *New Art New World: British Art in Postwar Society*, London: Yale University Press, 47; Architectural Review (1955), **118**, (708), 356; Banham, R.(1966), *The New Brutalism*, London: The Architectural Press, 10.

14 *Architectural Design* (1955), **25**, (1), (January), 1; Anon. (1955), 'Urban Reidentification', *Architectural Design*, **25**, (6), (June), 185.

15 Young, M., and Wilmott, P. (1957), *Family and Kinship in East London*, London: Routledge and Kegan Paul.

16 Nairn, I. (1955), *Architectural Review*, **118**, (702), (June), 365; republished as *Outrage*, London: The Architectural Press (1956).

17 Bean, D. (1987), The Golden Lane Estate, upublished M Sc thesis, Bartlett School of Architecture; Bacon, C.W. (1982), *Streets in the Sky: The Rise and Fall of the Modern Architectural Utopia*, unpublished PhD thesis, University of Sheffield.

18 Dannatt, T. (1959), *Modern Architecture in Britain*, London: Batsford, 11 (introduction by John Summerson).

19 Smithson, A., and Smithson, P. (1965), 'The heroic period of modern architecture', *Architectural Design*, (December); and The Heroic Period of Modern Architecture (1981), Milan: Idea Editions.

20 Banham, R. (1975), *The Age of the Masters*, London: The Architectural Press, 106.

21 Smithson, P. (1961), 'Class of 47', *Casabella*, (250), (April), 27 (translation, vii).

22 Pevsner, N., 'The anti-pioneers', radio talk 1966–7, quoted in W. Curtis (1994), *Denys Lasdun*, London: Phaidon, 78; *Architectural Association Journal* (1962), (January), 158.

23 *Architectural Review* (1963), **134**, (800), (October), 232.

24 Councillor T. Dan Smith, *Newcastle Housing and Town Planning Committee*, December 1959.

25 Banham, R. (1960), *Theory and Design in the First Machine Age*, London: The Architectural Press, 133.

26 Smithson, A., and Smithson, P. (1967), *Urban Structuring*, London: Studio Vista, esp. 50–9.

27 Sloman, A.E. (1964), *A University in the Making*, London: BBC, (April), 24.

28 *Archigram, Symposium zur Asstellung* (1997), Vienna: Ritter Verlag, 13 and 55; Cook, P. et al. (eds) (1991), *Archigram*, Basel: Birkhäuser Verlag; Crompton, D. (ed) (1998), *Concerning Archigram*, London: Archigram Archives.

29 Stirling, J. (1975), *Buildings and Projects 1950–1974*, London: Thames and Hudson, 68.

30 Harwood, E. (1994), 'Prestige pancakes', *Twentieth Century Architecture 1, Industrial Architecture*, London: Twentieth Century Society, 78–89.

31 Glendinning, M., and Muthesius, S. (1994), *Tower Block*, London: Yale University Press, 313–16.

32 Wigfall, V. (1997), *Thamesmead: Back to the Future*, London: Greenwich Community College Press.

33 *Architectural Review* (1967), **141**, (839), (January), 9–10; *Architectural Review* (1968), **142**, (851), (January), 9.

34 *Architectural Review* (1976), **159**, (947), 3.

35 Mikellides, B. (ed) (1980), *Architecture for People*, London: Studio Vista.

36 MacKean, J. (1989), *Learning from Segal*, Basel: Birkhäuser Verlag, 168–74.

CHAPTER 3
DEFINING AN APPROACH: A METHODOLOGY FOR THE REPAIR OF POST-WAR BUILDINGS

Susan Macdonald

The listing of post-war buildings raises particular philosophical and technical questions, but so far no specific guidance for the care and conservation of these buildings has been produced. English Heritage has been working on a case-by-case basis, using the existing codes of practice as a guide. Because we are at the cutting edge, there is no previous experience to draw upon; nor are there models to follow. English Heritage's post-war listing programme was one of the first in the world, but policies have only recently begun to be developed to include the specific issues raised by the listing of buildings from this era.

Attitudes to conservation are constantly reassessed and redefined according to the cultural climate and the technology available. The recognition of the value of post-war heritage requires a reassessment of the existing conservation philosophies; new methodologies must be found to tackle the specific problems of protecting these buildings. As the Government's adviser on heritage matters, English Heritage must set standards, find ways to resolve the more controversial issues, identify appropriate repair methods and break free from the control exercised by the repair industry over what can or cannot be done. In short, we must think more creatively about how to care for these buildings. Otherwise the icons and the yet-unrecognized heritage of the post-war era will not survive for the enjoyment of future generations (Figure 3.1).[1]

This paper revisits the principles of repair that form the basis of English Heritage's philosophical and practical approach to the conservation of buildings of special architectural or historical significance. It discusses deficiencies, highlights conflicts and reinforces the reasons why these principles remain relevant for buildings of any period, including those built after World War II.

Principles and practice

English Heritage's principles are outlined in Christopher Brereton's book *The Repair of Historic Buildings: Advice on Principles and Methods*.[2] This was written before the post-war listing programme began, and revised before the programme was completed. It includes a short, now outdated, section on reinforced concrete, but no references to, or illustrations of, post-war buildings. *Planning Policy Guidance: Planning and the Historic Environment* (PPG 15)[3] does not mention

*Figure 3.1   St Peter's Seminary, Cardross by Gillespie Kidd and Coia (1962) was aban-
doned in the mid-1980s and is now in a semi-derelict state. (Elain Harwood)*

any of the principal building materials of the twentieth century and contains no reference to post-
war buildings. In a very late draft of the controversial British Standard on principles of building
conservation, twentieth-century architecture was ridiculed and denigrated and considered to have
no cultural value. There is no mention of any conflicts that might arise when applying these
principles to the conservation of buildings from the more recent past. It could be assumed, therefore, that there is general consensus that all these documents adequately accommodate the range
of issues faced by an owner, manager or professional caring for a listed post-war building. Clearly
this is not the case, as the debate at international and local conferences indicates.

The failure of the key British conservation documents to address issues specific to post-war
buildings means that it is necessary to return for guidance to the more general principles contained within these and other well-known international documents, such as the Venice and Burra
Charters.[4] As a starting point these established principles are valid for any building type from
any period. Many of the case studies contained within this book embrace the existing principles,
but at the same time acknowledge that sometimes insurmountable and new problems require
innovative technical and philosophical solutions.

Conservation is demanding – it demands good practice. Good practice and conservation go
together. For most building owners, listing is a process that is perceived to reduce their rights to
develop or even repair the property in any manner they may wish. Listing is seen to threaten
higher maintenance and big repair bills. However, it has been shown that listing can increase a
property's value, and grant aid or heritage lottery funds have helped many owners look after
their buildings better than they were able to before they were listed.

Understanding the building

Common to all the conservation charters and treaties is the idea that any work to a listed building should be based on a detailed knowledge of the building to be conserved. Understanding a building's social and historical context, design and construction, and use of materials is fundamental to establishing its significance – an essential first step in any project. This will enable decisions regarding materials, design and aesthetics to be made, and if necessary balanced, so that the significance of the building is not diminished.

A conservation management plan, which identifies the building's significance and provides a forward policy for managing future changes, is the most useful way to ensure that all the relevant information has been assembled and synthesized so that logical and consistent decisions can be made on how the building is to be repaired and maintained in the future.[5] The forward policy establishes ways of managing change without compromising significance. The importance of the conservation plan has been brought to the fore by the Heritage Lottery Fund's (HLF) requests for a conservation plan in some instances as accompaniment to larger applications for funding. The HLF's commitment to the conservation plan methodology has been indicated by its willingness in certain instances to provide funds for the preparation of a conservation plan.

Understanding a building's materials and construction techniques, its prior use and maintenance history, how and why change has occurred, together with a sound knowledge of the potential repair options, is essential if appropriate conservation strategies are to be determined. This principle is the basis of both good conservation and good practice. English Heritage will query proposals for works to any building when there is concern that they will detract from or obscure the significance of the building. In the majority of problematic post-war cases, it is fair to say that the difficulty has been caused by the failure of the applicant to demonstrate that the building has been properly investigated, any problems clearly understood, and that the proposed repairs address the causes of the problems and not merely the symptoms.

Figure 3.2 illustrates a grade II listed building that has problems with its mosaic cladding. This prompted a proposal to apply an elastomeric coating over the mosaic, which was intended to prevent further deterioration, supposedly caused by the deterioration of the underlying concrete. English Heritage queried the proposal on the basis that the coating

Figure 3.2 The detachment of the mosaic cladding to the concrete is largely due to poor detailing around the balconies. (Elain Harwood)

would dramatically alter the appearance of the building, would require regular replacement and – most importantly – the cause of the mosaic detachment had not been correctly diagnosed and the proposed action did not address the problem. Subsequent investigations guided by English Heritage proved the concrete substrate to be in excellent condition. The mosaic detachment was found to be primarily a result of poor detailing around the balconies and parapets, resulting in water ingress. The consequent freeze–thaw action had dislodged the render on which the mosaic was laid from the concrete substrate. Neither this nor any of the other decay mechanisms characteristic of mosaic-clad concrete that are discussed in Part Three of this book would have been ameliorated by the application of a protective coating to the mosaic. The issues, which are far more complex than indicated here, have still not been fully resolved. Had the right consultants been involved and the necessary investigation work undertaken at the outset, a more satisfactory solution could have been identified and carried out much sooner.

Identifying problems

Correctly identifying the cause of decay is key to any successful repair. The successful identification of problems and the development of appropriate repair strategies depend on obtaining the right expertise. Architects are increasingly co-ordinators of specialists. The importance of structural engineers in the development of building materials and systems during the post-war era means that their advice will almost always be needed before repairs are begun. Industrialized system building relied on many additional specialists – licensed concrete or cladding contractors for instance – and specialist advice from someone conversant with the relevant materials and their construction techniques, and preferably someone with empathy for the aims of conservation, will probably be necessary when considering repairs. A product manufacturer, contractor, or even trade association's technical advisory service may be extremely helpful, but it should be remembered that they have a vested interest in using particular repair systems or products. Specialist contractors and product manufacturers can, however, play an important role in the development of site trials. Free investigations are rarely useful, and it is much better to formalize arrangements. Many traditional building conservation projects involve an extended team of specialists – timber consultants, paint, plaster and stone conservators and so on. Unfortunately many post-war buildings that English Heritage has recently been involved with were not being cared for by such comprehensive teams, but by a sole architect or surveyor, or even the building owner, with the product salesperson providing the only specialist input into the project.

The fact that the construction of these buildings is still in living memory offers the potential to understand them in a way that has never been possible before. The architect may still be able to explain the building's *raison d'être*, the construction process, why certain methods and materials were selected, the original maintenance expectations and so on. Drawings and specifications are valuable resources. The history of a building's maintenance, past problems and subsequent repair works also provides useful information for identifying problems and choosing repair options, and can inform future maintenance programmes. However, it is important to guard against the temptation to use this information to recreate or restore the building as new, rather than to acknowledge its history. Conservation is about managing change and it may be necessary to accommodate new requirements if a building's use is to continue in the future. Sir Denys Lasdun was consulted during the repairs to his Royal College of Physicians (1960–64). This ensured that decisions regarding the fabric and new design elements and details were made respecting the original design philosophy: the source of mosaics, for example, was easily located for the repairs. In contrast, Lasdun was not involved in the recent modifications to the interior of the National Theatre (1965), which he felt were invasive and compromised the building's spatial qualities. The architect's original maintenance plans for the building, which included a five-year cleaning cycle, did, however, inform the decision to clean the concrete, revealing the very high quality finish so important to the building's architectural character. Decisions regarding new requirements need to be balanced with the building's significance.

Avoiding unnecessary damage

Perhaps the most important principle described in the English Heritage document is avoiding unnecessary damage, which includes the concepts of conserving as found, minimum intervention and reversibility. It is the application of this principle that has prompted more controversy that any other. The seemingly short lifespan of some modern materials and the way they were detailed may make it difficult to conserve as found and with minimum intervention. But arguments about material and aesthetic authenticity are not confined to post-war buildings – a surprising number of similar dilemmas have been posed by buildings from other periods. Understanding the building and what makes it important ensures that decisions regarding the fabric, such as whether to repair or restore, are much more rational.

It is interesting to compare some well-known examples to contrast attitudes to conservation when dealing with buildings from different periods. Uppark, a National Trust property built in 1685–90 was devastated by fire in 1989. It was re-opened a few years ago following extensive and painstaking reconstruction. The decision to restore was taken on the basis of its importance as a fine seventeenth-century country house with an extensive collection of furniture and paintings. Despite a lively debate about the validity of reconstructing the house, there was overwhelming support for it. Compare with this the public reaction to the Zonnestraal Sanatorium in the Netherlands, a tuberculosis clinic designed by Jan Duiker and built 1926–8. It was abandoned in 1982 and fell into a ruinous state. The cultural importance of this building as an icon of the Modern Movement has only recently secured its repair or reconstruction, after a long battle by the building's supporters. There has been much debate over whether to reconstruct the building and thus retain the architect's philosophy of 'spiritual economy' at the expense of material authenticity, or to repair it, faithfully replicating the experimental materials and construction techniques that have proven so problematic and have resulted in its near ruination within sixty years. During the time the work has been under discussion, a period of nearly ten years, concrete repair technology has moved on, and now offers electrochemical methods that make it possible to conserve rather than replace the existing fabric. The work will still involve extensive reconstruction with the introduction of new materials, but the fact that new technology has ensured the structure is now salvageable has made it possible to consider saving it. Unfortunately, we do not yet place enough value on our post-war buildings to even consider reconstruction as a viable option – as attested to by the perilous state of St Peter's Seminary, Cardross, or the demise of the Brynmawr Rubber Factory of 1948–52 by the Architect's Co-operative.

The frequency of repair and the level of intervention depend on the lifespan of the materials and the technical efficiency of the design. There are durability problems with some of the materials used in the post-war period, due to limited knowledge of their long-term durability at the time they were specified, the importance of speed of construction and economy generally, and the lack of maintenance that seems to be common to many post-war buildings. That there might be durability problems with concrete was not properly acknowledged until the 1970s. The plantation-grown softwoods used for the windows of large-scale housing schemes have proved far less durable than the timber used in the past. The sealants that many cladding systems rely on as their defence against water penetration may not have been regularly maintained or replaced. There are precedents for the regular replacement of historic fabric once it has exceeded its lifespan. A stone slate roof, for example, will last at least a hundred years, thatch or shingle somewhat less, and a flat, membrane roof has its own lifespan. It is accepted and common practice to improve or amend details that are known to be technically defective, or to replace materials when they come up for repair, in order to lengthen their future life. Such changes should aim not to change the building's character, or detract from its essence or significance.

Many post-war materials had short-lived production periods. For example, the special glass used in many cladding systems may no longer be available. The Muroglas used to clad Chamberlin Powell and Bon's Bousfield School of 1965 was discontinued by Pilkingtons in the early 1970s (Figure 3.3). English Heritage's principles have always required that the life of the existing fabric be extended as long as reasonably possible. But once production of a particular material has ceased it becomes difficult to 'conserve as found' and to 'replace like with like'. However, it is important not to dismiss this principle too quickly. There is a fundamental flaw in the argument for preserving aesthetic over material authenticity. It is difficult and expensive to replicate an original aesthetic when the materials and construction techniques are obsolete. Replacement with similar (but not identical) materials and details results in the gradual erosion of authentic fabric and eventually the original will be so diluted that its value will have changed completely. Attempts to retain original fabric are far

Figure 3.3   Chamberlin Powell and Bon's Bousfield School, Chelsea (1956). (Elain Harwood)

Figure 3.4 Alexandra Road Housing by Neave Brown (1978), shown here during repair in 1997. (Elain Harwood)

more likely to ensure that the essence of the original is retained. The difficulties of sourcing scarce materials such as certain stone types, early window glass and so on are, however, frequently encountered in conservation practice.

'Less is more' is a catchphrase commonly cited by conservation practitioners. Many post-war buildings, however, have undergone radical interventions due to the technical requirements of the repair methods. This is not always necessary, as the following example illustrates. Alexandra Road housing in Camden, designed by Neave Brown, and completed in 1978, is listed grade II*. A large repair programme was carried out during 1997–8. Unfortunately, Brown has not been involved in the repair programme, and the original specification, which is available, has not been used to inform the work. The architect's specification identifies the original cement and aggregates to make the concrete, and describes the importance of the workmanship in achieving the required finish to the concrete, which is so fundamental to the design quality or what Alan Powers describes in his paper as the essence of the building.

When the repairs were first discussed, the intention was to restrict the works to those that were absolutely necessary, and to attempt traditional concrete repairs, matching the original concrete as closely as possible. English Heritage approved a number of sample repair panels in 1993, but subsequent changes in the repair mix, poor workmanship and the failure to limit repairs to what was technically necessary, have had a disastrous visual impact (Figure 3.4). All defects in the concrete were cut out to the lines of the original board marks to minimize visual disruption, and repaired using a proprietary bagged product. However, cutting-out included even the smallest rust stains left by small clips and nails, which were causing no long-term damage to the concrete, resulting in a total number of some 11,000 patch repairs. Aiming for minimum intervention would have reduced the visual disruption and the cost of the work considerably. The very disappointing results have less to do with the technical difficulties of achieving like-for-like repairs, and more to do with poor specification and workmanship, and poor communication. A conservation management plan would have been invaluable in establishing appropriate levels of repair and intervention before any of the work was undertaken.

Using proven repair techniques

The principle of using only proven repair techniques can be difficult to observe when many of the repair systems for modern materials – insofar as these exist at all – are fairly new, and there is no information on their long-term performance or any negative side effects. Decisions as to whether to use a repair method that does not have a proven track record depend on the importance of the material in question and what the alternatives are. The recent overcladding of the mosaic ribs of the Metropolitan Cathedral in Liverpool (Frederick Gibberd, 1967), for instance, is considered an interim measure. It is hoped that by the time the glass-reinforced plastic is due for replacement there will be better ways of retaining and repairing the mosaic cladding.

Maintenance

Maintenance is essential for any building, and the misconception that modern buildings are maintenance-free has resulted in the premature failure of the fabric of many post-war buildings. The maintenance cycle, like the repair cycle, is determined by the nature of the materials and the design of the building. Maintenance is a cost-effective way of prolonging the life of a building: well-planned and regular maintenance can extend the period between major repair programmes considerably.

Just as there are precedents for dealing with materials of a limited lifespan for ancient buildings, there are also means of coping with difficult maintenance problems for older buildings. The rainwater pipes at the seventeenth-century Chastelton House, West Oxfordshire, owned by the National Trust, require inspection and clearing out on an almost weekly basis, despite discreet modifications to introduce an overflow should they become blocked. The rainwater outlets on the roof of Denys Lasdun's Art Gallery at King's College, Cambridge (1964), suffer from similar problems, but in this case there is not the same willingness on the part of the owners to resource such a high level of maintenance. This means that a more radical intervention is required to solve the difficult drainage problem posed by the flat roof, which is surrounded by glazing. The solution likely to be implemented is to introduce internal rainwater pipes across the glazed edges of the gallery at ceiling level, which will be clearly visible.

One of the problems threatening the replacement of the large aluminium frame windows at Bousfield school was the difficulty of reopening them after the long winter months, when the felt runners stuck and often become detached on the first opening (Figure 3.3, *page 37*). Improvements to the runners and regular cleaning of the tracks is a much cheaper way of dealing with the problem and saving the windows. The perceived energy loss due to the large expanse of glazing could be solved by the discreet insertion of insulation within the section of the steel frame below the windows, between the coloured glass panels and the internal wall lining. Upgrading the original and inadequate heating would improve comfort levels further. The windows of Powell and Moya's Brasenose College (1959) were also threatened with replacement, for the same reason. The ground-level tracks tend to fill with dirt, causing the windows to stick. Regularly brushing out the tracks and an improvement to the runners will prevent the loss of these important architectural features.

Maintenance must include the maintenance of repairs. This is especially important for some of the repair techniques developed for modern materials such as concrete. A repair strategy that relies on the effectiveness of a coating, for instance, depends on the maintenance of that coating and its regular replacement. The long-term effectiveness of many modern repair methods is as yet unknown and therefore continuous monitoring of their performance should be built into the maintenance programme.

It should be established before a repair programme begins whether there will be money for maintenance. It is futile to carry out a repair using a technique that relies on regular maintenance if there will not be the money to sustain it. The fact that none of the grant-giving bodies can provide money for maintenance unfortunately does little to promote this approach.

Conclusions

English Heritage's principles reflect the current state of knowledge and technology and are open to review and change. They are fairly broad and, used with lateral thinking and creativity, are useful and important guides to the care and conservation of any building type, including those from the post-war era. Principles are not recipes; they need to be applied on a case-by-case basis with the building itself as the guiding factor. The discipline offered by the conservation management plan methodology is invaluable, in that it requires a building's significance to be determined at the outset and then ensures that any works retain, restore or enhance those values. As more buildings are listed and come up for repair, collective experience will grow and the relevance of these principles will be tested further. Ideas will no doubt change as our understanding of the buildings, materials and decay mechanisms grows, and as repair techniques are developed to address conservation aims.

References

1   English Heritage (1996), *Developing Guidelines for the Management of Listed Buildings*, London: English Heritage.

2   Brereton, C. (1994), *The Repair of Historic Buildings: Advice on Principles and Methods*, London: English Heritage.

3   Department of the Environment (1994), *Planning Policy Guidance Note 15: Historic Buildings and Conservation Areas*, London: HMSO.

4   ICOMOS Australia (1999), *Charter for the Conservation of Places of Cultural Significance* ('The Burra Charter'), Sydney: Australia ICOMOS; ICOMOS (1966), *International Charter for the Conservation and Restoration of Monuments and Sites* ('The Venice Charter'), Venice: ICOMOS.

5   Kerr, J.S. (1990), *The Conservation Plan*, National Trust of Australia (NSW); NSW Heritage Office and the Department of Urban Affairs and Planning (1996), *Conservation Management Documents*, Sydney: DUAP.

PART TWO

STRUCTURAL
ISSUES,
MATERIALS
AND SERVICES

CHAPTER 4
TOWARDS THE FULLY INTEGRATED BUILDING: SERVICING POST-WAR BUILDINGS

Jeff Parkes

When English Heritage asked me to contribute to the series of lectures on the preservation of post-war buildings, I was caught in something of a dilemma. As a services engineer, I spend a lot of my time replacing systems, not conserving them. The more I thought about the subject, the more it appeared to me that it was necessary to define the key word 'preservation'. One dictionary definition is 'to stop something decaying, to maintain and repair'. This reference to 'decay' is very apropos. Services systems do decay; like other mechanical engines, they contain moving parts – pumps, fans and pistons – which wear out. They suffer erosion from fluids travelling through pipes and ducts, and corrosion that makes pipes rust. And, of course, they suffer physical damage: grilles get battered and pipes are pulled from their brackets. It is therefore hardly surprising that a thirty-year-old services system is considered a senior citizen.

If thirty years is a good lifespan, then a building with a life of fifty years will have its services systems replaced at least once in its life. A listed building with a lifespan that could be considerably longer could have many changes of system. Hence attempting to preserve the building as a whole will ultimately lead to replacement for the vast majority of services systems. Moreover, as the services are a fundamental part of the way a building is used, any building refurbishment is likely to entail the replacement of large parts of the services system – and any need to refurbish the services system is likely to lead to considerable replacement of building components. All of which leads me to the conclusion that the words 'preservation', 'refurbishment' and 'replacement' are interchangeable in the context of services systems.

When, due to decay, services systems need changing, we need to address some important issues:

- accepting the need to change (refurbish or replace) in order to preserve;
- minimizing the intervention or builders' work needed when services are replaced;
- ensuring that buildings are used; a used services system is likely to have a longer life, especially if it is well maintained;
- the possibility of preserving, albeit in a non-working manner, services systems of historical importance;
- the part, if any, that the energy debate has had, and will have in the future.

I propose to discuss the above through a consideration of the history of services systems over the post-war period, followed by a case history that illustrates commonly recurring difficulties in refurbishment of buildings. Finally, I shall look at how the availability of energy in the post-war period has affected services design, and how it may affect it in the future.

Development of services since the war

The post-1945 period has been significant for building services, not only because it is the first period in the history of buildings in which services became extensively used, but also because of the acceleration of services development over that period. This development can be traced through three distinct periods: 1945 to late 1950s; late 1950s to early 1970s; and early 1970s to early 1990s.

Before we look at each, it must be added that there is a fourth period, from the early 1990s to the present, in which the design and installation of services systems has been affected by a need to conserve energy, not for financial or fuel conservation reasons, but for environmental protection. This period will be mentioned only briefly, as it is unlikely that these buildings will require active preservation so early in their lives.

The immediate post-war period (1945 to late 1950s) saw a need to build quickly to replace bombed-out structures in city centres and to house an expanding population. Architectural styles started to reflect new ideas, particularly in relation to social structures and housing. The techniques of construction were changing in response to the need to build quickly and cheaply. Prefabrication became the norm. The traditional architecture of stone or brick masonry facades was supplemented – even supplanted – by frame buildings faced with concrete panels and large expanses of glass. For services engineers, this was highly significant. Buildings were becoming far more responsive to the external environment: large areas of glass led to high summer heat gains, high winter heat losses and areas of discomfort around the perimeter glazing.

The services industry found it difficult to respond to these changes. The methods to analyse such thermal responses did not exist in general practice. The industry relied on installing traditional heating systems with openable windows for ventilation. Where air conditioning and ventilation was used, it was done in a limited way. Quite simply, there was not the space to install such large services systems; although plant rooms of the period are generous, riser space and, in particular, slab-to-slab heights are low.

The industry itself still tended to be craft-driven. Consulting engineers existed, but contractors undertook a large proportion of design work. Most graduates came from a mechanical engineering background and it was very common for any design office to be staffed by technicians rather than engineering graduates. Common design practice of the time was for the architect to design a building and hand fairly advanced drawings to the mechanical and electrical designers, who made the services fit. The buildings simply housed services rather than integrating them.

For services engineers, the late 1950s to the early 1970s was a catching-up period. The fundamental tools and research that allowed the calculation of rapid thermal response were developed, significant improvements were made in our understanding of the factors involved in creating a comfortable environment, and systems capable of responding to the new building forms were developed. It now became common to install cooling and ventilation systems. In this transition period, service engineering was developing on all fronts. The quality of engineers was improving. Designers began to use more sophisticated calculation methods, although they still relied upon manual calculation using what can only be described as 'fudge factors' to reduce the amount of iterative calculation (something that would later be done with ease by computers). It was only at the very end of this period that electronic calculators became available; computers were rare. More significantly, building professionals were recognizing that buildings could house the more sophisticated levels of servicing, such as air conditioning, only if more space was made available. However, simply providing more space to house services has never been something designers or clients have willingly done. It became obvious that clear and detailed study was needed to integrate services with structure and architecture in order to optimize volume. It was during this period that multi-discipline working came into vogue.

The oil crises of the 1970s significantly changed the way buildings were designed. Suddenly fuel was in short supply and hence expensive. The services industry set about responding to this by finding ways of reducing energy consumption. Two primary means were used in the 1970s and 1980s: constructing well-insulated buildings with small windows, and developing and using services systems with higher efficiencies, recovering energy where possible.

Services became more important, more extensive and larger. As buildings began to be designed to incorporate services, the emphasis turned to co-ordination and integration. In order to make these more intensively serviced buildings work, more space was allocated, particularly for ductwork in ceilings and electrical distribution under floors. This was further amplified through the building boom of the 1980s, during which increased use of IT led to yet further demands for space. The raised floor became an accepted part of building design.

In some respects, this period can be subdivided into the 1970s and 1980s. The 1970s focused more on energy reduction. Although system design was the primary method used to save energy, building fabric design also played its part. Buildings were designed using less glass, higher-mass facades and better levels of insulation. Few of these buildings were architecturally distinguished, yet their reason for existing, the conservation of energy, was often extremely elegant in conception. Building design, driven by services design, started to revert to a more traditional approach where buildings were built as environmental modifiers, not as purely functional or aesthetic objects.

The 1980s in many respects started to reverse this process, as energy became more available and cheaper, thanks to North Sea oil. The optimism and building boom of the period fuelled self-indulgent buildings. Services specifications were driven increasingly upward in the relentless push to attract larger and larger commercial rental values. As an example, allowances for electrical loads in offices started around the 15 watts per square metre region at the beginning of the period, increasing to 30–35 watts per square metre at the end. The excuse for such measures was a perceived need to service an increasing IT demand. In fact, today's IT systems consume far less power than their predecessors of the 1080s – but whether any building ever consumed in excess of 25 watts per square metre is highly questionable. The net effect of this over-indulgence was larger services, and although the industry had developed sophisticated methods of construction and integration, the areas provided for services tended to be generous. Typical floor voids would be 150 mm minimum, with ceiling voids of 450–600 mm. When these buildings come up for refurbishment in the next decade, replacement of services should be fairly easy.

To round off this brief history we need to mention the current period, the 1990s. During most of the period, the economy was in severe depression, and the building industry was badly hit. On the other hand, energy was cheap and the introduction of affordable computers allowed the calculation of previously difficult analysis to be done with ease. A new approach to design was adopted. Many buildings of the 1990s are pure external climatic modifiers. Put more crudely, buildings and their services systems are increasingly interdependent. The building fabric now acts as the primary environmental modifier, be it through increased thermal mass, passive daylight, solar control or natural ventilation. The services systems are often very simple, virtually like those of the 1950s: radiators with natural ventilation or small mechanical air systems. It is now quite common to have no false ceiling and for services to be exposed. These buildings will require very careful handling when refurbishment time comes around, due to the interdependence between the fabric and the system.

The development of buildings and their services systems in the post-war era, is analogous to a human being's development in reverse. An adult person is completely independent; there are still links to the parents, but the generations are not reliant upon each other (1945 – late 1950s). As a child, the person is an independent being, yet the relationship to the parent is one of dependency (1960s). As a baby, whilst the parent and child are separate beings, the child is totally dependent upon the parent (1970s and 1980s). In the womb there is absolute dependency and the child and mother are intrinsically linked (1990s).

The industry now faces a dual challenge: firstly, to design new buildings to conserve energy and secondly to refurbish many of the post-war buildings from the 1945 to 1972 era.

Refurbishment and revitalisation of post-war buildings

Until recently, many post-war buildings were demolished rather than refurbished. This is now changing. Designers and owners of buildings are recognizing that it is more energy efficient to reuse an existing building than it is to rebuild it. The embodied energy in building materials is great and should be retained wherever possible. Reuse of a building is quite easy in pre-war buildings, but the immediate post-war buildings of the 1950s and 1960s are a different matter. Owners, developers and designers have specific concerns that often lead them to question the viability of reusing a post-war building. Typically these primary concerns are:

- the building fabric: generally over-glazed, under-insulated, and very draughty;
- the restricted floor-to-ceiling heights available into which today's services can be installed;
- noise and vehicle exhaust pollution, especially in city centres.

These recurring themes appear whenever refurbishment or reuse of post-war buildings is considered. Taking into account the anticipated maximum lifespan of services systems (around thirty years), it is clear that most buildings built between 1945 and 1973 will be in need of refurbishment, if they have not already been refurbished. Many fine examples from this period have been under-used, unused or simply demolished due to the perception that they cannot be serviced to modern standards. This is not the case. With effort, co-ordinated design, teamwork and a little imagination, most buildings can be revitalized.

One such project was undertaken in 1997–8. It is on a very prominent central London site and demonstrates some solutions to the recurring problems of refurbishment. The building was built at the end of the 1950s. The floor plan is around eighteen metres wide by forty metres long with six floors and a basement car park. The roof is flat with an asphalt topping. Two separate, single-storey plant rooms are built above roof level. These housed lift motors, tanks and fans. The external facade consists of single glazed metal casement windows, occupying around 45% of the facade area. The cladding system is stone panelling. The internal floors were hollow pot supported in a concrete frame.

Built as an office, it had been occupied until the mid-1990s. The building remained vacant for several years, becoming increasingly derelict inside. The market perception was: good building; good site; services a problem. Modern offices have demands that were unknown in the 1950s, demands that tend to relate to services (IT, to name just one). This particular building suffered from a common problem, low slab-to-slab heights (Figure 4.1). One could have argued that there was more value in the site than in the building; however, though the building was not listed, its demolition would have been controversial.

In 1997 it was purchased with the intention of converting it into a hotel. Hotels can make excellent use of buildings from this era, as no raised floor is needed and services in the bedrooms tend to be vertically distributed. After purchase a potential tenant interested in leasing the building as a modern refurbished office space approached the owner. Plans were changed and we embarked upon the design of an office. The recurring problems hit us immediately. Firstly, the floor to soffit dimension was only 2,812 mm. The tenant required a 2,515 mm floor-to-ceiling height. As the potential tenant was an electronic publisher, the IT demands were going to be considerable and the occupancy levels high. This increased the cooling load to such an extent that air conditioning became a necessity.

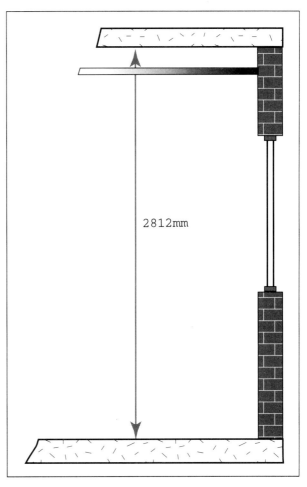

Figure 4.1 Original floor-to-ceiling height. (Jeff Parkes)

Secondly, the original openable windows could not be opened onto the external environment, which was very noisy and highly polluted by road traffic. Our approach was firstly to understand how the existing services worked, not because any of them could have been reused, but to point to how we could develop our ideas. The original design had induction units around the perimeter with large vertical risers on each perimeter column. Although there was a false ceiling, it was negligible. Because the building was originally designed to have openable windows, there were no fresh air or exhaust systems. The problem for us was that we needed to seal windows and introduce fresh air mechanically, but this was going to be very difficult with the restrictions upon the ceiling void. Typically the ceiling depth requirement quoted where air conditioning is installed in the ceilings is 450 mm. As the tenant needed underfloor electrical distribution, a raised floor was considered a necessity. Generally raised floors have a height of 150 mm. A floor-to-soffit height of 2,812 mm, less a 450 mm false ceiling and 150 mm raised floor, resulted in a floor-to-ceiling height of only 2,212 mm; this was unacceptable to the potential tenant and a deal breaker.

Our first step towards a solution was to recognize and explain to the client and design team the relationship between ceiling depth and vertical risers. If you have a generous ceiling void, you need fewer risers, as the ductwork that branches from a riser into the ceiling void can be large and hence serve a greater floor area. The converse is also true: the smaller the ceiling void, the smaller the branch duct and the more risers that are needed. In this building we needed to have many small risers. This was achieved not by inserting five or six additional risers in the centre of the building, but from following the original design intent of having many risers around the perimeter.

The original design from the late 1950s utilized a perimeter induction system, with risers at intermediate column positions. Induction systems are rarely used these days because of their high cost, and   relatively poor energy efficiency, and in particular because they require noisy room units. However, our modern replacement system was of the same generic type, i.e. one

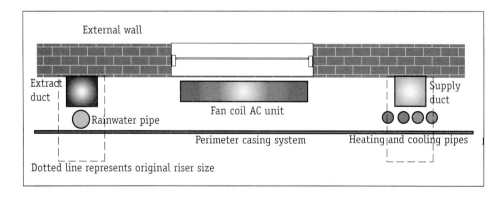

Figure 4.2   Perimeter AC system. (Jeff Parkes)

that could be placed around the perimeter in the same location as the existing system, allowing reuse of the original riser locations. In fact, because of our integrated approach and rerouting of rainwater pipes (the flat roof was re-asphalted and a syphonic rainwater system installed, reducing downpipe sizes considerably), we were able to make the risers significantly smaller.

With the air conditioning system on the perimeter, and its ductwork, pipework and electrical feeds also along the perimeter in vertical shafts, the ceiling void could be considerably reduced (Figure 4.2). The only ceiling void elements were lights and fire alarm systems. Even so, we still had to claw back every millimetre. The architect found a ceiling system that could be installed into a 37 mm depth, including the support and framing system. The luminaires were high-efficiency fluorescents of only 50 mm overall depth. The net result was more lettable area, a modern well-ventilated and cooled building, with the new air conditioning units replacing the old with minimal disruption to the original appearance, and minimum builders' work intervention.

This still left the question of electrical underfloor distribution. Buildings of the 1950s very rarely had any form of floor electrical system; those that did, generally embedded trunking in a screed or thick floor finish (such as parquet). The insertion of a raised floor poses several questions, the main one being what to do at staircases and doors. If a floor level is raised, the stair landings need adjustment. One approach is to ramp up and down to the stairs; this is often done, but rarely satisfactorily. Our approach was quite different. Over the years we have been looking at this problem and have found that buildings of this era often have floor screeds in the order of 50–70 mm. On top of that, they generally have an allowance for a reasonably thick floor covering. If you remove the screed and replace it with a raised floor, the making-up at the staircase can be eliminated. Removing screeds needs careful consideration, particularly by the structural and fire engineers. In this case, we found that the limiting factor was fire separation. The screed played no part in the structural stability. Fire engineers analysed the system and put forward a detailed analysis of the existing slab to show that it complied with the building regulations. This integrated design approach allowed us to remove the screed and free up the area.

The screed is about 50–75 mm high and raised floors are conventionally 100–150 mm high; that is, they are if you want them to be (Figure 4.3, *overleaf*). Modern cable management is becoming smaller. For example, why install cable tray for the client's IT wiring? He never uses it. Simply paint a route on the concrete floor and let him lay wiring on the floor, giving him a wider area of lay and hence, less floor void height. The raised floor we installed was 68 mm high. This type of thinking requires a change in attitude by many developers' advisers, who believe that 150 mm is a necessity, when really it is simply an outmoded guideline; 100 mm should be the norm.

The above example illustrates a single project. As all buildings have differences, the solutions proposed are not a panacea for all ills. The important aspects that should be drawn from the example are as follows.

▪ Don't take anything for granted, question and challenge perceived norms, e.g. the height of raised floors, luminaire and ceiling thicknesses.

- Work hard on your solutions, involve all disciplines and don't try to work in isolation, e.g. the removal of the screed involved services, structural and fire engineers as well as the architect in detailed studies.
- Study the original design concepts. Invariably you will never have all of the original technical information on the existing construction. The original designers had this information and probably embedded solutions to your problems within their designs, e.g. the reuse of perimeter vertical distribution.

In addition, you will find some recurring (if generic) elements in all services refurbishments:

- The plant rooms will be large enough for reuse; in fact they will often be too large. Generally plant areas will be in basements, or occasionally in rooftop plant rooms, and will be linked to a series of risers, often of adequate square metreage, but in the wrong aspect ratio. For example, you may need a one square metre riser sized at 1,500 × 650 mm to install ductwork into. The original riser, while it may be one square metre, may have been sized predominantly for pipework and be (say) 3,000 × 350 mm.

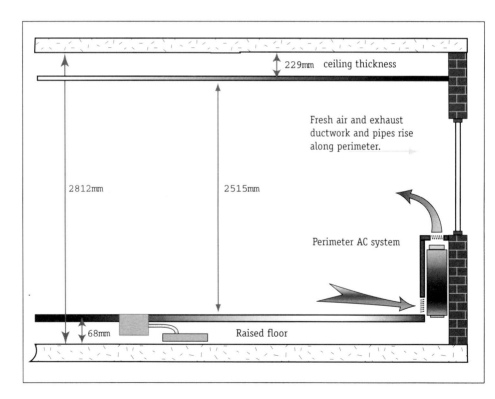

Figure 4.3   Final floor-to-ceiling heights following refurbishment. (Jeff Parkes)

- The provision of external cooling plant (chillers) will be difficult. If cooling was originally installed, there would probably have been a cooling tower. If not, there will be either nothing, or small plant scattered over roof areas. The provision of roof cooling plant often becomes a planning issue.
- There will not be a raised floor and any floor electrical system will be laid in the screed.
- The ceiling voids will be negligible.
- The overall slab-to-slab dimension will be around 2,600–3,200 mm.

Assuming that plant can be housed on the roof, it is clear that the location of plant will generally present few technical problems, or require much work on the fabric of the building. The difficulties come from the vertical and horizontal distribution. Contrary to perceived notion, vertical distribution is not limited by the size and number of risers that can be fitted into the space available, but by

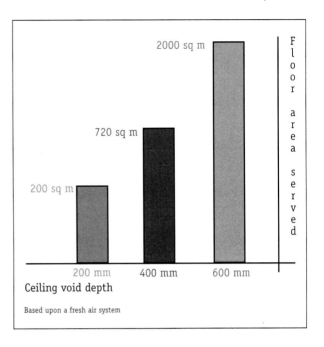

Figure 4.4 Floor area served in relation to ceiling void height. (Jeff Parkes)

the horizontal distribution. This is a very important technical issue, which must be understood. Figure 4.4 shows the floor area that can be served from a single vertical riser to different ceiling void depths (for a fresh air, not all air system). Put simply, the smaller the ceiling void, the smaller the branch duct from the riser, hence the less air it carries and the smaller the floor area it will serve.

In existing buildings with restricted ceiling voids, the number of risers often becomes ridiculously high and you either have to change the servicing strategy, use numerous small, easily hidden, strategically positioned risers, or increase ceiling void depth.

As mentioned at the beginning of the paper, services do not last forever, but require replacement in maximum thirty-year cycles. I believe that buildings should be used; they are living organisms and the most successful buildings are those that have served their occupants well. By continually upgrading the services, you are prolonging the life of buildings. The art of services replacement and refurbishment lies in minimizing the effects upon the fabric of the building, i.e. insertion. Some of the ideas discussed above illustrate that this can be done. It is, after all, a logical approach to reduce works to the fabric; not only does it conserve the aesthetic of the building, but it also makes refurbishing and giving extra life to the building cheaper. Most developers and building owners know and accept that services need frequent replacement. What often kills their plans is high levels of associated structural and building works. A good doctrine is to accept that services need replacement, plan for this, and undertake it in a manner that minimizes work to the fabric of the building.

Energy availability and utilization

Between 1945 and 1973, energy was cheap and little regard was paid to energy conservation. Between 1973 and the early 1990s, energy was generally expensive and often in short supply. Methods of saving energy were used in order to save money, and in the belief that energy sources would be exhausted before are just after the year 2000. In the 1990s, energy was plentiful and cheap; there was no reason to conserve it for either financial gain or to prolong its availability – but we are acutely aware of the need to reduce energy use in order to conserve our natural environment. As conservationists, we must look at the energy issues of post-war buildings in two ways:

■   any conservation measures or services replacements must be done in a way that reduces energy demand; and
■   we must recognize and celebrate post-war buildings that have been ground breaking or influential in their approach to energy conservation.

It is fair to say that most pre-1973 buildings will have had their services systems refurbished by now. At the very least, the main plant items such as boilers and pumps will have been replaced. Many of these refurbishments will have been done in the 1970s and 1980s. Plant items have become increasingly efficient over the last decade. In the 1970s and early 1980s, when many pre-1970s buildings were being refurbished, a typical boiler efficiency was 75%. Modern boilers have efficiencies of around 85% (and greater). This suggests that plant replacement now can be significant in reducing a building's energy take.

Paradoxically, while we are upgrading to more efficient systems, we are increasing the number of systems we install. Most pre-1970s buildings were naturally ventilated; the same buildings are now being refurbished with air conditioning. As everyone knows, air conditioning is a large user of energy. Not only is the cooling process costly, but the systems are operating throughout the year, heating in winter and cooling in summer. Compare this to a naturally ventilated building, in which the (heating) system stops running between April and October, leaving the building to respond naturally between spring and autumn. One of the great benefits of the UK climate is the long temperate spring-to-autumn period, which allows us to turn off our heating systems for much of the year.

How do we overcome this dilemma? With difficulty. The first response must be to retain (or use), natural ventilation wherever possible. If external pollution forces you to seal the building, you should consider adjusting the temperatures the building is cooled down to. General institutional standards specify a temperature of 22°C in summer for office space. In reality, most people can work comfortably in temperatures of up to 24°C. Accepting this two-degree difference considerably reduces the energy use (and plant size).

The other tool in solving the dilemma is trying to improve the building's thermal performance. Sufficient insulation and draught-proofing will reduce the building's energy take. Here lies a dilemma within a dilemma: how are we to improve the fabric and reduce energy take without unduly changing the aesthetic?

We need to touch briefly on facades here. Most buildings built before 1973 have shallow floor plates, which are excellent for providing daylight, but which reduce the available thermal mass of the floor and ceiling plates. The proportion of external wall to floor and ceiling area is high. The facade is therefore highly important; hence measures such as draught-proofing, double glazing, and adding insulation to facade panel systems should be done wherever possible, to reduce winter heat loss. In summer, solar reducing blinds can go a long way to improving the fabric's overall performance. You then need to look elsewhere to improve things. If possible, consider exposing soffits and using high mass materials such as blockwork for partitions. Increasing the amount of high thermal mass material, which acts like a 'heat sponge', reduces swings in temperature: heat is soaked into the structure and not absorbed by the services system.

Large areas of glass increase daylight and reduce the need for artificial light. However, increased areas of glass reduce the thermal performance. So it can be beneficial to investigate the balance between the benefits of increased daylight and the increasing need for cooling due to solar gain. Considering that around 25% of a building's energy goes in lighting, and lighting is used twelve months of the year, the annual energy take may be influenced to a greater extent by focusing on daylight rather than cooling.

It is fair to say that changing the building fabric, particularly the facade, is rarely done unless necessary. I would argue that if the facade can be improved without destruction, it should be.

Conclusion

The above notes only start to address the energy debate and probably raise more questions than answers, but I hope that they have increased awareness of some of the issues. A final thought: I believe we need to add a check box into the list of items that are crossed off when a building is considered for listing. This check box needs to address the quality of the environmental design. What is likely to transpire from this is an awareness of interesting and preservable advances in system design in the 1970s and 1980s, and holistic building designs in the 1990s. It will probably be easier to conserve holistic buildings of the 1990s, as their systems tend to be simple, the complexity being in the building form. For the system-based buildings of the 1970s and 1980s, conservation will be more difficult. One of the main premises of this paper is that systems do not last forever, and hence need replacement. Now I am suggesting that some systems are of such historical importance they should be retained. It is unlikely that we will be able to retain them all in working condition, so we need to address how preservation could take place. I have no clear answers to this, simply some thoughts:

- We need to recognize buildings that have environmental systems of historic importance and attempt to retain that heritage.
- All existing systems should be recorded in writing and with photographs and video before removal. Using modern methods of recording, very detailed records can be kept and published.
- Lower grades of system could be removed after recording.
- For medium-quality systems, an attempt should be made to keep the system operational by adding new equipment. Any equipment of historical importance should be preserved.
- Prime-quality systems should be preserved intact after decommissioning. A new system should be added to run in parallel.

One thing is clear: if we don't act, we could lose a very important part of our engineering heritage.

CHAPTER 5
PLASTICS: THE FIRST UNIVERSAL BUILDING MATERIAL
Anthony Walker

The emergence of the use of polymers in buildings marks the transition from an industry based primarily on traditional materials to one whose basic building blocks are malleable, infinitely adaptable synthetic products, the 'natural' materials of the era.

Natural and semi-synthetic polymers

The modern plastics industry was in its infancy at the beginning of the twentieth century. Natural plastics such as horn and shellac had been in use for many centuries, and during the nineteenth century gutta percha, bois durci and papier mâché, which were valued for their appearance and the ease with which they could be moulded,[1] were used for many decorative as well as functional building applications.[2] The first semi-synthetic plastic, Parkesine, a cellulose nitrate material developed by the prolific inventor Alexander Parkes, was exhibited at the London International Exhibition in 1862. Much of the impetus for the development of new plastics came from the desire to find substitutes for increasingly rare natural materials. Celluloid, a commercially successful exploitation of Parke's discovery, for which Henri van de Welde prophesied a great future,[3] is a good example: it was produced by Hyatt in America in response to a competition for a new material to replace ivory for billiard balls.[4]

Two other semi-synthetic materials were to be used in the building industry: cellulose acetate, known as 'non-flam celluloid' (1912), which provided lacquers and paints; and casein (1899), a semi-synthetic polymer based on milk, which was patented at the turn of the century to provide clear plastic coatings, and in 1909 as a solid material. The Erinoid company, formed in 1912, manufactured a range of casein products, including bathroom furniture, door handles, light fittings and many other small or medium-sized mouldings. Available in a wide range of colours, plain or mottled, the material readily absorbs water and is difficult to mould, so most products are machined from solid blocks or sheet material.

Synthetics and the arrival of tailor-made polymers

The first synthetic polymer, phenol-formaldehyde resin, was developed by Dr Baekeland in America, who registered a patent in February 1907 – beating Sir James Swinburne in the UK by just one day.[5] Swinburne turned to the development of lacquers under the trade name of Damard (because they were so 'damn hard'), while Baekeland's patents were to be the cornerstone for the development of high-pressure laminates such as Bakelite, Warerite and Formica (the latter so named because it was first developed as an electrical insulator which could be substituted for mica). The early phenol-formaldehyde dark brown and black laminates both complemented and contrasted with the chrome and glass streamlined designs of the 1920s and 1930s[6] and the resin was also used for a range of mottled doorknobs and other building products.

The British Plastics Trade Moulding Association was founded in 1929 and the Plastics Institute in 1931. Plastics were beginning to have an impact on building materials. In 1935, Grey Wornum lectured to the Society of Chemical Industry on the use of plastics in buildings, and the same year, following a lecture at the Architectural Association, he suggested that there was a great future in plastic wall linings. Cellulose paints were widely used and were recommended for their flexibility in covering cracks. Mollo and Egan, noted for decorative work in cinemas, used a novel technique, advertised as saving time on finishes, to provide an instant mural in the entrance hall at Embassy Court (Wells Coate, 1930s, Brighton) by projecting a monochrome image on to a light-sensitive cellulose coating.[7]

More colourful materials were also sought and British Cyanides displayed a new plastic at the Wembley Empire Exhibition in 1925.[8] Urea formaldehyde, unlike the phenolics, could be made in light plain colours or a in wonderful range of mottled patterns, to produce jewellery and small objects which were described as richly attractive with varied colouring and surpassing alabaster in brilliancy and depth.

It was both appropriate and ironic that the British Broadcasting Corporation should have been instrumental in the development of UK sources of these new materials for buildings: appropriate in that their new recording studios in Portland Place were symbolic of the new technology, and ironic because the studio designers' first choice of wallcovering was a German product, Trolit, first seen by McGrath in 1930 at Gropius' German pavilion in Paris.[9] It was only due to a ban on the use of foreign goods that McGrath, Wells Coates and Serge Chermayeff were forced to find a British substitute. The Beetle Products Company of Oldbury in England was then selected to provide a through-colour lining material mounted on a 9 mm plywood backing. This used a new urea formaldehyde resin produced by British Cyanide. Impressed with its success, British Cyanide had gone on to set up the Beatl ('beat all') company to market Beetle products.[10]

In 1861, the division between polymers and other materials had been recognized, and rubber, cellulose and proteins had been classified as 'colloids', whereas sugar and salt were termed 'crystalloids'. Colloids were believed to be exceptionally large clusters of molecules held together by an electrical or other force. It was not until 1922 that Hermann Staudinger, working on the production of synthetic rubber, and in the face of much opposition, postulated the theory that they were in fact long chains of many thousands of smaller molecules or monomers, and that it was this which gave them their unique properties. Working at Du Pont's laboratories in America,

Wallace Carothers developed this theory with the concept of functionality in polymer reactions – by which he meant the number of reactive groups: fewer than two will not polymerize, two lead to long chains and three give rise to three-dimensional networks associated with thermo-setting polymers. With this knowledge came the development of designed polymers, and the 1930s saw the introduction of a dramatic range of new plastics, including polymethyl methacrylate (acrylics) and polyethylene (polythene) in 1933; polyvinyl chloride (PVC) in 1935; polystyrene in 1937; and polytetrafluoroethylene (PTFE) and polyamide (nylon) in 1938.

Supported by this wealth of new materials, the plastics producers saw the building industry as a major market to be exploited. The House of the Future at the London Ideal Home Exhibition in 1928 had anticipated the use of a tough plastic panelling system for internal and external walls. Since such a material had not yet been produced, it was simulated by treating plaster with cellulose paint; it became reality in the Vinylite house at the 1933 Chicago Fair, one of the first of a series of 'all-plastic' houses demonstrating the universal nature of the materials.[11] Everything, including a prefabricated system of bolt-together wall panels (but excluding the plumbing), was made with Vinylite resins.

Manufacturers set out to woo the designers. Bakelite offered a deal whereby designers who helped to promote the new laminates would be supported with technical information and details. During the early 1930s, Bakelite ran a series of advertisements in *Modern Plastics* using well-known designers.[12] The June 1934 edition contained an advertisement that featured Raymond Dewey stating that Bakelite was invaluable to the designer in his search for simple, beautiful lines. At about the same time, Bakelite were using their own laminates for the interiors of their offices at Tyseley. The board room, reception and other prestige areas provided an opportunity to display the virtues of the laminates for interior design. Most of this has now been lost, but some sample sections have been saved by the Plastics Historical Society as part of their collection of plastic artefacts.

ICI adopted a similar approach with their Rexine range of cellulose nitrate leathercloth. Their 1937 promotional brochure was illustrated with building designs by leading architects of the time, including a milk bar by Maxwell Fry (Figure 5.1, *overleaf*), a school dining room by F.R.S. Yorke and, in a totally different style (possibly tongue in cheek), a fashion showroom by Raymond McGrath.

As the use of plastics grew, so did awareness of the new design opportunities they offered.[13] In 1934, Morris Saunders wrote in *Modern Plastics* of the inherent beauty and adaptability of decorative materials and, in 1935, Paul Frankl challenged designers 'to create the grammar of these new materials'.[14] The 1940 New York Museum of Modern Art exhibition displayed everyday objects priced at less than $10, to encourage the use of plastics in the home. In many ways, plastics were seen as a social equalizer, helping to overcome the high cost of scarce natural materials.[15]

In the same year, *Fortune* magazine ran a series of articles about the plastics industry and illustrated them with an imaginary continent called 'Synthetica'. The magazine described the new materials in extravagant prose as 'extending right out of the natural world' but, as Jeffery Meikle has pointed out, the same article reflected the confusion that commentators experienced in examining the new materials. On the one hand, it identified the potential of plastics, which made use of waste products, to offer social equality within an ordered and disciplined framework; while on

Figure 5.1   In promoting their artificial leathercloth range, Rexine ICI called on the services of several of the leading architects and designers of the day, including Maxwell Fry, Raymond McGrath, F.R.S. Yorke, and Grey Wornum, to provide illustrations of the use of the material. This illustration from their catalogue shows Maxwell Fry's Milk Bar proposals. (Courtesy of the Sylvia Katz collection)

the other plastics were shown as having their own artificial agenda, a 'carnival of material desire'.[16] This dichotomy was to be reflected in the development of plastics in buildings in the post-war period.

Post-war development

Plastics came into their own during the Second World War, when they were used for radomes, insulation for electrical cable, inflatable tanks, lightweight boats and moisture-resistant coatings. These applications accelerated the development of plastic products and established their acceptability in their own right as materials to suit new demands. Yarsley and Couzens wrote enthusiastically in 1941 of 'Plastic Man' coming into:

> *… a world of colour and bright shining surfaces, where childish hands will find nothing to break, or sharp edges or corners to cut or graze, no crevices to harbour dirt or germs …*

Andrew Saint has commented that architects returning from the war had become accustomed to working with these new materials and were willing and able to apply their knowledge to the development of new building solutions in post-war Britain.[17] Materials developed for serious wartime uses were called on to serve more light-hearted purposes; one example is the application of warship cocooning technology to the kiosk roofs at the Festival of Britain gardens.[18]

Despite some initial problems brought about by the use of inferior recycled materials in the immediate post-war period, plastics were seen as combining the virtues of durability and cleanliness[19] with colour and pattern, and they were widely used in hospitals, kitchens, ships and trains. The *Overseas Daily Mail* for 27 October 1945 reported that:

> *... because of the large stocks of aluminium and plastics left over from war jobs the following will be shortly available at low income prices: lime yellow plate racks that will never rust ... pastel shaded plastic cupboards; kitchen tables whose plastic top and aluminium legs need cleaning only with a damp cloth.*

The discovery of clear urea and thiourea formaldehyde resins had brought about a new range of laminates in the 1930s. These had a top layer of coloured and patterned paper on a core of kraft paper saturated in phenol formaldehyde. Production of these decorative laminates by Formica and Warerite ceased during the war, but the post-war period saw a rapid development of patterns, one-off designs and decorative effects.

Just before the war, Warerite produced what is claimed to be the first one-off laminated illustration, a Nicholas Bentley cartoon displayed at the 1939 New York Fair. In the post-war period, the production of individual laminates, in designs that ranged from maps to murals, became very popular. Sometimes drawn and painted by the designer or artist, and sometimes handmade under their direction, these have a value as original artefacts.

The Festival Pattern Group, set up under Mark Hartland Thomas, produced a unified series of patterns for a wide range of materials used at the 1951 Festival of Britain (Figure 5.2, *overleaf*). Contemporary photographs of the crystal structure of matter were seen as both a design inspiration and a reflection of the unity of art and science in the progress to a better future.

Design magazine, reviewing a new Warerite range in 1957, pointed out that the patterns should not be confused with those used for textiles, where the folds and pleats impose a different discipline; nor were they the same as wallpapers, being more formal because of their durability and rigidity.[20]

Advertising for both Bakelite and Warite laid as much emphasis on durability as on appearance. In the 1950s and 1960s, laminates had benefited from a general belief in synthetic materials as a way to a better environment; in the 1970s that trend was reversed, with a return to natural materials and earth colours reflected in the colour and pattern ranges of the main companies. The early laminates were all clearly layered sheets, which when cut displayed the darker resins used for the lower layers of the material. The introduction of post-forming grades and polyester decorative laminates in the late 1960s enabled curves to be achieved in one direction; but it was not until Formica introduced ColorCore, in a dramatic exhibition at the Museum of Modern Art in 1982, that a sheet with a single colour throughout allowed the material to be used in a fully three-dimensional way.

Figure 5.2   A bar top from the Festival of Britain designed by Leonard Manasseh in strong reds and greens. (Percy Reboul)

While the decorative laminates developed as the 'natural' material to be used for a wide range of linings, worktops and similar uses, other plastics were being used for cladding and walling, as in the Vinylite House. Holoplast panels, made from paper tubes saturated with phenol formaldehyde resin, which had first been used on ships before the war, now came into their own as a rapid and adaptable kit of parts. In Hertfordshire's post-war school building programme they were used as a universal system for internal and external walls, workbenches, kitchen tops and changing rooms.[21] In conjunction with a simple aluminium framing system, they were used internally and externally, hollow or with various fillings to achieve thermal and acoustic standards, and even fitted with internal heating elements. Their bright colours reflected theories of abstract design rather than the essence of the material involved.

The idea of a universal system for building had an intellectual attraction. Plastics, with their ability to be tailored to suit differing needs, offered the ideal material – but to achieve their full potential, their structural performance would have to be addressed.

During the war, Cotterell Butler had written in *The Builder* that fabric-reinforced and long fibre-reinforced plastics (FRP), which could be made by moulding or extrusion, offered extensive possibilities, but that the technique of production had not been fully developed and the cost factor was likely to be important.[22] Low-pressure cold-cured reinforced polymers had been developed rapidly to meet the wartime demand for radomes and other uses, despite problems of curing. These problems continued well into the post-war period. In 1949, Buckminster Fuller made one of the earliest attempts to use FRP as a structural building material. With his students at Black Mountain, he attempted to produce a dome using triangular sections cast in fibreglass. The sections were to be cast in plaster moulds, but the resin and chopped fibreglass mixture would not set and the components were thrown away.[23] Fuller did not abandon the material, however; FRP geodesic radomes seventeen metres in diameter were eventually developed for military applications and have been in use since 1956.

The potential to create self-supporting structures led to a series of dramatic and innovative forms particularly useful for exhibition structures, but the bulk of the material went into the production of corrugated translucent sheeting. Early glass-reinforced plastic (GRP) products showed fraying or blooming of the fibres within two or three years, combined with yellowing, dust accumulation and loss of light transmission.[24] By the early 1950s, the corrugated fibre-reinforced translucent sheets that were to dominate the use of GRP in the construction industry were on the market, and in Britain 30% of the total reinforced plastics production went into roofing and sheeting, a proportion equalled only by military uses and far exceeding that for boats and cars.[25]

A product that exploited this utilitarian material and its potential in buildings was the Kalwall system developed in the 1950s in America by Robert Keller, who had worked on the development of engineered woods from the mid-1930s. During the Second World War he had become familiar with GRP, and at the end of the war he started his company to exploit the material's potential. Initially using GRP supplied by others, the Kalwall system was developed as a translucent building panel that was self-supporting and could be used for large wall areas. Early examples shown at the twelfth conference of the Society of the Plastics Industry in 1956 included a dramatic end wall to a church in Woodstock, New York, by William Benshoton. The construction consisted of two sheets of $1/16$-inch (1.5 mm) reinforced plastic sheets bonded mechanically to an interlocking aluminium grid. Over 2,000 panels were used for the roof of the USA pavilion at the Brussels Expo, which covered 72,000 square feet (6,689 square metres) of floor area with a clear span of 302 feet (92 metres).[26] The end wall of the Assembly building at Cape Canaveral provided the opportunity to use the Kalwall system for a vertical window on a similarly large scale.

The 1950s saw the development of reinforced plastics in three-dimensional forms for complete room units or components such as bathrooms[27] and external cladding. Shell or folded plate structures were ideal for the development of GRP. The resins were expensive[28] and these forms could make the most efficient use of small quantities by taking advantage of the natural rigidity of the curved or folded plate forms. For many designers, the curve was symbolic of the inherent plasticity of the material, but the importance of both forms for the development of GRP was recognized by Professor Albert Dietz, who considered that plastics could play a significant part in providing solutions which would otherwise be impossible.[29] The famous Monsanto House, designed by Hamilton & Goody with Dietz as engineer, had four dramatic wings cantilevered from a central core, and was erected in Disneyland in 1957 using glass fabric polyester sandwich core construction.[30]

The 1959 American National Exhibition in Moscow, also designed by Dietz, used ninety GRP parasol shells, each twenty feet (6.1 metres) high and sixteen feet (4.9 metres) across, to provide a sheltered area for visitors to the exhibition. The translucent tulip forms had additional reinforcement at the edges and ribs, emphasizing their delicacy. Each 'tulip' was composed of six 'petals' $^1/_{16}$ inch (1.5 mm) thick with edge ribs of $^1/_4$ inch (6 mm) and supported on a central hollow tapered column with $^1/_4$-inch (6 mm) walls.

A spur to the development of the use of GRP in buildings was provided by a programme called *The Builders*,[31] broadcast on BBC television in 1966, in which it was implied that the process used for vehicle bodies being produced by Mickleover Transport could be applied to the low-cost housing market.[32] One of the first practical applications of GRP to buildings had been in 1961, with the rail relay switch-gear cabins Mickleover developed for British Railways.[33] By 1963, the system had been adapted to double-storey form for Bakelite's telephone exchange in Birmingham, and later that year another two-storey version was shipped to Sidney Island in the Antarctic as a fully equipped laboratory (Figure 5.3).

Three pavilions at the New York World's Fair provided another opportunity to show the virtuosity of GRP. The lightweight nature of the material has advantages for an exhibition building, in reducing the need for foundations, which are a costly element in a temporary structure, and

Figure 5.3   The telephone exchange at Tyesley under construction. The GRP panels are a development from the British Rail relay cabins. (Percy Reboul)

in cutting the cost of demolition. In the 7-Up pavilion, shallow vaulted shells with columns at each corner created a sheltered area, and in the Marina building a series of hyperbolic parabo-loids formed an enclosed space with infill glazing; both were of sandwich construction using simple butt joints between the shells.

The University of Michigan in 1966 advocated free-form structures created by spraying a rapid-setting foam onto a flexible membrane or mesh backing.[34] Felix Drury's foam houses illus-trated in *Progressive Architecture*[35] developed this method using a urethane foam on a heavy nylon fabric, closely related to the material used for the habitable sculptures of André Bloc.

In contrast, mass-produced plastic products exhibited simplicity of design, clean-cut lines and components that could be simply cast and moulded – benefiting from the 1960s interest in overall form rather than material surface.[36] Their lightness encouraged the use of large-scale pan-els with simple sculptural shapes and smooth surfaces, which emphasized the fact that build-ing elements could be produced as single mouldings, as opposed to an assembly of parts. Detailing was often unsophisticated and sometimes ill-conceived – for example, with joints at the point of maximum water run-off. Lack of fire resistance remained a problem: fire-retardant additives tended to reduce the weathering properties and durability of the material.[37]

Although a 'plastics aesthetic' was to prove illusory, polymers such as polyvinyl chlorides, acrylics and polystyrene provided many building materials, including cladding planks, gutters, glazing, finishes and insulation; their very ordinariness led to their acceptance as the right and 'natural' material for the purpose.

In the ICI house, built in 1963, an image of conventionality was conveyed by plastics used as substitutes for other materials, such as timber boarding, and for a range of wall surfaces, from laminates to vinyl papers, that could be easily cleaned. The house showed how plastics could be used to form a prefabricated bathroom or even provide a more revolutionary but unseen use as linking discs for mortarless blockwork.

These unostentatious uses of plastics were characteristic. A British Plastics Federation com-mittee reported in 1944 that the future for plastics in buildings was in resin-bonded laminated wood as a structural material, the development of sheet materials, trials of plastic piping and the manufacture of large components such as windows. By 1964, plastics had developed qui-etly but swiftly to the point where they dominated the related fields of coatings, claddings and coverings;[38] and in the late 1960s it was claimed that plastics in one form or another had invaded every building material market and every phase of the construction industry.[39] Detailing changed: no longer were overlapping or stepped configurations essential. Innovations such as silicone-jointed structural glazing made it possible to achieve a new sleek minimalist approach.

The ability of plastics to mimic other materials conspires with their diversity of finishes and properties to deny the material a specific image. At the second Iran International Congress of Architecture in 1974, Sir James Stirling dismissed the concept of 'truth to materials' and instead stressed the need to use forms and shapes with which people can identify, claiming that:

> … *according to what is appropriate for a particular building problem the building could be made of any materials … the whole spectrum of the past is available from earth works to plastics.*

Stirling's use of the material's image of plasticity at the Olivetti Training College in Haslemere might be seen as a form specific to the material – until we learn that he had earlier proposed carrying out the project in aluminium panels but could not do so for technical reasons. The 'plasticity' was more an expression of the building programme, which had called for extendibility, and which Stirling translated as an extruded form temporarily interrupted.[40]

In the 1970s, Professor Skolimowski argued in favour of the concept of a variable rationale as the basis of modern design. He contended that there was a change from 'form follows function' to a new rationale based on quality of life and the dictum that 'form follows culture'.[41] His argument was continued by Paola Antonelli in her introduction to the catalogue for the *Mutant Materials* exhibition, in which she quoted William Duncan:

> *The single most important material used by manufacturers in the future will be data*
> *... the raw materials will be chemical 'slurries' and raw elements that may be assembled and reassembled or restructured in replication processes.*[42]

Conservation

Which plastic is it?
The ability of plastics to adopt chameleon guises makes their identification more complex than the identification of traditional materials.[43] Historical evidence or chemical analysis will often be necessary before conservation repair can be attempted. The following tests can provide only a general guide for an initial assessment.

Transparency
Colour cannot be relied on for identification purposes, but the degree of transparency is reasonably reliable. Common transparent plastics are acrylic, celluloid and PVC, all of which tend to yellow with age, and cellulose esters and ethers, polycarbonates, cast phenolic, polyesters and polystyrene. The following will not be completely transparent:

- plastics with a partially crystalline nature: polythene, polypropylene, PTFE, polyformaldehyde and gutta percha;
- plastics which are toughened by alloying of a second phase: polystyrene and ABS;
- plastics which rely on a filler: moulded thermosetting plastics, phenol formaldehyde, hard rubber, shellac and bois durci.

Smell
Smell is very subjective and is best recognized by experiment with known materials. Rubbing, immersion in warm water or testing with a hot pin[44] can produce distinctive odours. Care must be taken when heating plastics, as some are very inflammable; it is recommended that reference be made to the techniques described in *Conservation of Plastics* and similar publications before carrying out tests.[45]

Feel

Relative hardness can be tested using a Barcol Hardness Tester or (for a rough guide) a fingernail. Melamine and urea formaldehydes are slightly softer than brass, with phenol formaldehyde close behind. Polymethyl methacrylate is halfway between brass and aluminium. Polystyrene and casein are almost the same as aluminium. Hard rubber, unplasticized PVC, polycarbonate, nylon, cellulose nitrate and acetate and polystyrene all lie between aluminium and lead, while polyethylene, gutta percha and plasticized PVC have very little resistance.

Polythene, polypropylene, nylon and PTFE all feel waxy. Polythene can be easily marked with a fingernail, as can expanded polystyrene, foamed polyurethane and polyisocyanurate. Polystyrene has a metallic ring. Phenolic resin, urea formaldehyde, unsaturated polyester, polymethyl metharcylate, polycarbonate, cast epoxy resin and polyacetal are all hard to cut.

Polymer structures and principal forms of degradation

Polymers are organic materials in the form of very long monomer chains. Their backbone is commonly a string of carbon atoms, each of which seeks to establish a stable octet of electrons by sharing those of hydrogen, chlorine, and fluorine, oxygen and nitrogen atoms.

The paraffin (alkane) group is the simplest of the hydrocarbon series and illustrates some of monomers formed by groups of just two different atoms (Figure 5.4).

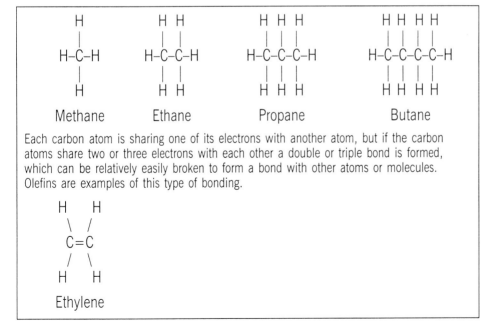

Figure 5.4   Simple hydrocarbons. (Anthony Walker)

Addition polymerization. In this process, an initiator molecule divides into two free radicals, which will then combine with a monomer (such as ethylene), unlinking the double bond and leaving a free bond at the end that will repeat the process again and again until it links with another chain or is terminated by a free radical formed by the initiator.

$$
\text{I- + } \underset{\substack{\diagup\ \diagdown\\ H\quad H}}{\overset{\substack{H\quad H\\ \diagdown\ \diagup}}{C=C}} \quad \text{becomes} \quad \text{I-} \underset{\substack{|\ |\\ H\ H}}{\overset{\substack{H\ H\\ |\ |}}{C\text{-}C\text{-}}} \quad \text{which can then repeat to become } \text{I-}\underset{\substack{|\ |\ |\ |\\ H\ H\ H\ H}}{\overset{\substack{H\ H\ H\ H\\ |\ |\ |\ |}}{C\text{-}C\text{-}C\text{-}C\text{-}}}
$$

This reaction typically will continue over 10,000 times until it meets another chain or an initiator fraction fragment forming an end.

Side branches are often formed with the same chain pattern. In another type of reaction where two monomers of different types combine there may be a repeating chain with a side branch formed by part of one of the monomers, for example the benzene ring (a group of six carbon atoms with attendant hydrogen atoms), which contains double bonds and may therefore readily link to other chains, thus producing a degree of rigidity.

Figure 5.5   Addition polymerization. (Anthony Walker)

Condensation polymerization. In this process, two different molecules are linked to produce a new molecule which is the basis of the chain. In order to produce the free valance for link-ing, atoms are removed and a small molecule (often water) is forced out, giving rise to the name 'condensation polymerization'. In order produce this reaction, polymers such as phe-nol-formaldehyde were processed at high temperatures, which could cause damage to the material from blistering by the conversion of the water into steam. To control this, the process was carried out under considerable pressure.

Polyesters are produced by the reaction of a dihydroxyl alcohol with a dicarbolic acid with little heat (they are exothermic) and so require little or no pressure, for example:

$$
\underset{\text{dicarbolic acid}}{\text{HO - }\overset{\overset{\displaystyle O}{\|}}{C}\text{ - }R_1\text{- }\overset{\overset{\displaystyle O}{\|}}{C}\text{ - OH}} + \underset{\text{dihydroxyl alcohol}}{\text{HO - }R_2\text{ - OH}} \text{ becomes } \underset{\text{ester}}{\text{HO - }\overset{\overset{\displaystyle O}{\|}}{C}\text{ - }R_1\text{ - }\overset{\overset{\displaystyle O}{\|}}{C}\text{ - O - }R_2\text{ - OH}} + H_2O
$$

Where R_1 R_2 are hydrocarbon groups

Figure 5.6   Condensation polymerization. (Anthony Walker)

Polymerization is the process of combining these monomers into long chains, often tens or even hundreds of thousands of units long. Carothers identified two distinct processes: 'addition polymerization' and 'condensation polymerization' (Figures 5.5 and 5.6).

Thermoplastic materials rely on van de Waals bonds (which are insignificant with small molecules) to hold their long molecules together at room temperature; heat provides the energy to overcome these weak bonding forces and allows chains to slide and the material to be moulded. Thermosetting materials have three-dimensional bonding between chains, increasing their rigidity; instead of being softened by heat, they will eventually degrade.

The performance of polymers with the same chemical formula can differ dramatically: chain lengths and therefore molecular weights vary, the sequence of atoms along the backbone can vary, and two molecules having the same chemical formula (called isomers) may have quite different attributes.

Attached to the polymer backbone are single atoms or even branches. The pattern of both the backbone and the branches can determine the characteristics of the polymer and its degradation behaviour. A chain with a single type of repeat is a homopolymer, and two or more repeat structures are described as copolymers. The side atoms may form a symmetrical pattern (syndiotactic), a regular but asymmetric pattern (isotactic) or no pattern at all (atactic). These side branches affect the bonding between molecules, increasing the mechanical interlocking but making it difficult to form crystalline structures; most branched polymers are amorphous.

Photodegradation

The bond energy between macromolecules is in the order of 300–500 kJ per mole while the energy emitted by the sun at the violet end of the spectrum (400 nm wavelength) is 300–400 kJ for ultraviolet (UV) radiation (energy levels above that are generally absorbed by the atmosphere). This will provide sufficient energy to break bonds between carbon and oxygen or chlorine, but insufficient to break those of carbon to hydrogen or fluorine.

For UV to cause photolysis, it must be absorbed by the polymer; yellowing is a common effect of the formation of conjugated structures. In carbon chain polymers with a repeat structure ~CH2CXY~ the general effect is a fall in molecular weight, which is due to chain scission; those of a repeat structure ~CH_2CHY~ tend to cross-link. Many UV filters work by absorbing the energy of the radiation through a gradual chemical change of the filter, and therefore there is a limit to their effective life.

Thermal degradation

There are two main forms of thermal degradation. In depolymerization, the backbone chain breaks down into small molecules and (unless other reactions take place) leaves no solid residue. Side group reactions occur where the molecules attached to the side of the main backbone interact and form new compounds.

Polymers do not burn, but under the action of heat they decompose to small molecules which may mix with air to form a combustible mixture. This then releases more heat and continues the cycle, unless at some stage the polymer releases a chemical flame quencher.

Atmospheric degradation

The commonest form of atmospheric degradation is due to oxygen, either on its own or (more usually) in combination with UV or thermal degradation. Nitrogen dioxide and sulphur dioxide in moist conditions will accelerate hydrolytic attack on some polymers, and nitrogen dioxide can also work as a photosensitizer, producing singlet oxygen that will act as a free radical and initiate breakdown of the molecular chain. Polyamides and polyurethanes are particularly sensitive to attack by nitrogen dioxide, resulting in chain scission and crosslinking.

Ozone acts on polymers such as polyethylene, polystyrene, rubber and polyamides to cause scission of the backbone, which can then undergo further degeneration.

Hydrolytic and biodegradation

Most polymers are hydrophobic. Hydrolysis, where it does occur, will proceed slowly and will generally require humid conditions and a pH factor <7. The results are breaks in the chains with a loss of physical properties. The main groups affected are polymers containing ester, amide, urethane and carbonate links, and natural proteins and polysaccharides.

Biodegradation and micro-organisms are specific in attack and may be able to adapt to new synthetic polymers. Materials sensitive to attack are aliphatic polyesters, polyethers, polyurethanes and polyamides. Fungi require oxygen, acidic conditions (a pH factor of 4–4.5) and a temperature of about 35°C. Actinomycetes and bacteria prefer less acidic conditions (pH 5–7) and will accept a wide temperature range, the optimum being 60°C. Biodegradation is influenced by chain length, and polymers that have been subject to photo-oxidation may be more susceptible to attack.

Dye reactions

Dyes are often affected by light, which causes degradation manifested by fading and colour change. The interaction between a dye and a polymer can be a cause of degradation not only of the dye but also of the 'carrier' material.[46]

Health hazards

Opinions vary widely as to the health risks posed by polymers. Some polymers are made from toxic monomers; when degraded, especially by heat, they can decompose to release these monomers. When polyurethane foam burns it produces hydrogen cyanide. Other polymers, such as urea, melamine and phenol formaldehyde resins, may release formaldehyde by slow decomposition at ambient temperatures; if continued over a long period, this can be a health hazard.[47]

Some plasticizers slowly leach out of plastics, evaporating from the surface or dissolving in cleaning agents. These can be toxic aromatic substances or carcinogens. It is now known that some of the solvents originally used in adhesives, including chlorinated hydrocarbons, are toxic, and that some aromatic solvents, such as benzene and toluene, are carcinogens.

Often the degree of exposure will be a critical factor in assessing risk, but the conservator should appreciate that a material that may now be considered risk-free could in its original formulation have contained hazardous materials – for example, some early vinyl tiles and sealants contained asbestos fibres.

Conservation methods and materials

Options for the repair of plastics, especially of the thermosetting variety, are limited,[48] although some materials, such as GRP, can be easily patched and recoated. There are, however, some simple actions that can be considered.

Repairs

Hard thermoplastics, such as acrylic, polycarbonate and polystyrene, can be bonded by solvent-cementing. Epoxy cements are suitable for thermosetting resins and PVA for polystyrene foam. The fumes from solvents may be an irritant and safety precautions should be followed. Thermoplastics can also be joined by heat, using a hot plate or warm air gun.

For all repairs, including patch repairs to GRP products using similar polyester resins, sample tests should be carried out to confirm compatibility between the materials.

Cleaning

Washing in warm water with a little non-ionic detergent is suitable for most plastics, with the exception of cellulose nitrate and cellulose acetate, which will show crazing. Harsh solvents such as acetone, benzene, toluene, carbon tetrachloride and lacquer thinners will all attack thermoplastics, as will many window-cleaning products. Yellowing can be removed from polycarbonates with Butyl Cellosolve, and they can be repolished with a polishing paste or wax. The use of solvents on cellulose acetates and PVC should be avoided, as they swell the material and leach out the plasticizer; nor should solvents be used on transparent polystyrene or acrylic, as there is a risk of stress crazing. There are several specialist polishes for specific plastics, and metal polish may sometimes be used to remove slight surface scratching. Shallow scratching may also be polished out with white toothpaste, and smoothing the surface of thermoplastics such as polycarbonate and acrylic can be achieved with methylene dichloride.[49] In all cases, the suitability of the cleaning material for the specific use must be checked and a test made on a trial area before any widespread work is undertaken.

Graffiti

Many of the cleaning gels and solvents used to remove graffiti are very aggressive and in some cases will result in more damage to the fabric than was caused by the graffiti. Some plastics are very resistant to graffiti, and indeed polyurethanes form the basis of many anti-graffiti paints. Others, including polycarbonates, clear PVC and vinyl claddings, have low resistance.

Removal of graffiti usually requires the use of a solvent, which must first be used on a test area to ensure that it does not react adversely with the polymer. Abrasive pads must not be used, as they will destroy the surface of soft plastics. On surfaces where there is a mixture of materials, it will be important to ensure, when washing down a surface to clean off a removal gel, that the run-off does not affect other materials, such as gaskets.

London Transport has issued a comprehensive guide based on practical experience and laboratory testing.[50]

Conservation of commonly used building plastics

Polyvinyl chloride

PVC is one of the most widely used polymers, with applications such as coatings, rainwater goods and windows. The unstabilized material is notorious for rapid discolouration and embrittlement, which are corrected by the use of stabilizers. Appraisals in the 1960s indicated a life of 15–20 years, which has been supported by studies by RAPRA.[51] Vinyl flooring was first developed as a vinyl-asbestos tile in 1933 and has been widely used since the war. The binder polyvinyl chloride degrades by the elimination of hydrogen chloride from the backbone, forming conjugated double bonds, a process that leads to gradual yellowing. Ultraviolet light will break down the carbon–carbon bonds, resulting in superficial fading and chalking of the tile surface. Moisture can also induce migration of plasticizers from within the tile and break down the adhesive/tile bond. Any repair should take account of hazards due to the release of fibres or vinyl chloride monomers.[52]

Rubber

During the 1930s and the post-war period, both natural and synthetic rubber were used in tile or sheet form (often, during the earlier period, as a coating to an asbestos core or as an undersurface to mats and loose rugs). It was seen as offering advantages of permanence, economy in use, noise absorption and hygiene,[53] and was therefore recommended as a wallcovering and even for draining boards. If it is in good condition, wax or polish finishes can reduce oxygen or ozone diffusion and limit damage from oils and acids, but care must be taken to choose a barrier containing no solvents that could attack the rubber.[54]

Decorative laminates

Decorative laminates[55] form a composite with a relatively high mechanical strength, available in various colours and textures, and with scratch/heat resistance, depending on the resins used. The fillers or reinforcement used will have a significant effect on the properties of the laminate: absorbent papers are used to obtain high resin content; non-porous layers will have a low resin content. Fabric reinforcement tends to have less tensile strength than paper but better resistance to impact or shock loads, and asbestos cloth may be used for heat-resisting laminates.

The first laminates were made from phenol formaldehyde with several layers of kraft paper saturated in the resin, allowed to dry, then assembled in whatever number was required to achieve the final thickness. These were then placed in a heated press, where they were put under a pressure of about 1,000 lbs psi at a temperature of about 300°C. Pressure is required to consolidate the material and to help contain the blistering that would otherwise occur. (The curing process is a condensation polymerization, producing water which converts to steam with the heat needed to facilitate the reaction.) These laminates are a natural yellow or brown and can be dyed to darker colours only, so the early ranges of laminate consisted of browns, dark greens or reds, and black. Mottled colours could be produced to imitate wood whorls or provide a general pattern, and some of these could be very attractive. Mechanization meant that the paper could be saturated in a continuous process, passing through a resin bath and then into a drying kiln before being cut into separate sheets. Premix materials were also developed, the bonding resin being added to the fibre before or during its formation into a sheet material, obviating the saturating process and enabling thick sheets to be produced more rapidly.

The development of clear urea and thiourea resins meant that plain colours could be achieved by dyeing the resin or by the use of coloured and decorated papers for the top layer, opening the way for patterned and decorative laminates. These resins tended to be more water-absorbent and less durable than the phenol varieties, and more expensive. The introduction of melamine in the late 1930s overcame the problem of durability, as it had high scratch and heat resistance. But melamine was very much more expensive than phenol, and the latter therefore continued to be used for the layers below the surface. The decorative layer can be of a real material, such as wood veneer or original artwork, and can incorporate fluorescent and phosphorescent materials, producing laminates that will glow and can be used for emergency signs.

Although the clear surface allowed a decorative finish, where the material was used at corners a characteristic thin dark line showed the underlying dark brown laminate and denied any impression of solidity, while emphasizing the surface nature of the material.

Different resins could be used in combination. A top layer impregnated with melamine provided a scratch-resistant surface that became transparent when cured and could be used over the decorative sheet. This would be impregnated with either a urea or a melamine resin and backed by layers of phenol-impregnated kraft paper, which is generally the cheapest filler material. Where uniformity of appearance was required, Alpha paper, produced from purified wood cellulose pulp in sheets .003–.007 inch thick, could be used for the top layers. Thin sheets of aluminium foil could be incorporated behind the patterned sheet to act as a heat conductor, protecting the surface finish, and textured surface finishes could be provided by the flat press plates. The overall thickness varied but standard thicknesses were $1/16$ inch (1.5 mm), although they could be reduced to $1/20$ inch (1 mm) or increased to $1/4$ inch (6 mm) or more.

With the advent of low-pressure resins that could cure at little above room temperature and at atmospheric pressure, continuous sheet materials could be manufactured. These were flexible and suitable for bonding to the backing on site, using either special packs of adhesive and brushes or a pre-applied adhesive on the rear face.[56] Development of phenol-formaldehyde resins allowed them to retain some plasticity, so that they could be shaped under heat and pressure. The extent to which these 'post-forming' grades can be shaped depends on the extensibility of the reinforcing fabric. Once heated in the press, the resin cures to a rigid sheet with the same properties as flat sheets.

The sheets of laminate are usually mounted on a backing, commonly of plywood, although after the war the shortage of plywood in the UK led for a time to the production of thicker sheets ($1/8$ inch/3 mm) of laminate, which were self-supporting. Other materials may be used to achieve particular properties: at one time asbestos was a commonly used backing, and in other instances sheet metal provided the support.

Laminates are generally tough and resistant to acids and alkalis, fats, alcohol, petrol and common organic solvents. They can be cleaned with warm water and soap or with most household non-abrasive cleaning materials. Knives and abrasive cleaning materials will scour the surface. Hot water does not immediately affect the laminate, but may leave a mark after prolonged contact. Damage will also be caused by very hot objects, which can cause local discoloration. Scratches can be removed by the use of wax made for that purpose, and major burns may be buffed with jeweller's rouge. Minor surface damage can be repaired with cellulose resins which are then recoloured; although this technique is appropriate to museum conservation, it is unlikely to be suitable for most building applications. The application of a clear seal to the surface may also be considered.

Failures are more likely to be related to the backing material or adhesive than to the laminate, and the application of a laminate to one surface will usually require a balancing veneer on the opposite face to avoid bowing. Adhesives are selected according to the environment in which they are to work and the conditions under which they are applied; some set rigidly, while others retain a degree of elasticity.

As long as it does not suffer impact damage, the surface is very durable, except for its tendency to fade in sunlight – the entrance to the ICI demonstration house was a classic example. Exposure to sunlight may also break down the surface sheen to give an overall matt appearance. Repeated wetting and drying can cause surface crazing and, although laminates are generally chemically inert, some solvents will cause deterioration – as will hydrochloric and sulphuric acids, hydrogen peroxide, acetone and sodium hydroxide.

Glass Reinforced Plastic: the material, manufacture and conservation

Plastics may be reinforced in a number of different ways, but in building Glass Reinforced Plastic (GRP) is probably the best known.[57,58] Various materials are used for reinforcement, including cotton, nylon, hessian, sisal, some types of kraft paper[59] and carbon fibres. The type of glass fibre used has a significant effect on the durability of the material. Fibres of E glass, a lime–alumina boroscilate glass low in soda (and so named because it was first developed for electrical installations), have the best resistance to weathering. For acidic conditions, A glass fibres can be used but they do not weather well. Weathering resistance can be improved by the use of neopentyl glycol and methyl methacrylate, and thermoplastic polymers can be added to reduce shrinkage.[60]

GRP is a thermosetting material that cures by catalytic reaction rather than by pressure or heat. Machine moulding is used only if there are long runs, as in boat building, in which case hot curing may be used to speed up the turn-around period. The most common method of manufacture is the hand or spray 'lay-up' process.

The mould is first coated with a release agent and a gel coat is then applied. The gel coat, which is a layer of resin, forms the outer layer of the GRP and protects the glass fibres and polyester lay-up resin. Various coloured pigments and fillers can be added to the gel to give specific properties. (Some gel coats include release agents.) Successive layers of resin and glass reinforcement are applied using mat, chopped mat, rovings or continuous thread, according to the stresses to be resisted by the moulding. The resin having been mixed with the catalyst shortly before use, the curing reaction will have started, so both the speed of the work and the need to ensure a bond between successive layers are critical factors in the quality of the moulding. Excessive amounts of the catalyst can lead to overheating of the material and cause cracking and crazing. As the lay-up proceeds, the materials are well compacted to ensure even dispersion of the resin and to remove entrapped air. After the initial hardening, the mould is released and the GRP is left in a stable environment to cure.

The density of the material and the presence of voids or contaminants depend on workmanship and have a significant effect on the durability of the material. Many early products were made in small workshops and their quality is very variable. Defects in the gel coat are of the greatest significance for the long-term durability of the product, since any breakdown of this layer can lead to water penetration, which will affect the glass reinforcement. A number of defects can occur during manufacture, most of which can be detected with good quality control. Invisible fracturing can occur when the component is released from the mould. This will not show up until later, when wicking occurs, conveying water along the glass fibres into the body of the material, where it leads to disintegration of the GRP.

The two most common forms of failure[61] are fibre 'pop-out' and surface micro-cracking, both of which will affect the appearance of the material and, if severe, will lead to other forms of breakdown. Fibre pop-out is believed to be due to differential volume changes in the glass and resin in the surface layer caused by environmental factors such as temperature and moisture. Stresses are set up, mostly parallel to the glass fibres, and can cause the resin surface to rupture. This may be aggravated by solar radiation, which causes crosslinking and thus makes the resin brittle, leading to micro-cracking.

The use of fire-retardant materials in the GRP results in a much lower resistance to weathering. A fire retardant based on tetra-chlorophthalic acid polyester has been shown to undergo both forms of degradation two and a half to three times faster than would a general-purpose polyester matrix.[62]

GRP became a popular material for prefabricated cladding panels during the 1960s and 1970s. In 1967, a GRP-clad panel was used as part of the SF1 system[63] developed by Indulux in conjunction with the GLC Architects Department and used in four tower blocks in Watney Market, Hackney and The Elgin Estate, Paddington.[64] A lightweight concrete filling provided the necessary fire resistance. The panels were erected in groups of six, each of which provided a three-storey section of cladding. The self-coloured GRP surface 2.286 mm thick was intended to provide a maintenance-free surface for twenty years. In fact, defects began to be evident much earlier, the repairs almost inevitably weathered differently, and the panels soon became a patchwork of different shades. The first panels had been manufactured in America by the Moulded Fiberglass Company, but later panels were produced at Indulux's works at Luton. By 1975 the panels had deteriorated significantly, and the GLC Scientific Branch *Buildings Report* of October 1975 stated that the GRP skin had separated from the filling, allowing up to 6 mm flexing. The mastic was sound but had hardened on the surface and lost adhesion. There were few cases of water penetration, which is rather surprising in view of the rather simple jointing detail.

Various inhibitors can be incorporated in the gel coat to achieve fire resistance, but at some cost in durability. An alternative was to use a fire-retardant gel coat with an outer coating to provide colour and a weathering surface. The panels used by Sir James Stirling in 1974 for the extension to the Olivetti Training College at Haslemere adopted this principle and are self-supporting, curving over the top of the two-storey blocks as a roof in a smooth extruded form.

The panels were finished with a polyurethane finish baked onto the surface, and after fifteen years showed considerable signs of weathering, with flaking of the coating, chalking and colour loss. Other defects include impact damage, some of it probably caused when knocking the panel out of the mould or during erection. Other areas have clearly been damaged in use. Studies carried out by RPA, GRP Design Consultants of Nottingham, led to proposals for repairs to damaged areas, filling pinholes and other surface defects to achieve a smooth surface, and recoating to provide a durable colour finish.

Tests were carried out with proprietary film coatings approximately 50 microns thick. Where these were applied around cracked areas of the previously applied polyurethane coating, this caused wrinkling, so a two-part polyester spray filler was used as an isolator over the existing degradation and followed by the film coatings. Tests complying with BS 3900 Parts E6 and F2 were carried out and demonstrated that the adhesion of the new coating would be as good as that of the the original coating.

The most significant conservation issue raised by this building is whether a raised joint should be formed between the panels to overcome leaks. This would significantly change the appearance of the building and compromise its 'extruded' quality.

The Herman Miller building at Bath, designed by Nicholas Grimshaw and Partners Ltd in 1979, were acclaimed in the architectural press. The GRP cladding panels provided a finished surface internally as well as externally, and were seen as the ultimate in high-performance cladding. Four types of panel were used in a double-insulated skin, with inner and outer leaves separated by an air cavity. The insulation is a polyurethane foam bonded to the GRP skins.[65] These full-height cladding panels, manufactured by Artech of Camberley in Surrey, were mounted in neoprene gaskets supported on an aluminium carrier system.

Generally the panels performed well, but an inspection carried out by Reg Pegg Associates in 1992 found three kinds of defect:

- impact damage, which was mainly due to vandalism;
- blistering, which needed no action;
- weathering of the surface.

The surface had largely lost its original gloss finish and there was general colour fading. Weathering of the polyester gel coat had also exposed the fillers, in particular aluminium hydrate, which formed a bloom (commonly known as chalking) on the panels. Although it could be rubbed off, it would return in a few days. Weathering had also exposed tiny air bubbles trapped in the gel coat. These had formed pinholes, which provided an inviting surface for algae growth, identifiable as a black stain on the panel surface. It was recommended that all affected areas should be abraded with P280 Grade Silicone Carbide paper and washed down with diluted Domestos, to give a clean mechanical key for two or three layers of a gun-applied, two-part polyester spray filler. This provided a smooth surface for the final coating, a two-part fluoropolymer paint, also applied by spray to a thickness of between 30 and 50 microns, and matched to the original gel coat for colour and gloss. A guarantee of twenty years was proposed for this treatment, subject to a satisfactory report on a sample panel. A year later, the sample was found to be surviving well.

Conclusion

In 1918 Garnier wrote, 'Truth alone is beautiful. In architecture, truth is the result of calculations made to satisfy known necessities with known materials.'[66] The sentiment was echoed in Le Corbusier's call for:

> ... the replacing of natural materials by artificial ones, of heterogeneous and doubtful materials by homogeneous and artificial ones (tried and proved in the laboratory) and by products of fixed composition.[67]

Plastics gave the designer this freedom. John Gloag spoke of the designer's limitless control of material.[68] The skin no longer represents the core, and the surface is free to exist in its own right.[69] Manzini took the view that:

> The Modern Movement, with its declared aversion to decoration and surface ornament, was just stressing the element of novelty in the new technologies of the nineteenth century – a hitherto undreamed-of capacity for controlling the surfaces of manufactured objects.[70]

The significance of plastics lies in their ability to free the designer from an image specific to the material, to allow the design to develop from the needs of the building programme rather than from the nature of the material, and in their capacity to be ordinary.

For the conservationist, plastics have a dual role: aiding the preservation of more traditional materials through the use, for example, of silanes and adhesives, and at the same time contributing in their own right to a significant and growing proportion of modern buildings.

Glossary of common plastics and their use

Acrylonitrile butadiene styrene (ABS)
ABS is rigid, tough, usually opaque with better heat resistance than polystyrene.
Uses: window fasteners, rainwater goods.

Amino resins
Common examples are urea formaldehyde (1926) and melamine formaldehyde (1934). These colourless resins have good resistance to photo-induced oxidation, but there may be some brown discoloration, particularly of the thiourea and urea groups, and all are affected by prolonged exposure to moisture and develop fine cracks. Melamine is the most resistant to moisture, chemicals and flames. Formaldehyde has now been identified as a hazardous material and its use is restricted.[71]
Uses: rigid moulded items such as electrical fittings, lavatory seats, 'unbreakable' tableware, sheet laminates and adhesives.

Cellulose acetate
Among the most common uses are photographic film (1912) and, with suitable plasticizers, as a moulding powder (1922).

Degradation of the acetate by moisture releases acetic acid, which acts as a catalyst in further hydrolysis, often producing a surface bloom but usually without crazing. Shrinkage stresses are set up due to the initial high water content and can lead to cracking.

Uses: mouldings, paints and coatings, insulation pads, handrail coverings.

Cellulose nitrate

Common trade names are Parkesine (1862), Celluloid (1869) and Xylonite.

Cellulose nitrate is affected by light and moisture, which cause it to become yellow and brittle. Oxides of nitrogen develop and will form acids, which in turn are catalysts in continuing reactions; the presence of metals can accelerate the process. The first signs of degradation are usually a surface bloom, but by that time failure of the plastic is already well under way. Regular washing with a very dilute ammonia solution to remove acidity from the surface will help to prolong life, although it will not affect internal acidity. The *India Rubber and Gutta Percha and Electric Traders Journal* of 8 July 1889 recommended rubbing with finely powdered pumice stone and water and exposing to the hot sun while still moist to prevent cracking.

Uses: early conservation lacquers, paint and coating systems capable of taking an applied texture, treatments for materials to produce leather cloth and similar textiles, fibres for artificial silk (1889), photographic films up to 1940s, sculpture (it was used by Naum Gabo, among others) and decorative items.

Elastomers

These are natural, modified and synthetic rubbers, including polychloroprene (Neoprene), butyl rubber, silicone rubbers and polysulphides.

In natural rubber the most common causes of ageing are crosslink reversion, oxidation, ozone and light. With less than 5% sulphur, rubber is very flexible, but at more than 30% it becomes rigid and forms ebonite.

Synthetic rubbers include styrene-butadiene (SBR) and butadiene acrylonitrile (NBR), the latter being widely used for gaskets, seals and contact adhesives. Butyl rubber is a copolymer of isobutylene and isoprene and has good resistance to sunlight and oxidation; it is used as a mastic and sealant. Silicone rubbers have a siloxane link as the basis of the polymer, since pure silicone backbones are unstable and in some forms cross-linking can be activated by atmospheric moisture.

Epoxy resins

These were first produced in Europe in 1955. They are chemically complex, involving phenolic compounds that form a linear polymer which cures by coupling of the end epoxide groups, and their polymerization differs from that of other polyesters as the resin and hardener act as a series of 'hooks and eyes'. They have good chemical resistance, particularly to alkalis.

Uses: adhesives, resins for reinforced plastics and coatings.

Phenol formaldehyde

Phenol formaldehyde is a hard, brittle, heat-resistant, thermosetting plastic. When cast without fillers, it can be transparent or coloured; but when used as a resin in rigid thin laminates and other mouldings produced with heat and pressure, the colours are limited to dark browns, greens and black.

It is very stable, although prolonged exposure to moisture may result in absorption, and sunlight and UV cause brown discoloration. Some surface degradation and loss of gloss may occur and it will blister or crack if exposed to heat. It will burn only with great difficulty.
Uses: electrical goods, high pressure laminates and adhesives.

Polyacrylonitrile

The fibres are often referred to as acrylics (not to be confused with acrylics based on acrylate esters). Acrilan, Courtelle and Orlon (1950) are unaffected by bacteria, and show good resistance to sunlight, atmospheric oxidation and moisture, but may discolour when heated.
Uses: soft furnishings.

Polyamide – Nylon

Nylons produced from amino acids or lactams (1940) are followed by a single number indicating the number of carbon atoms in the repeat unit. A double number indicates that the polymer is derived from a diamine (1938), the double number indicating the number of carbon atoms in the two components.

Nylons generally have high melting points. They are strong, flexible and tough, as well as being abrasion- and solvent-resistant, but become brittle in sunlight unless stabilized and are subject to photo-induced oxidation in the hydrocarbon sections, while the amides are subject to hydrolysis and moisture absorption.
Uses: catches, rollers, central heating tubes, rope, fibres and bristles.

Polycarbonate – Makrolon and Lexan

Polycarbonates came into use in the mid 1950s. They are naturally clear, transparent materials, which are rigid up to 100°C. They have high resistance and generally weather well, but will yellow and become brittle with age, and may suffer from atmospheric abrasion.
Uses: glass substitute.

Polyesters

Polyester was discovered by Berzelius in 1847 but not exploited until 1928. The fibres are used for fabrics and resins that can be moulded at low temperatures. It has good electrical and mechanical properties and chemical resistance, and a wide colour range.
Uses: GRP, in which form it is used for building shells and components, pipes, ducts and furniture; resin cements, 'plastic metal' and wood fillers.

Polyethylene – Polythene

Polythene was discovered 1933, and came into full production as an essential part of the war effort for electrical and radar protection in 1942. A high-density version was discovered in 1953, a tougher material used for structural and non-structural foams. It has a wide range of different densities and softening temperatures, is chemically stable, does not dissolve in solvents at room temperature, is unaffected by acids and alkalis and is a very good electrical insulator. A translucent material, it can be pigmented, and biodegradable versions are available for packaging.

Some polar liquids, such as chloroform, ether, silicones and detergents, can cause stress cracking. Polythene is susceptible to photo-oxidation if exposed to UV; auto-catalytic once started. The first signs of failure are yellow or brown discoloration followed by cracking. Exposed polythene is usually black to help absorb UV. It can be attacked by rodents and subject to surface growths. *Uses:* water pipes, buckets, tanks, damp-proof membranes and vapour barriers.

Polymethyl Methacrylate – Acrylics – Perspex, Lucite and Diakon

These were developed in the 1930s. Perspex (1934) is clear, hard, capable of taking a gloss finish, and has good weathering properties, including resistance to moisture and UV light. In 1957 ICI started adding a trace of UV absorber, claiming that it significantly improved the material's performance and reduced its tendency to yellow. Acrylics are susceptible to burns and some organic solvents, and can develop stress crazing. They can be coloured, although early pastel shades are subject to fading in strong light. Cleaning with ethanol and propan-2-ol are believed to be safe and there are proprietary polishes that can be used to restore surface gloss and remove scratches. *Uses:* signs, illuminated ceilings.

Polypropylene

Polypropylene dates from 1959 and is similar to polythene, but has greater rigidity and a higher softening point. It is more susceptible to photo-oxidation, but it is not subject to environmental stress cracking.
Uses: rigid mouldings, such as manholes, stacking chairs and parts of cars, and as a reinforcing fibre in composite materials.

Polystyrene

This was first polymerized in 1839 using sunlight, and converted into polystyrene in 1845. Large-scale production was possible when a high purity monomer became available (1937). High impact grades (1948) have largely been replaced by ABS plastics. Polystyrene's brittleness can be overcome by blending it with rubber. It is not subject to oxidative degradation in sunlight or UV, but the rubber additives in high-impact and ABS grades can accelerate degradation. Exposure to high temperature causes degradation. Exposure to light causes yellowing, sometimes accompanied by crazing. Early coloured material is prone to fading. Polystyrene can be stressed by alcohol, white spirit and fats and may also be affected by solvent-based adhesives or lacquers, as well as polishes.
Uses: insulation, and void formers in concrete.

Polytetrafluoroethylene (PTFE)

PTFE was discovered in 1938 and was produced commercially 1948. It has a very low friction, is chemically inert and is resistant to high temperatures and weathering. It is degraded by UV and will creep under load. PTFE is now included in some lists of hazardous materials, due to its performance under fire conditions.

Uses: pipe linings, tape for threaded joints, bearings for plant and bridges.

Polyurethanes

Polyurethane was first discovered in 1937. It is produced in many thermoplastic and thermosetting forms, of which the more flexible dissolve in some organic solvents and acids.

Uses: insulation and upholstery foams, sealants and caulking, paint and one-part coating systems.

Polyvinyl Chloride (PVC)

PVC was patented in plasticized form in 1912 and first produced commercially in about 1935. Relatively unstable, it degrades at the temperature required for processing, so it is always used with a stabilizer. The plasticized form may be processed at lower temperatures.

Grades suitable for extrusion and injection were developed in the 1950s, allowing a substantial increase in the range of products related to building. Later developments include modified unplasticized PVC and chlorinated PVC. *The Weathering and Performance of Building Materials* (1970) puts the anticipated life of PVC products at between ten and thirty years.

Under prolonged heating the material degrades, liberating the acidic gas hydrogen chloride and instigating an auto-catalytic reaction, which proceeds quite rapidly. A similar effect can be caused by the action of UV. The first sign of degradation is the development of a brown colour. Polyvalent metals can also instigate degradation; thus insulated copper cables may attack their casing and cause it to become brittle. In the plasticized material, the plasticizers are quite volatile and the material hardens, while the plasticizer may be absorbed into other materials, such as polystyrene, which can be adversely affected. Vinyl chloride, which is released from PVC at a very low level, is defined by Curwell and March as a hazardous material; PVC should be conserved with care once it becomes degraded.

Uses: unplasticized PVC: rainwater goods, window frames and, in a translucent form, for roof lights and corrugated roofing. Plasticized PVC incorporating a stabilizer: flooring, electrical installations, and paints.

References

1 Williamson, C. (1992), '150 years of plastics degradation', in N.S. Allen, M. Edge and C.V. Horie (eds), *Polymers in Conservation*, Cambridge: Royal Society of Chemistry.

2 Gutta percha was used for speaking tubes, floor coverings (British Patent No. 1302, 8 May 1857), mouldings (British Patent No. 24, 1 October 1852 and British Patent No. 623, 3 November 1852) and even patented for roof tiles (British Patent No. 383, 14 February 1853). Shellac was used for paints and varnishes and in conjunction with fillers for moulded objects. Vulcanized rubber produced mouldings and rubber seals and waterproofing patents abounded. Papier mâché was used for mouldings.

3 Pevsner, N. (1960), *Pioneers of Modern Design*, Harmondsworth: Penguin, 30.

4 An extract from a statement by Hyatt in 1885, quoted in Mossman, S.T.I. (1994), 'Parkesine and celluloid' in S.T.I. Mossman and P.T.J. Morris (eds), *The Development of Plastics*, Cambridge: Royal Society of Chemistry, 19.

5 Fielding, T.J. (1940s), *The History of Bakelite Limited*, London: Bakelite.

6 Bertram, A. (1938), *Design*, Harmondsworth: Penguin, 43.

7 *Architects' Journal* (1936), **84**, (19 March), 463–464.

8 Katz, S. (1985), *Classic Plastics*, London: Thames and Hudson, 11.

9 The designs produced for the studios, in particular those by Raymond McGrath, Wells Coates and Serge Chermeyeff, relied extensively on a new German cellulose material, Trolit, which had been introduced by Walter Gropius. *Architects' Journal* (1931), **83**, (4 November 1931), 598; Yorke, F.R.S. (1932), 'Details', *Architectural Review*, **72**, (429), (August), 65; Yorke, F.R.S. (1932), *British Plastics and Moulded Products Trader*, (October), 205. Yorke reported on 'a laminated sheet made from white paper impregnated with a liquid synthetic resin obtainable in almost any colour but never before

manufactured as a wall covering. I understand, however, that since its inception at Broadcasting House it has become a standard product.'

10 Hayes, J. (1994–5), 'From cyanide to beetle', *Plastiquarian*, (Winter), **7**, 14.

11 Davidson, J.G.and McClure, H.B. (1933), 'Applications of vinyl resins', *Industrial and Engineering Chemistry*, **25**, (6), 645–652.

12 Cook, P., and Slessor, C. (1992), *Bakelite*, London: Apple, 107.

13 Meikle, J.L. (1994), 'Materia nova: plastics and design in the US, 1925–1935' in S.T.I. Mossman and P.T.J. Morris (eds), *The Development of Plastics*, Cambridge: Royal Society of Chemistry, 40–41; *Modern Plastics* (1934), (September), 14.

14 *Listener* (1935), (9 January).

15 Meikle, J.L. (1992), 'Into the fourth kingdom: representations of plastic materials 1920–1950', *Journal of Design History*, **5**, (3), 178.

16 Meikle, J.L. (1992), 'Into the fourth kingdom: representations of plastic materials 1920–1950', *Journal of Design History*, **5**, (3), 178.

17 Saint, A. (1987), *Towards a Social Architecture*, London: Yale University Press, 22–24. Experience of inflatable tanks and other new materials and structures were to prove invaluable in the post-war period.

18 *Architectural Review* (1952), **112**, (July), 667.

19 Anon. (1937), 'Plastics in Architecture', *Architectural Forum*, (February), 147; Lewin, S.G. (ed) (1991), *Formica and Design*, New York: Rizzoli, 50.

20 *Design* (1957), (100), (April), 36.

21 Singer, J. (1952), *Plastics in Building*, London: Architectural Press, 81.

22 Butler, C. (1940), 'War-time building practice', *The Builder*, (24 May), 611–614.

23 Pawley, M. (1992), *Design Heroes: Buckminster Fuller*, London: Grafton, 120.

24   Scott, K.A., and Matthan, J. (1970), 'Weathering' in B. Parkyn (ed) (1970), *Glass Reinforced Plastics*, London: Iliffe, 229.

25   SPI 12th Annual Meeting, Chicago (1956). In France the differential was even larger, with 810 metric tons of laminates being used for corrugated panelling, more than double that for the next category, which was electrical laminates. Western Germany had only started producing flat and corrugated sheets in 1954 and showed more interest in self-supporting structures and concern about the fire resistance and colour-stability of the materials. Japan was also expanding the manufacture of sheet materials and with only 100 scientists and engineers engaged in development of reinforced plastics experienced severe limits on the degree of innovation.

26   Morgan, P. (1961), *Glass Reinforced Plastics*, (3rd edn), London: Iliffe, 298 and 304.

27   Anon. (1969), 'Prefabricated bathroom units', *Architects' Journal*, **149**, (18), (30 April), 1191–1198; Clark, B.A. (1965), 'Using plastics in heart units', *Industrialised Building Systems and Components*, (July).

28   'Salesman's briefing' Rollosrank glass reinforced plastics products.

29   Deitz, A.G.H. (1972), 'Contemporary shell structures', *Modern Plastics*, (March), 91–187.

30   Deitz, A.G.H. with Goody, M.E., Heger, F.J., McGarry, FJ. and Whittier, R.P. (1957), 'Engineering the plastics house of the future', *Modern Plastics*, (June), 143.

31   *Radio Times* (1966), (31 March), 49 and 52. The programme was broadcast on BBC 1 television at 9.30 on 7 April and examined building techniques of the nineteenth, twentieth and possibly twenty-first centuries.

32   Roach, E.C. (1974), 'Manufacturer's view of the general use of plastics panels as structural and non-load bearing units', *The Use of Plastics for Load Bearing and Infill Panels Symposium*, University of Surrey.

33   Quarmby, A. (1974), *The Plastic Architect*, London: Pall Mall Press.

34   Kirby, D. (1967), 'The application of polyurethane foam to developments in building in Great Britain', International Conference on Building Materials, Warsaw.

35   Anon. (1971), 'Foam Home', *Progressive Architecture*, (May), 101.

36   Dormer, P. (1993), *Design Since 1945*, London: Thames and Hudson, 168.

37   Dietz, A.G.H. (1956), 'Paper and plastics in building', paper presented to the 7th Conference of the Technical Association of the Pulp and Paper Industry, in *Tappi*, **39**, (12), (December 1956), 38a–50a.

38   Platts, R.E. (1964), 'The role of plastics in house structure' Technical Paper No 176, (April), Ottawa: National Research Council Canada, 1.

39   Platzker, J. (1968), 'Why plastics are not used in greater quantities in buildings', paper presented to the 26th Conference of the Society of Plastics Engineers, New York.

40   *Architectural Plastics* (1974), (11), (May), British Plastics Federation, 6.

41   Skolimowski, H. (1978), 'Rationality in architecture and the design process', in D. Sharp (ed), *The Rationalists*, London: Architectural Press, 160–172.

42   Antonelli, P. (1995), *Mutant Materials*, New York: Museum of Modern Art,19.

43   Katz, S. (1985), *Classic Plastics*, London: Thames and Hudson; Morgan, J. (1991), *Conservation of Plastics*, London: Plastics Historical Society and The Conservation Unit of the Museums and Galleries Commission.

44   Katz, S. (1985), *Classic Plastics*, London: Thames and Hudson, 146; DiNoto, A. (1984), *Art Plastic*, New York: Abbeville Press, 215.

45   Morgan, J. (1991), *Conservation of Plastics*, London: Plastics Historical Society and The Conservation Unit of the Museums and Galleries Commission, 37.

46   Allen, N.S. (1992), 'Action of light on dyed and pigmented polymers' in N.S. Allen, M. Edge and C.V. Horie, *Polymers in Conservation*, Cambridge: Royal Society of Chemistry, 193.

47   Brantley, L. Reed, and Brantley, Ruth T. (1996), *Building Materials Technology*, New York: McGraw Hill, 212.

48   DiNoto, A. (1984), *Art Plastic* , New York: Abbeville Press, 216

49   van Tulleken, K. (1982), *Working with Plastics*, Amsterdam: Time Life Books, 35.

50   Whitford, M.J. (1992), *Getting Rid of Graffiti*, London: E. & F.N. Spon.

51   Simpson, J., and Horrobin, P. (1970), *The Weathering and Performance of Building Materials*, Aylesbury, Buckinghamshire: Medical and Technical Publishing, 239

52   Konrad, K., and Kofoed, P. (1995), 'Vinyl Tile' in T. Jester (ed), *Twentieth-Century Building Materials*, New York: McGraw-Hill, 241–245; Curwell, S.R., and March, C.G. (1986), *Hazardous Building Materials*, London: E. & F.N. Spon, 35 and 85.

53   Wollacombe, J. (1935), 'You need not have a noisy house', *The Ideal Home*, **32**, (October), 249.

54   Park, S. (1995), 'Rubber Tile' in T. Jester (ed), *Twentieth-Century Building Materials*, New York: McGraw-Hill, 222–227.

55   Walker, A., Konrad, K.A., and Stull, N.L. (1995), 'Decorative plastic laminates' in T. Jester (ed), *Twentieth-Century Building Materials*, New York: McGraw-Hill, 126–131.

56   McCann, H. (1955), 'Surface and decorative uses of plastics in building', *Plastics in Building*, Building Research Institute USA, (April), 63.

57   Walker, A. (1995), 'Fiber reinforced plastic' in T. Jester (ed), *Twentieth-Century Building Materials*, New York: McGraw-Hill, 142–155.

58   Sonneborn, R.H. (1954), *Fibreglass Reinforced Plastics*, New York: Reinhold. The first American technical handbook. In this publication the material is referred to as FRP, but GRP is the more usual term as Fibreglass is a proprietary material.

59   Bader, Scott (n.d.), *Crystic Polyester Handbook*.

60   *Industrialisation Forum* (1978), **9**, (1), 29.

61   *Ibid.* 27–32.

62   *Ibid.* 31.

63   Sharp, D. (1991), *Twentieth Century Architecture Visual History*, London: Lund Humphries, 292; Webb, M. (1969), *Architecture Today*, Hamlyn/Country Life, 94.

64   Reply at the Council Meeting 24 October 1967 to a question from Mr H. Ferguson.

65   Brookes, A J. (1990), *Cladding of Buildings*, London: Longman Scientific and Technical, Chapter 2.

66   Garnier, T. (1918), *Une Cité Industrielle*, Paris, 8.

67   Le Corbusier (1946), *Towards a Modern Architecture*, London: Architectural Press, 214.

68   Gloag, J. (1943), 'The Influence of Plastics on Design', *Journal of the Royal Society of Arts*, **91**, (23 July), 462–470.

69   Manzini, E. (1985), *Domus*, (666), (November), 54.

70   Manzini, E. (1990), 'Objects and their Skin' in P. Sparke (ed), *The Plastics Age*, London: Victoria and Albert Museum, 118.

71   Curwell, S.R., and March, C.G. (1986), *Hazardous Building Materials*, London: E. & F.N. Spon, 35.

CHAPTER 6

THE USE OF CONCRETE IN THE POST-WAR ERA

Michael Bussell

Our theme is the post-war heritage, which in broad terms covers the last half century. In the perspective of architectural history, this is a relatively short period. However, the timescale is very different within the context of concrete – a shorthand term for what we are taking here to be the use of the material (usually reinforced, less commonly prestressed) as a major element of a building or other structure.

In the UK, the first major architectural and structural use of reinforced concrete was in 1897. Weaver's Mill in Swansea, South Wales, was a large utilitarian structure built on the French Hennebique system, only three years after the first large-scale use of this system for a refinery in Paris.[1] (Redundant, its fabric deteriorating, not at all readily adaptable to new use, and – it has to be said – of debatable aesthetic merit, the building was demolished in 1984, despite being listed.)

From 1897 to the end of World War II is 48 years; from 1945 to our conference is 53 years. So, chronologically if not necessarily in landmark events and structures, more than half of the modern history of concrete in building already belongs to this post-war era. (Of course the Romans had been earlier users of concrete.[2,3] They exploited the natural cementitious properties of volcanic ash, known as 'pozzolan' from its discovery at Pozzuoli in Italy. They also discovered that the addition to lime mortar of burnt clay, and crushed brick and tile, enhanced its compressive strength significantly. They built many fine large domes and vaults as well as using concrete in more straightforward uses such as walls and foundations.)

My task here, is to review half a century of the extensive use of concrete in building – a daunting task in any event, and a paper of this length requires a broad-brush approach. I propose to consider the basic ingredients of concrete and the process of concrete construction, then to pick out some key technical developments since World War II and examine the architectural treatment of exposed concrete, before considering some of the problems encountered with concrete in this period.

If there were no technical problems to be dealt with in concrete structures, then there would be no call for the papers that follow this one, dealing with the deterioration and repair of concrete. But it is not necessary to argue that there have been problems. They have largely been associated with durability, which I define here as the ability to perform in service over a substantial period without failure and without major repairs being necessary. Most durability problems arise from one or more of these factors:

- use of unsuitable materials – unsuitable either in themselves or in combination with other materials;
- poor workmanship;
- inadequate supervision;
- inadequate understanding or experience.

While I will be considering problems encountered in the last half-century, it is neither my wish nor my intention to denigrate concrete, which is an excellent and versatile constructional material that has been used to achieve many notable buildings and other structures. But, as with every other building material, to use it successfully we must understand its properties, its strengths, and its weaknesses.

Concrete: materials and process

Concrete and its components
Concrete is an artificial stone in which discrete particles (the filler) are cemented together by a binder material. In concrete the filler comprises aggregates, coarse and fine, which should be graded in size and mixed in proportions so as to form a dense, closely packed material. The binder material, typically cement, should ideally fill all voids within the aggregate mixture. The cement is activated by mixing with water to initiate a chemical setting reaction.

Like natural stone, concrete is strong in compression but relatively weak in tension or when sheared or twisted. However, it can be reinforced to overcome these weaknesses, and reinforced concrete has found wide use as a versatile structural material.

The various materials and processes involved in concrete construction are now considered in more detail.

Cements
The story of modern cement begins in 1824, when Joseph Aspdin secured a patent for Portland cement (so named because its pale grey-white colour when set resembled that of some Portland stone).[4] This comprises limestone and clay burnt together at high temperature and subsequently ground into powder which, when mixed with water, reacts chemically and sets hard. Cement, water, and aggregate will produce concrete.

Subsequent material developments have been numerous. The original Portland cement was classed as 'ordinary' or OPC, to distinguish it from purpose-designed varieties such as rapid-hardening or sulphate-resisting cement (the latter being particularly useful in groundworks where sulphate-bearing groundwater and soils attack and damage OPC). White cement has attracted the attention of architects keen to exploit the material's potential to create an unadorned 'honest' structural envelope.

High alumina cement (HAC) was much used from the 1950s until the mid-1970s in the manufacture of precast structural components, particularly prestressed floor and roof units, as its very rapid strength development allowed faster turn-round and consequently more efficient use of the formwork or moulds in which the concrete was cast. However, investigations following three roof failures in 1973–4 showed that a long-term strength reduction took place in normal environments. It had previously been believed that this occurred only in warm, humid environments. As a result, HAC was effectively banned for new construction.

More recently, other materials have been used partially to replace Portland cement. These can have technical advantages in some situations, as well as recycling abundant (and cheap) industrial waste products.[5] Their use also reduces demand for the basic constituents of Portland cement – limestone and clay – the extraction of which impacts on the landscape. An example is blast-furnace slag, a by-product of the smelting of iron ore to make steel.

Additives may be included in the cement–water paste for specific purposes: calcium chloride was found to accelerate the setting reaction in cold weather, and was accordingly used for winter working. Its use is now restricted following the realization that its chloride content aggravated reinforcement corrosion.

Water for concrete should ideally be clean and free from chemicals or impurities that could affect durability. The use of sea water should be anathema, as it is rich in chlorides. Nevertheless, it has sometimes been used, often with all-too-evident results such as massive corrosion of the reinforcement and spalling of concrete.

Aggregates

Aggregates from natural sources have been used in much post-war concrete work. For coarse aggregate, typically of a nominal $3/4$ inch (20 mm) size, crushed rock or river gravels have been commonest. Fine aggregate is typically sand. Architects have exploited the wide choice of crushed rocks and sands available for concrete when designing exposed concrete finishes. Pressure from increasing demand, however, has led to use of dredged marine aggregates, which have not always been adequately washed to eliminate their potentially damaging salt content.

More recently, 'artificial' aggregates have been developed. A notable example is pulverised fly ash waste (PFA) from coal-fired power stations, which is formed into pellets and marketed as Lytag. Various other industrial waste-products have been similarly employed,[6] harking back to the nineteenth-century use of clinker, broken bricks, and 'rubbish' (a term used to describe demolition waste) as aggregates. Often, the working of these into suitable forms for aggregates yields a material of lower density than natural aggregates. This has led to the development of lightweight concrete,[7] which has been exploited with particular success where reduced dead-weight is beneficial, such as in cantilevered roofs.[8] One example is the grandstand roof at Sandown Park, Esher (Figure 6.1, *overleaf*).

Some natural aggregates have proved physically or chemically unstable in concrete. Physically unsound aggregates undergo significant volume changes with variation in their moisture content and/or temperature, and particularly during cycles of freezing and thawing. An example is the so-called 'expanding' shale.[9] Adverse chemical effects include, notably, 'alkali-aggregate

Figure 6.1   The cantilevered grandstand roof at Sandown Park Racecourse, Esher, Surrey (1972, Fitzroy Robinson & Partners with Jan Bobrowski & Partners). (Michael Bussell)

reaction' (AAR) or, more precisely, 'alkali-silica reaction' (ASR).[10] In this, alkalis in the cement combine with 'reactive' silica, as found in some silica-bearing rocks such as cherts and siliceous limestones. The resulting gel is hygroscopic and swells, creating bursting forces within the concrete that lead to cracking and spalling.

Reinforcement

Reinforcement to improve the strength of concrete in tension was initially of iron and subsequently of steel. The reinforcement forms include rods, bars, wire, and woven meshes. Grip is essential: the reinforcement must bond to and/or mechanically attach to the concrete. If it does not, then the two materials cannot work together. The ends of plain reinforcing bars have been bent up or hooked to provide anchorage, and various ways have been developed of twisting or deforming reinforcement in order to improve bond. Before World War II, however, the more exotic forms had effectively gone out of use, leaving what we recognize today: plain mild steel bars, hot-rolled ribbed and cold-worked 'deformed' (i.e. twisted) high-yield bars, and rectangular mats of small-diameter rods welded together to form sheets of mesh.

By fortunate chance, the coefficients of thermal expansion of a typical concrete and of steel are virtually the same, about $1 \times 10^{-5}/°C$, so that the two materials can work together without significant distortion.

In addition to its primary role in strengthening concrete, reinforcement is also effective at controlling the width of cracking in concrete. It is perhaps important to point out that, unless it is prestressed (as discussed below), concrete must crack if the reinforcement is to work at the stresses it can safely carry. This is because the tensile strain in the steel and the adjacent concrete must be the same, as they are bonded together. At the safe working stress in the steel, the strain in the concrete exceeds its cracking strain. Thus, for economic design, cracking in the concrete must be permitted – within limits.

Reinforcement will control cracking, keeping crack widths within acceptable limits for appearance and durability, if the steel is relatively closely spaced. Thus, even when reinforcement is not needed for strength, so-called 'anti-crack' reinforcement is commonly provided in walls, slabs, and other elements to control the width of cracks arising from loading, temperature effects, small structural movements, and so on. And 'distribution' or 'nominal' reinforcement is provided in slabs and elsewhere to distribute concentrated loads over a larger area.

In recent years, galvanized and stainless steel have been used in an effort to counter corrosion problems, particularly in cladding panels. Epoxy-coated steel is a still more recent development in this field.

Prestressing

A later development, associated with the French engineer Freyssinet,[11] was prestressing. In 1928, Freyssinet recognized that cracking (apart from risking exposure of the reinforcement directly to airborne moisture, with possible consequent corrosion) reduced the efficiency of a given section. An uncracked section would be stiffer, allowing use of thinner and/or shallower members for a given load and span. Cracking could be prevented by precompressing the section.

There are basically two ways to prestress concrete. In one, the concrete is cast around pre-tensioned rods or wires anchored in the moulds. These are released when the concrete has hardened, so that the concrete is compressed by transfer of force from the bonded steel. Because pre-tensioning is a factory process, the quality of materials and workmanship can be closely controlled.

Alternatively, in post-tensioned work, the concrete is cast first, with tubular holes or sheaths formed along its length. Into these are inserted bars, rods, or cables, which are then post-tensioned to compress the concrete. The steel is anchored at its ends by wedges, nuts on threaded bars, or purpose-formed grips.[12] The void between the steel and the concrete may be grouted to provide enhanced anchorage and to increase corrosion protection. Post-tensioning is a site activity, with the attendant potential problems of poor workmanship and supervision.

An advantage of post-tensioning is that sheaths can be profiled to match the distribution of bending action within a beam or slab. In the case of a uniformly loaded member freely supported at each end, this distribution varies parabolically, rising from zero at each end to a

maximum at midspan. Giving the post-tensioned steel a matching profile will minimize the quantity of steel required, hence improving structural efficiency. Pre-tensioned steel is by its nature
straight (it can be deflected within the moulds, but only into straight sections with expensive
anchorages needed to resist the out-of-balance forces at changes in direction).

It was quickly discovered that prestressed concrete would shorten under load, from three
causes. One is elastic shortening, which happens instantaneously when any material is subject
to compression. The other causes are peculiar to concrete: shrinkage, as the concrete slowly
loses moisture; and creep, which is time-related shortening under load. The combined effects of
these are such that steel of ordinary strength would lose much of its effectiveness, so prestressed
concrete is invariably made using high-strength steel.

Placing reinforcement

The reinforcement, usually cut and bent to shape off site, has to be placed in the correct position and at the required spacings to satisfy the design intentions. It must also have the correct
cover from the concrete face to ensure both durability and fire resistance. To achieve this, spacers of the appropriate thickness are used. These can be precast concrete blocks with projecting
wires for attaching the steel or, more commonly now, proprietary nylon or plastic spacers notched
to hold the steel bars by a press-fit.

Occasionally the reinforcement cage is suspended from above to eliminate the risk of any
spacer markings on the bottom or side faces. However, this does not ensure that the correct
cover is automatically maintained on these faces. Also, the reinforcement must not move about
while being worked on and while concrete is being placed. This requires an adequate number
of spacers, and the wiring together of the bars to form a rigid entity.

Formwork

Whether the concrete is precast off site or poured in place, formwork is needed to define the
concrete element's shape. Together with supporting props and other members, the formwork must
also be strong and stiff enough to support the weight of wet concrete until it has hardened, without failure or distortion. A further role for formwork, discussed under 'Architectural concrete'
below, may be to provide a particular surface finish to the formed concrete faces.

The traditional formwork material has been timber, particularly plywood. Other suitable materials include steel (especially for mass-production precasting), and glass-reinforced plastic (for
sculptural profiles). Large cardboard tubes have been used for circular columns.

Whatever the material used, some form of surface treatment is usually necessary to ensure
that the formwork comes away cleanly when removed or 'struck' after the concrete has reached
the necessary strength to allow this. Mould oil is a commonly used bond-breaker; it is important that the oil does not find its way onto the reinforcement, where its debonding properties
would be distinctly unwelcome. Retarders applied to the formwork delay the setting of the cement
paste, allowing subsequent architectural treatment of the concrete surfaces after formwork is
stripped, such as exposure of the coarse aggregate by wire-brushing.

Concrete mixes

In the post-war period, concrete was customarily batched by volume, using proportions that were known by experience to give adequate strength. A 1:2:4 mix (one part of cement, two parts of fine aggregate, and four parts of coarse aggregate) could be expected to give a cube crushing strength of 3,000 pounds per square inch (about 21N/mm^2) at 28 days. Water was added, often 'by eye', to achieve the required workability.

In the 1960s there was a shift towards specifying concrete by strength. This allowed the concrete supplier (increasingly a ready-mixed firm, mixing off site and delivering by lorry) to use a previously proven economical mix design with a lower cement content. Unfortunately, durability was not addressed explicitly by such a specification, any more than it had been by the volume basis.

Research, and the study of corrosion-damaged concrete in various exposure conditions, has shown clearly that increased cement content produces improved durability.[13] So, too, does reduced water–cement ratio; this had been known since 1918, when Duff Abrams found that concrete strength increased as the water-cement ratio was reduced, but durability had not been linked in the same way. Not until BS CP110:1972[14] appeared was specific consideration of durability required as a design issue, additional to the question of strength.

Transporting, placing, compacting and curing

Once mixed, concrete must be placed before initial set has begun. Difficulties can occur with ready-mixed concrete when the depot is distant from the site and/or deliveries are delayed by heavy traffic. While the concrete will be kept in a plastic state by the rotation of the truck's drum, it will start to stiffen as time passes. A well-known but unfortunate practice was to add sufficient water on arrival to 'refresh' the mix. This increased the water-cement ratio. The consequent reduction of strength might be noticed in lower cube test results, but the longer-term effect on durability was less apparent.

The introduction of quality assurance systems has done much to improve the general standard of ready-mixed concrete.

Placing needed care. Pouring the concrete from too great a height could lead to 'segregation': the coarse aggregate would sink to the bottom and produce a concrete of uneven strength and (if exposed) visibly stratified appearance. This was particularly likely with poorly graded or 'over-wet' mixes. A more recent development has been the use of concrete pumping. With a suitably designed concrete mix, pumping reduces the risk of segregation and allows concrete to be delivered as closely as possible to its required location.

Compaction, driving out trapped air from the mix to produce a dense concrete with only small voids, is now recognized as an essential process for both strength and durability. In the early years of this century, concrete was often made 'self-compacting'. This in practice meant using a high water content to produce a 'runny' mix that would flow readily into spaces between congested reinforcement and into all corners of the formwork, with unwelcome consequences for durability. Any compaction would be carried out by hand, using rods or variously shaped 'punning' tools to expel trapped air from the concrete.

In 1924 Freyssinet demonstrated the benefits of mechanical compaction. In the post-war period mechanical vibrators, internal or external, were increasingly specified for structural concrete. However, congested and inaccessible sections made compaction difficult, for example at the base of tall columns, with a resultant risk of 'honeycombing' or voiding, visible only when the formwork was stripped.

Curing is an essential part of the concreting process. After-initial set, concrete needs to be kept moist and insulated against cold and drying winds if it is to develop its strength, achieve a dense microstructure, and minimize surface cracking. This is achieved in various ways, typically by leaving the formwork in place on formed faces, and by applying hessian, plastic sheet, sprayed membranes, or other treatment to exposed top surfaces to control moisture loss. In cold weather, expanded foam boarding or other protection is added to protect the 'young' concrete against freezing, which would drastically reduce its strength.

The final process is stripping or removal of the formwork, not to be undertaken until concrete strength is adequate for the new construction to support itself. Formwork must be stripped gently to avoid shock loading of the concrete.

The importance of knowledge and experience

It is clear from the above description that concrete construction involves numerous tasks calling for a variety of skills. Many things have to be got right in the design, specification and construction to ensure sound performance. The designer and the reinforcement detailer can influence the quality of construction by ensuring that the design is buildable. For example, it should avoid unnecessary changes in section profile and congested reinforcement. Practical detailing allows easier formwork manufacture and steel-fixing, with plenty of room in and around reinforcement to permit concrete flow and the insertion of mechanical vibrators. And (human nature being what it is) the easier it is to build something, the greater is the chance that it will be built properly.

On site, three principal trades are needed: the carpenter for formwork; the steel-fixer for placing reinforcement; and the concretor for the placing of concrete. Lack of training and experience, pressures of time and money, and inadequate supervision can all contribute to poor-quality work that leads to subsequent problems. Many instances have found their way into the literature. On the other hand, a sound design properly built will perform satisfactorily (and attract no attention).

Mention must be made of the Cement and Concrete Association, funded by the cement manufacturers, which made a major contribution to the informed use of concrete during the post-war period through its training courses and publications. A substantial reduction in funding in 1986 was regretted by many practitioners, although its successor, the British Cement Association, continues its predecessor's valuable work, albeit on a smaller scale.[15] Other bodies furnishing guidance include the Concrete Society[16] and the British Precast Concrete Federation and its several trade association subsidiaries concerned with various aspects of precast concrete, including cladding.[17]

More recently, there has been growing recognition that the trade of concretor is of vital importance to successful concrete construction. Concreting is a task seen as 'messy' and is all too often delegated to the least-skilled labourers. At least one company has gained a high reputation through specializing in this work and providing well-trained concretors and supervisors, while a joint initiative by the Concrete Society and the Concrete Industry Alliance is seeking to improve training and enhance the image of this essential trade.[18]

Concrete since the war: techniques and building types

Inevitably the Second World War focused the efforts of the building industry on military construction and works related to defence and civilian protection, such as air-raid shelters. Concrete is an excellent 'defensive' material when used in the mass, as witnessed by its widespread adoption for shelters, submarine pens, the German 'Atlantic Wall' along the north French coast, pillboxes, and other structures in which resistance to shells and bombs was crucial.[19]

Concrete also played a key role in the Allied invasion of Europe in 1944. This relied on supplies and equipment for its continued success. The first essential, therefore, once a beachhead had been secured, was a harbour to receive shipping and to protect it from storms. The invasion was to be directed against beaches rather than existing harbours, which were too heavily defended. Accordingly, an 'instant harbour' was needed. For this the Mulberry Harbour was developed, employing large precast floating concrete units that could be towed across the English Channel and installed on the Normandy coast.[20] This was highly successful, resisting a fierce storm and serving for many months until more orthodox harbour facilities had been captured.

Wartime activities are not irrelevant to an account of the post-war period, for several reasons. Industry had geared up on a massive scale for the wartime effort, so that when peace came many factories were available to switch to peacetime tasks. Large wartime projects such as the Mulberry Harbour had demanded new approaches to large-scale organizational planning, which could be applied to post-war rebuilding. Many parts of the UK, particularly London and many other cities and towns, had suffered heavily from air raids, which left large tracts of buildings destroyed or uninhabitable and in need of reconstruction. Moreover, a major social programme, including the Welfare State and the National Health Service, was conceived during the war; this would evidently require new housing to replace those demolished in slum clearance, as well as new hospitals, schools, and other communal buildings.

With the war over, work on reconstruction and new developments could, in theory, begin. Practically, however, there was a desperate shortage of many construction materials, not least steel and bricks. However, the raw materials for concrete (clay and limestone to make cement, and stone and sand for the aggregates) were fairly freely available, as were labour and factories newly freed from war work. As a result, there was an upsurge in concrete construction, which took advantage of the available resources while trying to reduce dependence on those that were scarce (and usually rationed). Some of the most significant developments are considered next.

Housing

Traditional housing used bricks, which were in short supply. Consequently, much effort was put into developing concrete for housing, making use of the available factories by prefabricating the dwellings. Numerous housing types, at this time mainly of one and two storeys, were built with precast units, which could be rapidly assembled on site.[21,22]

At the same time, larger inner-city housing projects needing greater densities were constructed, generally using *in situ* concrete. Some experience of such construction had been gained before the war, a notable example of which was the collaboration between the Tecton group of architects and the structural designer Ove Arup. This team had produced several memorable structures in the 1930s, in particular Highpoint, the private development of large flats in Highgate, north London. This experience was applied and developed to meet the demand for high-density affordable council dwellings. The Rosebery Avenue flats for Finsbury Borough Council in Central London (1949) rose to eight storeys, as high as was then permitted in the London County Council area because of limitations on the reach of fire brigade ladders.

Such multi-storey blocks in concrete could exploit the characteristics of the material, with internal cross-walls, party walls and floor slabs all made of concrete placed *in situ*. This contrasted with the steel-framed building, the structure of which is inevitably based on columns and beams; non-load-bearing partitions had to be added as a subsequent task. Thus concrete provided not only the load-bearing structure and the building's stability, but also the fire and acoustic separation between adjacent dwellings. At Rosebery Avenue a novel system was employed to fix and strip the formwork, greatly speeding up the work. The formwork was reusable too, countering the criticism sometimes levelled against *in situ* concrete structures that they are built twice, once in timber (the formwork) and then in concrete, when the first attempt is demolished and cleared away.

Shells and vaulted roofs

The shortage of reinforcement after the war had a particular influence on the design of large-span roofs. Since Roman times concrete had been used in arches, domes and vaults, which took advantage of its good compressive strength long before reinforced concrete had been developed. Now designers turned to the shell and the vault when large-span roofs were needed for factories, bus stations, canteens, market halls and the like.

Two strands can be identified: the 'standard' solution and the 'one-off'. The standard solution typically comprised multi-bay cylindrical barrel vaults or 'saw-tooth' roof profiles with north-light glazing, supplemented by the occasional hyperbolic paraboloid. Roofs were supported on columns, the out-of-balance thrusts at vault and shell edges being resisted by edge beams. Some reinforcement was necessary in the valleys, columns, and beams, but overall the amount of steel needed was very much less than for the principal rival in this field, the structural steel trussed roof. And, of course, the concrete formed the roof decking too; whereas the steel trussed roof required the addition of a deck, typically of profiled metal, corrugated asbestos or translucent sheet plastic.

Two British companies dominated the market for standard concrete roofs, Twisteel Reinforcement Ltd (later known as GKN Reinforcements) and British Reinforced Concrete Ltd (BRC).[23] Such roofs are very much a product of the circumstances of the time, when steel was in short supply but labour was relatively cheap and abundant, especially for the formwork. Today, the economics would be different.

The same argument applies to the one-off shell or vaulted concrete roof. A number of memorable examples remain in use, although perhaps the finest now stands empty, with consent to demolish. This is the listed Brynmawr factory in South Wales with its nine shallow rectangular domes, each spanning 25 by 19 metres (Architects' Co-Partnership and Ove Arup & Partners, 1947–51).[24,25] The genesis of such roofs lay usually in active architect–engineer collaboration, often encouraged by an enlightened client. Ove Arup & Partners, with several very mathematically talented engineers, were a leading force. Their collaborations included the Bank of England Printing Works (1953–56, with architects Easton & Robertson)[26] and the later dome roof following the destruction by fire of the original Smithfield Poultry Market in central London (1960–62, with architects Sir Thomas Bennett & Son).[27,28]

Other notable shell or vault roofs of this period include the Commonwealth Institute of 1960–62 (Robert Matthew, Johnson-Marshall & Partners and Harris & Sutherland) (Figure 6.2), and Felix Candela's c.1962 hyperbolic paraboloid roof for a John Lewis warehouse in Stevenage.[29] Other architects and engineers designing one-off shell roofs included Edward Mills, Felix Samuely, and Sir Frederick Snow.[30]

One further form of shell may yet attract the conservation lobby's interest – the power station cooling tower, a thin-walled lightly reinforced concrete shell whose strength comes from its hyperbolic paraboloid shape.

Applications of prestressed concrete

Prestressing was patented by Eugene Freyssinet in 1928, but found little use in the UK until the immediate post-war period, when there was recognition of its merits in reducing the amount of steel needed. It received the active support of the Ministry of Works, and early applications

Figure 6.2   The hyperbolic paraboloid roof of the Commonwealth Institute, Kensington, London (Robert Matthew, Johnson-Marshall & Partners with Harris & Sutherland, 1960–62). (Michael Bussell)

included a Stationery Office building in 1948, and the 1953 Kilburn Telephone Exchange in north London (recently converted to flats).

Precast, prestressed concrete found wide application in standard bridge beams and in flooring units for buildings. Both applications benefited from the reduction in depth afforded by a prestressed section compared with its reinforced concrete counterpart. Flooring units are invariably pretensioned, to reduce the risk of damage in handling as well as offering factory standards of quality control and rapid incorporation on site. Profiles have included thin slabs, deeper hollow-core slabs (nowadays usually extruded), inverted tee and trough sections, and the so-called X-joists (of rectangular section with scalloped sides resembling a fat letter X) which are used with infill blocks. As an indication of success, the production of prestressed flooring units rose from nil in 1950 to about 1.1 million square metres just ten years later, and to 2.75 million square metres in 1996.[31]

Prestressing offered benefits also as a joining method by which smaller components, precast off-site, could be stressed together in situ. This again gave the advantage of factory production quality and quick site assembly, where only the filling of joints was needed prior to the stressing. Two 'off-the-shelf' systems using this approach were Laingspan and Intergrid,[32] both of which provided truss sections for floor and roof beams.

Another application of prestressing to elements is in the cantilevered grandstand roof, for which, as already noted, lightweight concrete offers advantages in reducing dead weight. Prestressing strengthens and stiffens the section, and the result is both elegant and functionally efficient.

Innovative forms: the Festival of Britain

The Festival of Britain, held in 1951, was consciously conceived as 'a tonic to the nation' after the war and the drab immediate post-war years of rationing and slow reconstruction. It provided the building industry with a showcase for innovation, and the industry seized the opportunity to show what it could do.[33] Apart from the well-known steel Skylon landmark tower with its 76.2 metre-high vertical lattice tube, and the aluminium-trussed Dome of Discovery with its span of 111.2 metre (both, alas, demolished), there was much concrete construction to admire. Also now lost, the Fairway Café (Architects' Co-Partnership and Ove Arup & Partners) had a slender prestressed diagonal lattice grid roof. The UK's first prestressed concrete footbridge, part of the infrastructure of the Festival site, was designed by Ove Arup & Partners. Its testing to destruction after the Festival provided valuable data on the performance of such structures.

A survivor from the Festival, albeit with remodelled elevations, is the Royal Festival Hall (Robert Matthew and Leslie Martin of the London County Council, 1948–51). This exemplifies the plastic and mouldable qualities of concrete, with its auditorium box supported on columns within the building envelope to give maximum acoustic shielding against the adjacent busy Charing Cross railway lines on their viaduct. This arrangement also frees the concourse to improve circulation. The concrete is not expressed externally. In this respect it differs conspicuously from the Hall's later neighbours, the Queen Elizabeth Hall, Purcell Room and the Hayward Gallery, and the enveloping raised walkway. Regrettably, these now illustrate the less appealing side of London weather acting on boardmarked and other forms of exposed concrete surfaces.

Bridges

Thousands of concrete bridges have been constructed since the war.[34] Most have been built to meet the apparently insatiable demands of the road-building programme from the late 1950s, including new motorways, upgrading of main roads, and the inner ring roads and other 'improvements' inflicted on so many towns and cities.

The typical concrete bridge has a single-span or multi-span deck, carried on vertical or raking columns. Deck elements include pre-cast, prestressed standard beams with an *in situ* deck; a wholly *in situ* construction, often itself prestressed by post-tensioning; and pre-cast segments, stressed together, as in the Hammersmith Flyover (London County Council, 1962). Welcome variety is provided by single-span arched structures, as on the M2 and M62, and haunched multi-span bridges such as the Medway Viaduct, south of Rochester in Kent (Freeman Fox & Partners, 1960–3).

Ove Arup's Kingsgate footbridge at Durham, of 1963 (Figure 6.3), is a small but distinguished structure, notable both for its simple logical form and for the thought given to its construction. To avoid the need for substantial and expensive temporary works across the River Wear, the bridge was cast in two halves, one on each bank and parallel to the river. Their supporting columns incorporated bearings, allowing the two half-spans to be carefully rotated and turned through 90° to join at mid-span.

In terms of performance, corrosion of reinforcement has been the largest problem for bridges, just as for buildings. De-icing salts have entered the concrete surface either directly or via expansion joints. Corrosion of column reinforcement has also occurred where columns stand in salt water. This corrosion, its repair, and the effects of weathering, often in harsh environments, have all taken their toll on the exposed concrete surfaces.

Figure 6.3   Kingsgate Footbridge, Durham (Ove Arup & Partners, 1963). (Michael Bussell)

Slipform construction

A development originating in the construction of chimneys was slipforming, a technique that increased the speed of vertical construction. In traditional concrete construction, columns and walls are built typically in storey-height lifts of about three metres. The formwork is then stripped and refixed for the next lift, followed by fixing of reinforcement and pouring of concrete. In slip-forming, speed is achieved using either a 'leapfrog' system or continuous climbing forms. In the leapfrog system, the formwork is successively moved up the concrete so that construction proceeds in steps of perhaps one metre. With continuous climbing forms, the equipment is supported on the already built structure and lifted by jacking against it. This method requires a continuous supply of concrete and labour to maintain progress. Falsework down to ground level is eliminated by suitable design of the climbing frame. The method has been used to advance the cores of buildings (allowing an earlier start on installing plant in the rooftop plant room), for tall bridge piers, for chimneys and cooling towers; in some instances, whole buildings have been successfully slipformed, including the floors, walls, and columns.

Later housing developments

Early post-war housing projects such as Rosebery Avenue (London, 1949) paved the way for later, much larger-scale housing developments, in which whole areas of low-rise Victorian terraced housing were pulled down, to be replaced by 'point blocks' of twenty storeys or more. These usually employed precast concrete floor and wall units, often with textured concrete external faces, as the components of a so-called large-panel 'system building' method. The panels, cast at a distant factory or in a site-specific smaller facility, were craned into position and joined by *in situ* stitching.

System-building was seen from the 1950s until the late 1960s as a rapid and acceptable way to replace housing as part of the slum clearance programme. The housing 'numbers game' was practised by Government and Opposition, especially approaching general elections, when each party would pledge a greater number of housing starts in the next year if elected. This poker-like raising of the stakes was accompanied by enthusiastic technical and financial support for industrialized housing from government departments and agencies (notably the National Building Agency, established to 'vet' systems), and from local authorities. The proliferation of designs for such work can be judged from the 1965 edition of *The Comprehensive Industrialised Building Systems Annual*, which describes no fewer than 224 different systems.[35]

Architectural concrete

This term is arguably synonymous with exposed concrete. Inspiration for making concrete the visible and finished surface came from architects such as Le Corbusier and the argument for 'structural honesty', as well as the more mundane but practical belief that a self-finished concrete surface would be cheaper and more durable, and require less maintenance than an applied finish such as plaster or paint. Regrettably, the enthusiasm for these arguments sometimes outran the reality of the building process, knowledge of material performance, and the aggressive, damp British climate.

Early post-war use included the cladding panels of prefabricated housing, from which developed the much wider use of concrete cladding as the outer leaf of the building envelope, often a storey or more in height and six metres or more in length. The panels were applied to housing, offices, factories, hospitals, schools, and many other building types.[36] There was no obligation for the structure to be of concrete: it was often of steel or even masonry. Indeed, in the notable CLASP system, developed initially for the Consortium of Local Authorities Special Programme in areas prone to mining subsidence, the concrete cladding panels were but one choice for the envelope of an essentially light steel-framed, low-rise system, later applied to other uses besides schools.[37,38]

Precast cladding had the advantage that it could be made under factory conditions to a consistent quality, and inspected and approved before it was incorporated into the building. A variety of treatments could be applied to the exposed surfaces, as they could to *in situ* work. In the latter case, however, 'you only got the one go'; if the result was not satisfactory there was little to be done, except to bodge. In contrast, a poorly finished or damaged precast panel could simply be rejected.

Nevertheless, *in situ* concrete was often exposed. Concrete is generally placed in discrete pours, separated by (nominally) horizontal and/or vertical construction joints. If the exposed concrete surface is left as 'fairface' (meaning usually that it bears the faint imprint of ply grain from the formwork), then even slight colour changes between adjacent pours, the often slightly 'wavy' joint lines, and any surface blemishes such as blowholes, will be conspicuous. While this did not (regrettably, in my opinion) deter bridge engineers and others from often specifying a fairface finish, there were numerous surface treatments that could be applied to the concrete to produce a more textured surface that would often mask such imperfections. To avoid corrosion risks it was essential, when specifying cover to the reinforcement, to take into account any loss of surface concrete resulting from such treatment.

The following are some common treatments used on both *in situ* and precast concrete faces. Notable London buildings to which such treatments were applied are identified.

Boardmarked

Bearing the imprint of rough-sawn timber; requiring ideally very close co-ordination between architect and contractor to achieve pleasing results by incorporating necessary features such as shutter ties at regular and planned locations. This finish, used almost exclusively on *in situ* work, was a key component of 'New Brutalism'.[39]

Used at: the Royal National Theatre, Queen Elizabeth Hall, Purcell Room, Hayward Gallery, and adjacent walkways and terraces at the South Bank Centre, London.

Exposed aggregate

Grit-blasted, washed or wire-brushed after use of retarder to delay surface set, or acid-etched to expose the coarse aggregate, giving a 'stony' appearance.

Used at: Ernö Goldfinger's Trellick Tower, Westbourne Park, West London, and to be seen in almost every town and city street with a 1960s building (also the long-term effect visible on many concrete surfaces after exposure to British weather, as a result of wind scour and so forth

– for example, the Mappin Terraces at London Zoo and the Citadel at the junction of Horse Guards Parade and The Mall.)

Bush-hammered

Surface mechanically hammered, loosening coarse aggregate, which falls out to leave an irregular reticulated surface with pockets up to 50 mm deep, depending on the size of coarse aggregate used.

Used at: Barbican Estate and Arts Centre, City of London.

Finned and/or rope-marked

Formed using a serrated surface to the formwork, e.g. by rubber mouldings, to produce fins; laying coarse rope in the back of the fin moulds, or hammering the tips of the fins when still relatively young and weak, to result in projecting rough or jagged fin faces between smooth (usually vertical) re-entrant troughs.

Used at: the Elephant House at London Zoo and the Czech Centre in Notting Hill, West London.

Blockwork and reconstructed stone

Two further finishes should be mentioned. One is exposed concrete blockwork, the other is reconstructed stone (also encountered under the names of cast stone and reconstituted stone).

Concrete blockwork has been very widely used structurally in low-rise buildings.[40] It is available in various densities; the 'normal' weight, suitable for external use, was also commonly employed for inner leaves of external cavity walls until the upgrading of thermal insulation requirements to aid energy conservation in the mid-1970s made it unsuitable for such use without filling the cavity. Such blockwork is produced with a plain pressed face, which has a coarse porous structure. It is also available with a denser smooth face, more like the reconstructed stone described below. A novel use is in the Church of Our Lady of Lourdes and St Vincent de Paul in the Harrow Road, West London (Clive Broad, 1973–5) (Figure 6.4).

Reconstructed stone, cast stone and reconstituted stone are technically correct terms to describe precast concrete produced with a smooth dense surface (and often coloured, since both the cement and the aggregates are usually derived from natural stones), achieving a stone-like appearance at lower cost than natural stone. The name, however, clearly strives towards identification with a better class of building material – stone rather than precast concrete. Specialist precasting firms have been active in this field during the post-war period and have produced many excellent cladding schemes, for example Centrepoint in Central London (R. Seifert & Partners, 1962–5).

Regrettably, such firms have proved especially vulnerable to the economic downturns since the war, in which the British building industry is invariably among the first to suffer. In recent years Shawells, Dean Jesmond and Empire Stone, to name but three respected firms, have failed, and we have lost the benefit of their very skilled employees and their practical expertise.

Problems and solutions

The rapid and large-scale adoption of concrete after the war meant, perhaps inevitably, that designers and builders did not always have the experience needed to ensure successful performance. Codes of practice for design and construction were either out of date or nonexistent.[41] And in some respects, notably durability and differential movement between building materials, there was a lack of understanding of the issues.

Damp
Unfortunately, large-panel housing was often built with scant attention to thermal insulation or the avoidance of cold bridging, so that on cooler days the residents might be obliged to turn up the central heating and close the windows to exclude draughts. The result was condensation and mould growth.

Structural robustness
A more serious structural issue was the robustness of large-panel construction. The partial collapse in May 1968 of a 23-storey tower block, Ronan Point in East London, killed five people.[42] The subsequent investigation revealed deficiencies in the joints between panels, which had been unable to resist the lateral pressure on a load-bearing wall panel as a result of a (relatively) small gas explosion in a kitchen on a corner of the block.

Figure 6.4   Concrete blockwork in the Church of Our Lady of Lourdes and St Vincent de Paul, Harrow Road, West London (Clive Broad, 1973–5). (Michael Bussell)

Unfortunately, regulatory design guidance had not kept up with the rapid growth of such systems. Building regulations had no explicit requirement, as they now do, to consider such events, designing to ensure that, if an accident or explosion were to occur, there would not be 'disproportionate' structural failure. There was at the time no code of practice for large-panel precast structures. And codified wind pressures for high-rise buildings were found to be on the low side.

Site failings

On the construction side, hair-raising tales were told of essential bars and bolts, intended to help connect precast panels together, being cut off when they were found to snag the lowering of the next panel waiting on the tower crane hook. And steel fixing was all too often slipshod, leaving the steel with inadequate cover. This resulted in corrosion as described below. These and similar failings arose from poor understanding and inadequate supervision on site.

Durability

Early practice had correctly acknowledged the importance of concrete cover to the reinforcement in terms of fire resistance, but did not appreciate its significance in protecting the steel against corrosion. The papers that follow deal with this issue in detail, so that only a short account is appropriate here.

Fresh concrete is naturally alkaline, and accordingly protects embedded steel against the corroding effects of oxygen and moisture present in the atmosphere. With time, however, atmospheric carbon dioxide reacts with the concrete in a process known as carbonation. This begins on the surface of the concrete, and moves inwards at a rate that is roughly proportional to the square root of elapsed time. Thus it takes about four times as long for the carbonation to penetrate 20 mm as it does to penetrate 10 mm. Thereafter the steel is more vulnerable to corrosion. Oxygen and moisture react electrolytically with iron in the steel, producing iron oxides; these occupy a larger volume than the original metal, so that expansive forces develop that lead to cracking of the surface concrete around the reinforcement. The cracks allow readier ingress of oxygen and moisture so that the corrosion process accelerates. Eventually the concrete spalls off.

Clearly, the process is less likely to occur if the concrete cover is thicker, denser, and less porous. It is now understood that the best protection comes from a well-graded, well-compacted concrete with a low water–cement ratio and a sufficient cement content for the exposure conditions. Regrettably, this knowledge was, at best, thinly spread in the years after the war.

Complementary problems arose from chlorides, which aggravate the corrosion process. These could be present in poorly washed marine aggregates, or in additives such as calcium chloride, used to accelerate hardening of the concrete in cold weather. Chlorides could also enter the concrete from de-icing salt used on roads; from direct contact of structures such as jetties and bridge piers standing in sea-water; and from wind-blown salt spray along the coast. (There are numerous case histories of seafront buildings suffering seriously from the effects of salty spray.)

Present-day codes of practice demand proper attention to durability issues, so we are entitled to hope that these problems will be much rarer in future.

Differential movements

Probably the most serious consequence of differential movements between building materials has been associated with brick-clad medium and high-rise buildings.

Concrete, as already explained above in considering prestressing, shrinks and creeps, becoming shorter with time. The movement is modest, typically 1–2 mm over a storey height. However, it is cumulative, so that a twenty-storey tower block may eventually shorten by some 20–40 mm at the top.

Concrete-framed buildings were commonly clad with brick, with the outer leaf supported on the edge of the floor slab and built tight up to the underside of the slab above. Architects often wished to mask the slab edges, so that the brickwork was carried past these as thin 'slip tiles', mortared against the slab edges. Unfortunately, new bricks fresh from the kiln are very dry, and are prone to expand as they absorb atmospheric moisture over time.

The picture, then, is of a concrete frame that is gradually shortening, and a rigid skin of brick panels that, if anything, want to expand, but are restrained from doing so by being pinned into the frame at each floor level. In such a situation, it has not been uncommon for the brick panels to bulge outwards and for the brick slips to be loosened or even detached from the slab edges. This is both potentially dangerous and actually expensive to remedy.

The problem does not seem to have been made public until the late 1960s. Since then, guidance documents and subsequent codes of practice have urged the use of 'soft joints' at floor levels, to allow the movements to occur without distressing the fabric.

Conclusion

Reinforced concrete is still, in historical terms, a relatively new material. Treatment of its problems demands an awareness of the processes by which the structure was originally produced. While many aspects of the post-war use of concrete have barely received a mention in this review, I hope that enough has been covered to provide at least a sketch of the more important aspects of the development of concrete construction during this period.

The main conservation problems presented by post-war concrete fabric will generally be due to deterioration of exposed concrete – corrosion of the reinforcement and associated spalling of concrete. These are still relatively novel problems, whose diagnosis and treatment are discussed in the papers that follow this.

References

1   Cusack, P. (1984) 'François Hennebique: the specialist organisation and the success of ferro-concrete 1892–1909', *Transactions of the Newcomen Society*, **56**, 71–86.

2   Adam, J.-P. (1994), *Roman Building: Materials and Techniques*, London: B.T. Batsford.

3   Davey, N. (1974), 'Roman concrete and mortar', *The Structural Engineer*, **52**, (6), 193–195.

4   Francis, A.J. (1977), *The Cement Industry 1796–1914: A History*, Newton Abbot: David and Charles.

5   Neville, A.M. (1981), *Properties of Concrete*, (3rd edn), London: Pitman.

6   *Ibid.*

7   Institution of Structural Engineers (1988), *Structural Use of Lightweight Aggregate Concrete*, London: IStructE.

8   Bobrowski, J., Bardhan-Roy B.K. and Maciag, T. (1974), 'The design and analysis of grandstand structures', *The Structural Engineer*, **52**, (2), 37–56.

9   Neville, A.M. (1981), *op.cit.*

10   Institution of Structural Engineers (1992), *Structural Effects of Alkali-silica Reaction: Technical Guidance on Appraisal of Existing Structures*, London: IStructE.

11   Walley, F. (1996), 'Prestressing', *Proceedings of the Institution of Civil Engineers: Structures and Buildings*, **116**, 390–403.

12   Walley, F. (1985), *Post-tensioning Systems for Concrete in the UK: 1940-1985*, London: Construction Industry Research and Information Association.

13   Neville, A.M. (1981), *op.cit.*

14   British Standards Institution (1972), *British Standard Code of Practice 110, The Structural Use of Concrete*, London: BSI.

15   British Cement Association, Century House, Telford Avenue, Crowthorne, Berkshire RG45 6YS.

16   The Concrete Society, Century House, Telford Avenue, Crowthorne, Berkshire RG45 6YS.

17   British Precast Concrete Federation, 60 Charles Street, Leicester LE1 1FB.

18   Bennett, D. (1998), 'Time to raise standards for the lowly "concretor"', *Concrete Quarterly*, (Summer), 13.

19   Mallory, K., and Ottar, A. (1973), *Architecture of Aggression: A History of Military Architecture in North West Europe*, London: Architectural Press.

20   Institution of Civil Engineers (1948), *The Civil Engineer in War, Volume 2*, London: ICE.

21   White, R.B. (1965), *Prefabrication: A History of its Development in Great Britain*, London: HMSO.

22   Finnimore, B. (1989), *Houses from the Factory: System Building and the Welfare State 1942-74*, London: Rivers Oram Press.

23   Anchor, R.D. (1996), 'Concrete shell roofs, 1945-65', *Proceedings of the Institution of Civil Engineers: Structures and Buildings*, **116**, 381–389.

24   Arup, O.N. and Jenkins, R.S. (1953), 'The design of a reinforced-concrete factory at Brynmawr, South Wales', *Proceedings of the Institution of Civil Engineers*, **3**, 345–397.

25   Perry, V. (1994), *Built for a Better Future: The Brynmawr Rubber Factory*, Oxford: White Cockade Publishing.

26   Robertson, Sir H., Arup, O., Jenkins, R.S., and Rosevear, H.F. (1956), 'Design and construction of the printing works at Debden', *The Structural Engineer*, **34**, (4), 137–151.

27   Ahm, P., and Perry, E.J. (1965), 'Design of the dome shell roof for Smithfield Poultry Market', *Proceedings of the Institution of Civil Engineers*, **30**, 79–108.

28 It is perhaps surprising that, after establishing his consultancy practice, the late Sir Ove Arup wrote or co-wrote only four papers on particular projects (although he spoke and published widely on broader issues, notably the approach to building design and architect-engineer collaboration). Of the four, two are on Brynmawr and the Bank of England cited above – both shell roofs – while the other two deal with the Sydney Opera House, popularly but incorrectly regarded as a shell roof structure.

29 Sharp, D. (1995), 'Umbrella shells mark a watershed in Stevenage', *Concrete Quarterly*, (Winter), 15.

30 Morice, P.B., and Tottenham, H. (1996), 'The early development of reinforced concrete shells', *Proceedings of the Institution of Civil Engineers: Structures and Buildings*, **116**, 373–380.

31 Walley, F. (1996), 'Prestressing', *Proceedings of the Institution of Civil Engineers: Structures and Buildings*, **116**, 390–403.

32 Saint, A. (1987), *Towards a Social Architecture*, New Haven and London: Yale University Press.

33 Collins, A.R. (ed) (1983), *Structural Engineering – Two Centuries of Achievement*, Chislehurst: Tarot Print.

34 Smyth, W.J.R. (1996), 'UK concrete bridges since 1940', *Proceedings of the Institution of Civil Engineers: Structures and Buildings*, **116**, 432–448.

35 Deeson, A.F.L. (ed) (1964), *The Comprehensive Industrialised Building Systems Annual 1965*, London: House Publications.

36 Morris, A.E.J. (1966), *Precast-concrete Cladding*, London: Fountain Press.

37 Saint, A. (1987), *op. cit.*

38 Lyall, S. (1996), 'New Era for CLASP', *Architects' Journal*, (7 November), i–vii. Includes a concise history of the system with guidance on recognizing the various versions.

39 Banham, R. (1966), *The New Brutalism*, London: Architectural Press.

40 Gage, M.. and Kirkbride, T. (1980), *Design in Blockwork*, (3rd edn), London: Architectural Press.

41 Bussell, M. N. (1996), 'The development of reinforced concrete: design theory and practice', *Proceedings of the Institution of Civil Engineers: Structures and Buildings*, **116**, 317–334.

42 Ministry of Housing and Local Government (1968), *Report of the Inquiry into the Collapse of Flats at Ronan Point, Canning Town*, London: HMSO.

CHAPTER 7

THE DETERIORATION OF REINFORCED CONCRETE: AN INTRODUCTION

Jimi Fadayomi

Durability and deterioration of concrete

Since first being used in ancient Greek and Roman times, concrete has been widely acknowledged as a versatile and economical construction material that offers speed and cost-effectiveness in a diversity of building applications. Normally, concrete would also be expected to be durable, but this is not always the case. All concrete structures are subject to physical and chemical changes. A durable concrete can be thought of as 'one in which these changes occur at a rate which does not detrimentally affect its performance within the intended life'.[1] One certainty is that it would be unwise to think of concrete (or indeed, any other construction material) as 100% maintenance-free. However, the nature and extent of any necessary maintenance will vary greatly with circumstances.

The underlying causes of deterioration of reinforced concrete can be assigned to four main categories: design, construction, materials and maintenance.

Design

It is important that the likely exposure conditions are properly anticipated; the correct mix must be used; allowance should be made for sufficient concrete cover to the reinforcing steel – the actual cover for 'mild' conditions of exposure should never be less than 15 mm for most grades of concrete; and thermal and differential movements must be catered for by the provision of sufficient movement joints of appropriate dimensions and location.

Construction

Compromises at site must be minimized by ensuring proper supervision, since quality control is a vital factor in the construction of durable structures. Commonly occurring faults include:

- poorly compacted concrete, which is therefore not in continuous close contact with the reinforcement;
- inadequate curing;
- incorrect use of spacers, resulting in low cover to reinforcement;

- porosity due to the addition of too much water;
- honeycombing due to mix design, grout loss or inadequate compaction.

Materials

Injudicious selection of the components of the concrete can exacerbate its subsequent deterioration. An example of this is the incorporation of calcium chloride as an accelerating admixture in order to provide rapid setting and improved formwork utilization. This practice is banned for reinforced concrete structures.[2]

Another example is alkali–silica reaction (ASR). This is a chemical process in which alkalis, mainly from the cement, combine with certain types of silica in the aggregate when moisture is present. The reaction produces an alkali–silica gel that absorbs water and expands to cause cracking and disruption of the concrete. A third example is the inclusion of iron pyrites among the aggregates, leaving unsightly surface staining after local corrosion of the aggregate.

Maintenance

Problems associated with maintenance can be derived from two sources: lack of maintenance and a technically incorrect approach to maintenance. The former is self-explanatory. An example of the latter might be using epoxy resin mortars for concrete repairs on building facades. Epoxy resin mortars possess a different coefficient of thermal expansion from concrete's, the likely outcome being cracking around the repairs. However, it is acknowledged that epoxy resin mortars may be technically preferable for temperature-stable or corrosive environments.

A wide spectrum of causes and mechanisms for reinforced concrete deterioration has been documented in the literature. The underlying causes mentioned above can all be developed significantly under greater scrutiny. Moreover, consideration might be given to unanticipated occurrences such as fire. However, this paper restricts its focus to one particular problem, the corrosion of reinforcement in concrete. Further information regarding the other mechanisms of deterioration is available from sources such as Neville.[3]

Steel corrosion

Fundamental principles

The production of steel from iron ore requires a process that converts it from its oxidized condition (its state in nature) to that of the pure metal. Laws of physics and chemistry dictate that, consequently, the metal will have a strong inclination to revert to its naturally occurring form (i.e. it will have a tendency to rust).

Corrosion engineers think of corrosion as the degradation of a metal by an electrochemical reaction with its environment. Indeed, Broomfield defines corrosion as 'the process by which a refined metal reverts back to its natural state by an oxidation reaction with the non-metallic environment (e.g. oxygen and water).'[4]

The 'unwelcome battery'

In simple terms, steel corrosion is due to the formation of an 'unwelcome battery'. As with any battery, three electrochemical components are required for the steel corrosion to propagate:[5]

- an anodic reaction (i.e. a positive terminal);
- a cathodic reaction (i.e. a negative terminal);
- ionic conduction through an electrolyte (i.e. a connecting wire).

All three components must occur simultaneously for corrosion to be active. The omission of any one of these processes will cause the corrosion reaction to stop.

Environmental factors

Several factors affect the rate of corrosion. Firstly, the presence of moisture from the atmosphere or, say, a marine environment will accelerate corrosion. Oxygen acts as a fuel in the corrosion process, so its ready availability will speed up the corrosion rate. As with all chemical reactions, the higher the prevailing temperature, the faster will be the rate of the corrosion process, and vice versa. Finally, it should also be noted that the presence of pollutants (e.g. industrial atmospheres) can alter the conductivity and pH of the electrolyte.

Passivation

As we have seen above, steel has a natural tendency to corrode in the presence of water and oxygen. It would therefore seem to follow that steel embedded in concrete would also corrode, as concrete is porous to air and contains moisture. However, such corrosion is not necessarily automatic.

The reason for this is that steel reinforcement in concrete is protected from corrosion by a passivating layer that forms on its surface. Chemically, this layer comprises iron oxides and it is formed as a result of the very highly alkaline environment (pH approximately 13) generated in concrete during cement hydration. This passivation is effective despite the presence of air and moisture. It is also worth noting that the concrete cover to the reinforcement will itself offer some protection, purely as a physical barrier.

The passivating layer around the steel has the ability to regenerate itself in the event of localized damage occurring – as long as the surrounding environment remains unchanged.

In order for reinforcing steel to corrode in concrete there must first be a breakdown of the passivating layer. The major causes of this are a reduction in the alkalinity of the concrete around the reinforcing steel, for example due to a reaction with atmospheric carbon dioxide (carbonation), and attack by depassivating chloride ions at the surface of the steel. Secondly, as with the earlier battery analogy, there is the need for an electrolyte to provide electrical continuity. In the case of reinforced concrete, this role would be played by the continuous pore water. Finally, the corrosion reaction would need a fuel to sustain it. Oxygen, available via the concrete pores, would act as the fuel.

The extent and rate of breakdown of the passivating layer around the reinforcing steel will be determined by the interrelationship between the contributory environmental conditions outlined above. For the purposes of this paper, I shall focus upon the two major causes of loss of passivity of steel in concrete and hence its corrosion – carbonation of the concrete and chloride attack.

Corrosion of reinforcing steel

We have seen how reinforcing steel within concrete is normally protected by a passivating layer on its surface, which has been generated as a result of the highly alkaline environment. This layer may be broken down by carbonation of the surrounding concrete matrix or attack by chlorides, which may have been present in the original mix, or may have penetrated into the concrete from the environment.

The subsequent corrosion of the reinforcing steel can be understood in terms of simple electrochemistry using the analogy of an 'unwelcome battery' cell formation. The corrosion products (rust) are produced at the anode, oxygen provides a fuel for the reaction at the cathode and the pore water acts as the electrolyte.

Carbonation

Carbonation is considered to be the most common cause of the loss of passivating alkalinity in reinforced concrete. In this process, carbon dioxide from the atmosphere penetrates the concrete through its capillary pores. It reacts in the pore liquid of the concrete with the soluble alkaline calcium hydroxide (produced during cement hydration) to form insoluble calcium carbonate (Figure 7.1).

Carbon dioxide dissolves in the pore water to form a weak carbonic acid. The reaction of acid with alkali leads to a reduction in the overall high alkalinity of the cement matrix, until the pH falls below the level required for the passivation to remain effective around the embedded steel reinforcement (typically pH 10–11). The 'carbonation front' will move into the concrete following the principles of diffusion. The process occurs from the surface inwards, its rate of penetration depending primarily upon the permeability of the concrete and the atmospheric humidity.

The diffusion will occur more rapidly if the concrete has an open capillary pore structure in the cement paste matrix. At a macroscopic level, this can be combatted by ensuring good compaction. At a microscopic level, good curing will result in smaller pores and fewer connections between the pores, thereby reducing the mobility of the carbon dioxide. Also, additives such as silica fume may be used in the original construction to block pores or reduce pore size.

$$Ca(OH)_2 \quad + \quad CO_2 \quad \rightarrow \quad CaCO_3 \quad + \quad H_2O$$

CALCIUM   CARBON   CALCIUM   WATER
HYDROXIDE   DIOXIDE   CARBONATE

Result: progressive loss of passivating alkalinity in the pore liquid

Figure 7.1   Carbonation of concrete. (Sika Ltd)

Carbonation is most rapid at relative humidities between 50% and 75%. Below 50%, the moisture content of the pores is insufficient for enough calcium hydroxide to dissolve and react with atmospheric carbon dioxide in the reaction zone. Above 75%, the situation is reversed – the calcium hydroxide freely dissolves, but the pores are effectively blocked with water, retarding the ingress of carbon dioxide.

Carbonation damage will tend to manifest itself most rapidly when there is insufficient depth of concrete cover over the reinforcing steel. However, it can still occur, even when the concrete cover is very thick. Typical reasons might be the presence of a very open capillary pore structure with the pores well connected together, or low alkaline reserves in the concrete matrix. Contributory factors here might include poor curing of the concrete, a low cement content and a high water–cement ratio (it is impossible to preclude continuous capillaries in cement paste with a water–cement ratio of more than 0.7).[6]

It should be noted that the process of carbonation *per se* has no adverse structural implications. Indeed, carbonated concrete will normally have a slightly higher compressive strength than previously. The significance of the process relates to its impact upon the passivation of the embedded reinforcing steel.

The carbonation-induced corrosion cell

We shall now take an overview of some of the electrochemistry underpinning the corrosion of reinforcing steel due to carbonation of the surrounding concrete.

The carbonation-induced corrosion cell can be explained as a series of chemical equations that form the components of a battery (Figure 7.2). Once the passivating oxide layer has broken down, an electrochemical cell is set up, due to differences in electrical potential along the reinforcing steel within the concrete. Anodic and cathodic sites are formed, connected by the electrolyte in the form of the pore water within the hardened cement paste.

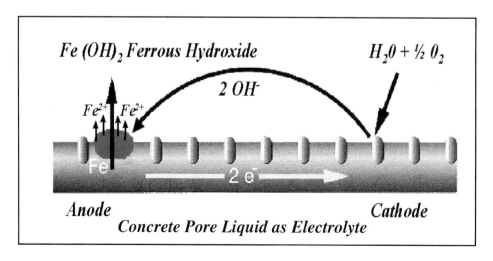

Figure 7.2   The carbonation-induced corrosion cell. (Sika, Ltd)

At the anode, the steel surface dissolves into ferrous ions (Fe^{2+}) whilst the free electrons (e^-) pass through the steel to the cathode. At the cathode, the electrons are absorbed, combining with water and oxygen to form hydroxyl ions (OH^-). These travel through the electrolyte (pore water) to the anode, where they combine with the ferrous ions in an initial anodic reaction to form ferrous hydroxide.

A series of subsequent reactions will then occur at the anode, involving the further oxidation of the ferrous hydroxide to form rust products. One typical product is ferric oxide (Fe_2O_3), but other more complex rust forms will also be generated.

Overall, this 'unwelcome battery' comprises the oxidation of steel at the anode, with oxygen fuelling the reaction by being reduced at the cathode. The pore water acts as the electrolyte.

When the concrete surrounding embedded steel reinforcement becomes carbonated, the likelihood is that a series of corrosion cells will be formed along the bar in the affected areas. Their close proximity will normally result in uniform corrosion of the whole of the steel surface to produce the ferric oxide (rust). The rust products will have an increased volume of up to ten times that of the steel which they replace. The expansive forces that are generated result in the cracking and spalling of the concrete cover. These symptoms, combined with a red–brown flaky rust on the bar and rust stains exuding from cracks, are all typical visible indications of carbonation-induced corrosion.

The stages of carbonation-induced deterioration

Our understanding of the impact of carbonation on the deterioration of reinforced concrete can be assisted by considering the stages of the damage development (Figure 7.3).

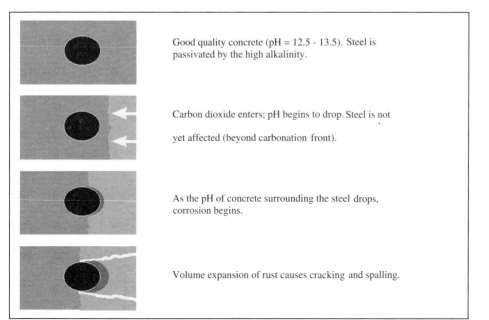

Good quality concrete (pH = 12.5 - 13.5). Steel is passivated by the high alkalinity.

Carbon dioxide enters; pH begins to drop. Steel is not yet affected (beyond carbonation front).

As the pH of concrete surrounding the steel drops, corrosion begins.

Volume expansion of rust causes cracking and spalling.

Figure 7.3   Carbonation: stages of damage development. (Sika Ltd)

Initially, freshly cast, good quality concrete will have an approximate pH of 13. In this environment, the reinforcing steel will have a passivating layer on its surface due to the highly alkaline environment.

As atmospheric carbon dioxide permeates into the concrete and begins to react with the calcium hydroxide, the degree of alkalinity is reduced. Gradually, the pH will become lower as this process of carbonation affects the concrete from the exposed face inwards. A carbonation front is established, but until this front reaches the reinforcing steel, the steel remains unaffected.

Therefore, carbonation of a concrete facade may not necessarily result in corrosion of the steel reinforcement. If the ingress of the carbonation front can be arrested before it reaches the steel, there should be no need to break out and treat the reinforcement, with the subsequent need for patch repairs.

For this reason, it is imperative that the progressive survey, which is necessary as part of a concrete repair project, should entail a careful cross-correlation of the results of a cover meter survey (to assess depth of cover to steel reinforcement) with the results of carbonation depth testing. This will enable the accurate identification of all locations where reinforcing steel is actually in contact with carbonated concrete. Too many specifications still require the contractor to break out all carbonated concrete, without regard to whether there is any reinforcing steel within the carbonation zone.

The next stage of damage development is when the carbonation front reaches the reinforcing steel. The pH around the steel will drop, resulting in the breakdown of the passivating layer and the initiation of corrosion. During this early phase of the corrosion process, there may be no obvious external symptoms.

Finally, however, volumetric expansion of the rust will cause more noticeable cracking and spalling, which may be visible, as well as audible when the surface is tapped with a hammer.

It should also be noted that carbonation can occur along the faces of cracks present in the concrete surface, because superficially 'minor' fissures represent an easy route of ingress for a gas such as carbon dioxide. This may result in a localized carbonation depth much greater than the depth of the general carbonation front. For this reason, cracks in the surface should be investigated to ensure that they do not coincide with steel reinforcement, resulting in the potential for corrosion beyond the apparent depth of carbonation.

Corrosion of reinforcing steel: chloride attack

Sources of chlorides

Chloride ions can destroy the protective passivating layer that occurs on embedded steel reinforcement. They arise from a number of sources and may be cast into the original concrete during construction or diffuse into the hardened concrete from the external environment.

A typical source of cast-in chlorides is the use of calcium chloride as an accelerating admixture. This was commonly added to the mix before the 1970s, before its use in reinforced concrete was prohibited. Chlorides might also be added in the basic components of the concrete itself (e.g. sea water or poorly washed sea-dredged aggregates).

The two most common external sources of chlorides that may subsequently diffuse into the concrete are de-icing salts and marine environments, the latter causing exposure to sea salt spray and/or direct wetting by sea water.

Within the concrete, chloride ions may exist in solution in the pore water or may be loosely bound to the crystalline hydration products of cement. Chloride ions in solution are relatively free to move. Proportionately, more of the chloride ions will tend to be bound if they were cast in than if they have penetrated from the environment. Thus, for a given chloride ion concentration, the chloride ions will be more mobile and, therefore, provide a greater threat to the steel, if they have penetrated from the external environment.

BRE Digest 264 categorizes the risk associated with various concentrations of chloride contamination (see Figure 7.4). Generally, the threshold chloride values above which corrosion is deemed likely to occur are 0.4% chloride by weight of cement for cast-in chlorides and 0.2% if they diffuse in. However, individual circumstances may significantly affect the risk levels associated with different chloride concentrations.

Chloride penetration mechanisms

While the risks from cast-in chlorides should not be overlooked, it is external chlorides penetrating into the concrete that cause most problems. Chloride ions achieve their mobility through concrete primarily by dissolving in water and moving by diffusion. High concentrations of chloride ions will have a tendency to spread out into surrounding areas of lower concentration, as the system strives to achieve an equilibrium.

A number of factors affect the rate of penetration of chloride ions. These are similar to those which affect the rate of penetration of carbon dioxide (i.e. the permeability, water–cement ratio and the curing regime). Additionally, chloride penetration rates can be affected by the type of cement used (increased tricalcium aluminate content reduces the mobility of chloride ions).

Risk of Corrosion	Chloride Ion Content by Wt. Cement
LOW	UP TO 0.4%
MEDIUM	0.4% TO 1.0%
HIGH	ABOVE 1.0%

N.B. This categorization particularly applies to chlorides present in the original mix. Lower limits may apply if the chlorides have penetrated from outside the hardened concrete.

Figure 7.4 Categorization of chloride ion content. (From the Building Research Establishment (1982), BRE Digest 264: The Durability of Steel in Concrete, Part 2 – Diagnosis and Assessment of Corrosion-Cracked Concrete, Watford, BRE)

The chloride-induced corrosion cell

As earlier with carbonation, we can now take on overview of some of the electrochemistry under-pinning the corrosion of reinforcing steel due to chloride attack (Figure 7.5).

Once again, an 'unwanted battery' comprising an anodic region, a cathodic region and an electrolyte is created. However, the initial depassivation method is different to the carbonation process. Localized, sufficiently high concentrations of chloride ions attack the passivating layer, causing a breakdown irrespective of the prevailing pH level.

The steel dissolves to form ferrous ions (Fe^{2+}) at the anode, with electrons passing through the steel to the cathode. The chloride ions then act as a catalyst in a preliminary anodic reac-tion, forming ferrous chloride ($FeCl_2$) due to their very strong affinity for ferrous ions. However, ferrous chloride is extremely unstable, reacting with the hydroxyl (OH^-) ions generated at the cathode to produce ferrous hydroxide ($Fe(OH)_2$) and regenerating chloride ions, which may then re-attack the steel.

Then, as with carbonation-induced corrosion, a series of subsequent reactions will occur at the anode, resulting in the generation of rust products.

Additional considerations

Chloride-induced corrosion tends to result in a localized breakdown of the passivating layer, as opposed to the widespread deterioration which is typical with carbonation. The cathodic areas are much larger than the anodic areas. The reaction rate is driven by the size of the cathode in

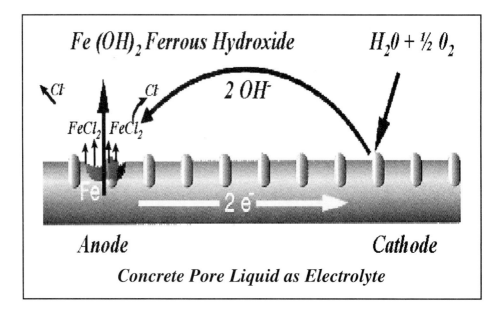

Figure 7.5   The chloride-induced corrosion cell. (Sika Ltd)

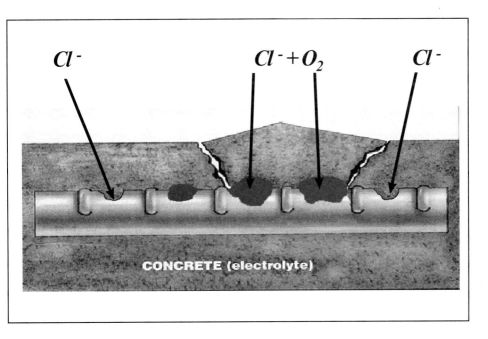

Figure 7.6   Chloride-induced pitting corrosion. (Sika Ltd)

relation to the anode, leading to the rapid corrosion of the anode and 'pitting corrosion', i.e. a localized significant loss in cross-sectional area.

With chloride attack, corrosion may still occur in conditions of low oxygen availability, albeit very slowly. In such circumstances, the corrosion products will be less voluminous than under normal conditions, and may not result in expansive stresses and cracking of the cover. Instead, the rust products tend to be non-expansive, or even soluble, and may penetrate into the concrete matrix. As a result, deterioration of the reinforcing steel may occur with no outward indications of problems, although sometimes rust staining may become noticeable (Figure 7.6).

Chloride attack can also be stimulated by an increase in the free chloride–hydroxyl ratio. This may lead to chloride-induced corrosion in concrete containing low concentrations of chloride that might not otherwise have caused corrosion. For this reason, carbonation of the surrounding concrete (thereby using up hydroxyl ions) may cause previously 'low risk' chloride levels to exacerbate the corrosion.

The free chloride–hydroxyl ratio is also important in explaining another problem associated with chloride attack. This is the possibility that patch-repairing a structure with extensive chloride attack can lead to deterioration in the adjacent areas. This phenomenon is known as 'incipient anode' formation in the surrounding areas. It occurs because patch repairing the corroding area effectively stops the anodic reaction. This, for reasons of electrochemical balance, also results in the generation of hydroxyl ions at the cathode being stopped (Figure 7.5). Therefore, areas that had been protected from corrosion because they were acting cathodically next to the now-repaired anode, may have a sufficient increase in free chloride–hydroxyl ratio to initiate corrosion. This will typically take place in close proximity to the patch repair.

Corrosion control strategies

Several strategies exist for treating deteriorating reinforced concrete structures, the most judicious approach depending on the nature and extent of the damage and the prevailing aesthetic, financial and technical constraints.

The correct approach

Several factors should be taken into account before choosing products or techniques for the repair of defective reinforced concrete. Firstly, sufficient investigations should be carried out to ascertain the nature and extent of the deterioration. This will ensure that the underlying cause is correctly identified and that any treatment addresses that cause, rather than merely the symptom.

The objectives of the building owner and any constraints upon the remedial approach should also be given due regard. At this stage, an appropriately sympathetic treatment of post-war heritage can be accommodated. Techniques such as the use of surface-applied corrosion inhibitors are proving invaluable in reducing aesthetic compromises when repairing listed structures.

A detailed specification can then be drawn up, specifically tailored to the structure in question.

Repair options

Notwithstanding the above comments, the traditional approach for a long-term repair has been to break out contaminated concrete around corroding reinforcement, or where the steel is likely to corrode, and to replace it with an alkaline repair mortar. Normally, it is a technical prerequisite that further ingress of carbon dioxide or chloride ions is prevented by the application of a protective coating over the entire exterior surface of the concrete. However, aesthetic considerations may sometimes preclude this, resulting in a considerable technical compromise.

In recent years, there has been greater awareness of techniques that utilize the principles of electrochemistry as the basis of remedial approaches. The most established amongst these is cathodic protection (primarily used for chloride attack on civil and marine structures). Chloride extraction and realkalization provide alternative methods for treating chloride-infected concrete and carbonated concrete, respectively.

In the context of preserving post-war heritage, an exciting development in recent years has been the advent of corrosion inhibitors as part of the remedial strategy. Corrosion inhibitors penetrate the concrete and act directly on the steel reinforcement to inhibit the corrosion process. In structurally or aesthetically sensitive areas, they offer the potential for less break-out and, moreover, may reduce the need for an overall coating treatment.

Whilst such products are by no means 'miracle cures', responsible manufacturers of corrosion inhibitors will be able to provide independent testimony from third parties as to the effectiveness of their product. For example, Mott MacDonald conclude that the Sika corrosion inhibitor,

FerroGard, can 'improve resistance to the initiation of pitting corrosion in chloride contaminated concrete and reduce the risk of general corrosion in carbonated concrete', as well as 'reduce the risk of incipient anode corrosion occurring in areas adjacent to the repair.'[7]

The overriding principles when finalizing the remedial approach are that the rule of 'horses for courses' should be observed and that common sense is paramount.

References

1   Concrete Society (1984), *Technical Report No.26: Repair of Concrete Damaged by Reinforcement Corrosion*, London: Concrete Society.

2   British Standards Institution (1972, amended 1997), *CP110. Code of Practice for the Structural Use of Concrete*, London: BSI.

3   Neville, A.M. (1995), *Properties of Concrete*, (4th edn), Harlow: Longman Group.

4   Broomfield, J.P. (1997), *Corrosion of Steel in Concrete: Understanding, Investigation and Repair*, London: E. & F.N. Spon.

5   Shaw, M.A. (1997), 'Penetrating corrosion inhibitors for reinforced concrete protection', paper presented at Structural Faults Conference, Edinburgh.

6   Building Research Establishment (1982), *BRE Digest 264: The Durability of Steel in Concrete, Part 2 – Diagnosis and Assessment of Corrosion-Cracked Concrete*, Watford: BRE.

7   *Sika FerroGard 901 and 903 Corrosion Inhibitors: Evaluation of Test Programme* (1996), Mott MacDonald.

CHAPTER 8

REPAIRING REINFORCED CONCRETE: AN OVERVIEW
Paul Lambert

Through an appreciation of the materials of construction combined with prudent maintenance, many ancient and traditional structures have remained serviceable over hundreds of years. The record of durability of many more recent reinforced concrete structures has been less impressive. During the twentieth century, the rapid development of reinforced concrete coincided with the specialization of the professions involved in building. One result appears to have been a failure to appreciate the characteristics of structural materials in respect of durability; this has led to the design and construction of unattractive structures that have suffered from premature staining, cracking and spalling, all of which has helped to undermine the reputation of reinforced concrete.

Reinforced concrete is essentially specified and judged on average, but fails in particular – especially when problems arise from corrosion of the reinforcement. Corrosion problems are typically the result of either loss of alkalinity due to carbonation of the cover, or the ingress of significant levels of chloride ions from some external source. Factors such as low cover, locally misplaced steel, honeycombing and cracking can all have a profound effect on how long the reinforcement can resist the urge to return to its oxide roots. In general, structures do not exhibit reduced serviceability due to the average or typical characteristics, but as a consequence of local deficiencies and defects.

Some of the most interesting and innovative approaches to increasing the durability of reinforced concrete are associated with the repair of existing structures. Techniques such as cathodic protection, re-alkalization, chloride extraction and corrosion inhibition have all become quite widely accepted and increasingly applied. Cathodic protection and the application of corrosion inhibitors have both been comprehensively employed by other industries for a long time.

Durability of reinforced concrete

The majority of reinforced concrete around the world performs adequately and gives few problems. A minority of structures have deteriorated due to either the action of aggressive components from the external environment or incompatibility of the mix constituents. Problems can arise as a result of incomplete or inaccurate site investigation, poor design, badly specified concrete, poor workmanship and a range of other factors. The mechanisms of deterioration are primarily chemico-physical in nature, i.e. a chemical reaction with the formation of products greater in volume than the reactants, producing physical damage. Deterioration may occur due to a number of mechanisms on which a large body of literature already exists. These include:

- corrosion of reinforcement, due to chloride ions, carbonation or change in the reinforcing bar environment (e.g. impinging cracks);
- sulphate attacking the concrete;
- salt recrystallization (exfoliation);
- soft water/acid attacking the concrete;
- alkali–aggregate reaction (AAR);
- frost damage.

Steel reinforcement embedded in good-quality concrete is in a highly alkaline environment (generally >pH 13), produced by the hydroxides of sodium, potassium and calcium released during the various hydration reactions.[1] In addition, the bulk of surrounding concrete acts as a physical barrier to most of the substances that may lead to degradation of the reinforcement. Provided this environment is maintained, the steel remains passive and any small breaks in the stable protective oxide film are soon repaired. However, if the alkalinity of the surroundings is reduced, for example by reaction with atmospheric carbon dioxide (carbonation), or if depassivating chloride ions are made available at the surface of the steel, then corrosion may be initiated, resulting in loss of steel section and spalling of cover concrete.[2]

To understand better how the repair or modification of reinforced concrete structures can enhance long-term durability, it is essential to understand how exposure conditions influence the following factors:

- the rate of breakdown of protection and initiation of corrosion or other deterioration;
- the rate of corrosion or deterioration;
- secondary deterioration processes.

For example, carbonation develops much more in dry internal conditions than in wet, near-saturated conditions.[3] Once carbonation has reached the steel, corrosion rates are negligible when dry and most rapid when near saturation or subject to wet-and-dry cycling.[4] Once sufficiently developed to crack the cover, corrosion is accelerated. Spalling of the cracked cover by frost action further accelerates the deterioration. In the case of chloride-induced corrosion, chloride ion ingress can occur only through the liquid phase of the concrete. The maximum rate of ingress occurs during cycles of wetting and drying. Chloride-induced corrosion is a distinct function of temperature, humidity and cycles of wetting and drying.[5] For alkali–aggregate reaction, the most damaging condition is from 95% relative humidity (RH) to near saturation. Total immersion may leach alkali and ameliorate the reaction; while at 80% RH, AAR proceeds very slowly until rewetting occurs. AAR is effectively dormant below 75% RH.[6]

Improved durability can be achieved by resisting the ingress of aggressive substances through the use of 'high-quality' concrete. A thick cover depth of low-permeability concrete will greatly assist in preventing depassivation of the reinforcement; however, structural factors may limit the maximum cover. The composition of the cementitious matrix is clearly important, and the use of cement replacement materials such as fly ash, blast furnace slag and micro-silica can also be beneficial, particularly when improving the resistance to chloride ion ingress.[7] The corrosion rate of steel in concrete depends on the presence of an ionically conductive aqueous phase in contact with the steel, the existence of anodic and cathodic sites on the metal surface in contact with this electrolyte, and the availability of oxygen to enable the reactions to proceed. This indicates an additional route to restricting corrosion and hence improving durability, through control of one or more of the reactants. While it is possible to stifle corrosion by restricting oxygen availability, the amount of oxygen required to maintain corrosion is very small and may be difficult to limit, other than by complete immersion in water.[8] Alternatively, limiting water access and encouraging the concrete to dry may control reinforcement corrosion through the associated increase in electrical resistance, which limits the magnitude of corrosion currents.

Moisture and structural degradation

The control or exclusion of high moisture levels represents one of the oldest and most widely used methods of protecting and extending the service life of structural materials. The passivating effect of the alkaline environment generated and maintained in Portland cement-based reinforced concrete will generally overcome the need to maintain a dry environment. However, unrestricted access to moisture can result in damage to the concrete, to the reinforcement or to both.

Corrosion of steel

In the presence of moisture and oxygen, steel rusts. The rate and nature of the process depends on alloy composition, environmental factors, and the design and nature of additional protection. In its simplest form the corrosion process can be represented by two dissimilar metals in an aqueous electrolyte, joined to allow electrons to pass from anode to cathode. In reality, when a metal corrodes, anodic and cathodic areas can be formed on a single surface in contact with the aggressive aqueous environment. As a result, corrosion can occur at a large number of sites over the surface of the metal. Dissolved metal ions react with hydroxyl ions to form corrosion products. Production of hydrogen at the cathode can lead to failure in some materials, e.g. high-strength, low-alloy steels, due to hydrogen embrittlement in areas that are stressed.

The relative humidity of an environment has a profound effect on the rate of corrosion of steel. There is a critical level of relative humidity below which corrosion does not occur and often secondary and tertiary levels above that, at which the corrosion rate increases significantly. In the case of steel, corrosion commences at a slow rate at approximately 60% RH. The rate increases at 75–80% RH and again at 90%. Contamination of the environment has a tendency to reduce the relative humidity at which corrosion is initiated.[9]

Concrete resistivity

The rate at which steel corrodes in concrete is strongly affected by the resistivity of the concrete, as this determines the degree of current flow. Resistivity is effectively a measure of resistance to the passage of current. When the resistivity is high, >12 kÛ cm, the resistance to current flow is high and the rate of corrosion is minimal. Conversely, when the resistivity is low, <5 kÛ cm, the resistance to current flow is low and it is possible for a high rate of corrosion to be sustained.[10] The relative humidity of the concrete has a significant effect on its resistivity. As the relative humidity/moisture content of the concrete increases, its resistivity decreases. Thus, as indicated for atmospheric conditions, increasing the relative humidity of the concrete has a tendency to increase the rate of corrosion of the steel. Increasing the concentration of chloride ions also reduces the resistivity and it may therefore be assumed that, for a given relative humidity, corrosion rates increase with increasing chloride content. Variation in concrete age and composition can effect the degree to which a change in relative humidity alters resistivity, but the general trends remain constant.

Rate of carbonation

The rate of passage of carbon dioxide into concrete is controlled, in part, by the permeability of the concrete; high permeabilities result in more rapid carbonation. It has been shown that the optimum relative humidity for carbonation lies in the range 50–70%.[11] Below these values the reaction is stifled by lack of moisture, and above them the passage of carbon dioxide into the concrete through the pore structure is impeded. Where reducing relative humidity is employed as a means of controlling corrosion rates, it may be advisable to apply a protective anti-carbonation coating to minimize the risk of increased levels of carbonation, particularly with highly porous concretes and low covers. Once carbonation has reached the steel, corrosion rates are negligible at 50% RH but most rapid at 95% RH.[12]

Wetting and drying

Concrete exposed to the atmosphere is subjected to cycles of wetting and drying, which tend to affect the cover concrete, most significantly where the corrosion process is active. Repetitive cycles of wetting and drying have a significant effect on the rate of corrosion, typically resulting in higher corrosion rates than those encountered under stable conditions.

Moisture control

The durability of reinforced concrete can be significantly affected by its relative humidity. It has been shown that there is a limiting level of relative humidity, below which corrosion will not normally occur. For steel in concrete this appears to be in the range 60–70% RH and is influenced by factors such as the level of chloride contamination. As relative humidity increases so does the rate of corrosion, although at full saturation the corrosion rate is significantly reduced as moisture fills the concrete pores and acts as a barrier to oxygen transfer. Controlling the relative humidity of reinforced concrete should therefore provide an effective means of controlling reinforcement corrosion, particularly where the removal or exclusion of excess moisture also removes or prevents the ingress of potentially aggressive species. As most of the moisture and mobile species that influence the durability of reinforced concrete must cross the boundary between substrate and atmosphere, the application of coatings and surface treatments can be highly effective in limiting or preventing degradation.[13]

Repair methodologies

By employing a combination of experience, good engineering sense and the body of information reported in the literature, it is usually possible to identify the areas in a reinforced concrete structure where destructive reinforcement corrosion is most likely to be occurring. Where the primary cause of corrosion is the ingress of chloride ions, any detail where salt-laden water can gather and concentrate is at greater risk. Little can be achieved without actually examining the structure and performing simple tests to target the risk areas and select appropriate techniques for further examination. Similarly, those areas under the greatest threat of loss of structural integrity can usually be identified in advance, so allowing any investigation to be correctly targeted. Where both the risk of corrosion and the loss of structural integrity coincide, the potential for serious failure is so high that the prospective investigator must ensure the problem can be adequately identified and quantified.

Having identified what is corroding, why it is corroding and how fast it is corroding, it is then necessary to decide what, if anything, can be done to stop the corrosion and make good the damage. When selecting a method of repair it is essential to know whether the 'owner' expects the renovated structure to be:

- better than new;
- as good as new;
- not quite as good as new but better than it was;
- prevented from going worse; or
- made to degrade more slowly.

Typically, the first option is expected and the last option specified. Each of the five approaches is valid in the appropriate context, and a large part of the skill in concrete repair is in correctly identifying and matching methods and service requirements, usually within restricted budgets.

Options for repair

The first and most regularly employed concrete repair option is to do nothing at all. Provided that the structure and those who use it are not put at risk, many reinforced concrete elements can be allowed quietly to degrade and disintegrate (subject to some form of monitoring or periodic inspection), until they are eventually replaced. True repair starts with patching – the removal of cracked, delaminated or contaminated concrete and reinstatement with a repair material, usually cementitious. In their simplest form, patch repairs may be little more than aesthetic exercises. Successful repair of carbonated or chloride-laden concrete requires the complete removal of affected material adjacent to reinforcement. Chlorides are particularly difficult to deal with, as corrosion tends to occur in the areas of maximum chloride concentration, which in turn protect adjacent areas.

Repairs to areas of corrosion and delamination often result in subsequent corrosion to the adjacent, previously protected areas – the so-called 'incipient anode effect'. Patch-repairing chloride-contaminated concrete can therefore become an expensive option, with large volumes of sound but chloride-contaminated material having to be removed, with possible structural implications. The limitations of patch repairs, particularly with respect to chloride attack, have been important in driving forward the development of alternative approaches to repair.

Cathodic protection

Although the beneficial effects of cathodic protection have been recognized since the middle of the eighteenth century, it is only during the second half of the twentieth century that the technique has been seriously employed, predominantly in the protection of pipelines, ships and oilfield structures. More recently, the technology has been refined and applied for the protection of structural steel elements, particularly those embedded in concrete, but also those encased in mortar, plaster or masonry.

Corrosion of steel is an electrochemical process that results in the formation of anodic and cathodic sites on the surface of the steel. Under typical atmospheric conditions, metal is dissolved at the anodic sites while the cathodic areas remain unaffected. By applying a small externally generated current to the steel, it is possible to make all the steel cathodic and therefore non-corroding, hence 'cathodic protection'. The externally applied current can either be produced by a material that will corrode preferentially to the steel – a 'sacrificial' anode such as zinc – or provided by a low-voltage DC source via an effectively inert material to provide an impressed current to the steel.

Cathodic protection is a means of protecting steel from aggressive chloride-laden environments. It is also, but less commonly, used for carbonated concrete. The steel is maintained as the cathode in an electrical circuit driven by either an impressed current or (more unusually for reinforced concrete), a sacrificial anode. Cathodic protection systems must be carefully designed and account must be taken of many different factors, such as the aggressiveness of the environment, the area of steel to be protected, the resistivity of the surrounding material, the positioning of any external metallic objects that could be affected by the system, and the type of anode used.

The initial design requirements and the application of a current throughout the service life of the structure being protected can make cathodic protection more expensive and complex than conventional repair systems. A careful evaluation of cathodic protection systems relative to other repair options should be made in order to ascertain whether cathodic protection is the best route to follow. Besides being used for repairing corrosion-damaged concrete, cathodic protection is being developed for the protection of new structures, including post-tensioned members. Because passivated steel requires less polarization to achieve protection, stressed tendons can be included without giving rise to the usual concerns about hydrogen embrittlement. Continuing developments in the method of application and the anode systems available, such as sprayed conductive overlays and an increasing range of discrete anode geometries, promise to extend the use of this technique in both new and existing structures.

Re-alkalization

As previously discussed, steel reinforcement is passivated (protected) by the alkaline environment created by the surrounding concrete. Carbonation of the concrete by the acidic reaction with atmospheric carbon dioxide results in the conversion of the normal concrete constituents, calcium hydroxide and calcium silicate hydrates, to calcium carbonate. This is accompanied by a reduction in alkalinity and loss of protection to the reinforcement, which can then corrode in the presence of oxygen and water. In the past, the only remedy for this type of deterioration was to remove and replace the affected concrete to restore the alkaline environment; in the majority of cases, this will continue to be true.

The electrochemical technique of re-alkalization restores the alkaline environment around the reinforcement without removal of the carbonated cover concrete. In the re-alkalization process, a temporary mesh electrode contained within a reservoir of alkaline sodium carbonate solution is attached to the surface of the concrete. An electrical connection is made between the surface mesh and the reinforcement and a current is applied, such that the reinforcement becomes cathodic and the mesh anodic. The migration of water by electro-osmosis toward the reinforcement results in a suction pressure being established in the network of capillary pores, and the alkaline solution is drawn into the concrete. Electrolysis at the cathode results in the generation of hydroxyl ions necessary for re-passivation of the steel surface. When the cover zone is saturated (and this has been confirmed by testing) the current is disconnected and the external electrode and reservoir are removed. The concrete surface is then coated with a conventional anti-carbonation coating to prevent re-carbonation of the now-alkaline pore solutions.

This technique has advantages where disruption has to be kept to a minimum. Research into the effects of re-alkalization on the materials and engineering properties of reinforced concrete is continuing, in particular into its effects on reinforcement bond strength and alkali–aggregate reaction, e.g. the potential use of lithium salts to limit the production of expansive gels.

Chloride extraction

Chloride extraction (desalination) makes use of the same electrochemical principles as re-alkalization, except that the primary aim is to remove negatively charged chloride ions from within the concrete, by ion migration to the surface anode. The current density required for chloride extraction to be effective is generally much greater than that required for re-alkalization. The time required to reduce the chloride concentration at the reinforcement to acceptable levels depends upon a number of factors.

Corrosion inhibitors

Corrosion inhibitors are widely used in the protection of metals. There has long been interest in their potential use for the protection of concrete reinforcement, generally as admixtures of calcium nitrite. A more recent development has been in the availability of inhibitor systems that can be applied to the surface of reinforced concrete or directly introduced into the body of the concrete (e.g. by injection or by means of an inhibitor-rich implant) and which will then migrate to and protect the steel. These materials have very high vapour pressure and are capable of migrating through concrete to form a film on the surface of the reinforcement and thereby protect it.

Migratory corrosion inhibitor systems have the potential to reduce significantly the rate of chloride-induced corrosion in structures. With increasing availability of such materials, it is hoped that further independent research and trials will be initiated to assess their performance and effectiveness in comparison with other remedial techniques for corrosion control. There is particular interest in their use with prestressed and AAR-susceptible structures where the use of active electrochemical techniques may be undesirable.

As inhibitors are often specified for use in parallel with some form of corrosion monitoring, this is also proving to be an effective way of encouraging the monitoring of structures over significant proportions of their service lives.

Protective coatings

Coatings can be used to protect concrete substrates in several ways. They can form an impermeable barrier between the environment and the substrate, affording almost complete protection (provided that the coating is continuous). Coatings can also protect the substrate by slowing down the rate at which aggressive components from the environment penetrate the substrate; i.e. they provide partial protection, which may be adequate to allow the structure to fulfil its design life.

There are at present a large number of mainly organic coatings available to protect structural materials such as reinforced concrete from many different service environments. In addition to epoxies, polyurethanes and bituminous systems, there is now an increasing use of penetrating water-repellent pore liners. Water repellents in current use are generally based on silanes and siloxanes, which can be applied to fair-faced concrete surfaces without significantly altering their appearance, and are therefore of particular interest with respect to historically important structures.

Silane and siloxane

Water repellents based on organic silicon compounds offer a convenient route to enhancing the durability of new and existing reinforced concrete structures, particularly where these are exposed to chloride environments. Alkylalkoxysilanes or silanes have been in use for many years for the treatment of mineral-based materials such as glass fibres and powdered stone. Because of their smaller molecular size, they can penetrate far deeper than silicone resins and it is not essential for the treated material to be completely dry, so they can be used with concrete.

It should be noted that none of the silicon-based materials can be used on saturated substrates, where the water-filled pores prevent the water-resistant treatment from being effectively absorbed. Silane reacts with moisture to produce a silanol intermediary, which in turn produces the polysiloxane or silicone resin. An alkaline environment is required to catalyse the reaction and so, in neutral materials such as brick and carbonated concrete, no water-resistant compounds are formed. Alkylalkoxysiloxanes or siloxanes are produced when silane reacts with water. In practice, they are produced directly from Cl-silane. They consist of chains of silane groups, linked by oxygen atoms, and the length of the chains is determined by the amount of water added. Oligomeric (fewer than four groups) and polymeric (more than four groups) forms of siloxane can be produced, but the large size of the polymeric form makes it difficult to apply and prone to remain tacky and attract dirt.

Oligomeric siloxanes retain most of the advantages of silanes with regard to penetration and moisture tolerance. They have the added advantage of a low vapour pressure under normal conditions of application, which results in far lower evaporation losses compared with silanes. While conventional siloxanes still require an alkaline environment for full reaction to occur, modified materials are now available with a suitable catalyst already added. Such materials will react even in neutral materials, provided that moisture is present. It is also possible to produce modified siloxanes, which can be exposed to heavy rain after only a few hours. For alkaline materials such as concrete, it is still necessary to use long alkyl group siloxanes. Methyl siloxanes perform best with natural stone and where pore systems are coarse and more open. Because of their low evaporation loss, siloxanes can be applied as low concentration solutions (6–8%) in hydrocarbons such as white spirit or aromatic solvents, but the solvents must be anhydrous. As with silanes, they can be dissolved in alcohol (again, anhydrous), but with a certain loss in performance.

Sprayed concrete

Spray-applied cementitious materials are increasingly specified for use in major reinforced concrete repair programmes. Spray application offers a number of advantages in the successful placement of repairs, especially on soffits and vertical faces. Large volumes of such materials have been used for reinstatement of carbonated or chloride contaminated cover, in strengthening works and as overlays for cathodic protection systems. The performance of any repair material is clearly critical to the long-term success of the remedial works in which they have been employed. While it should be relatively straightforward to identify and specify the appropriate performance characteristics required by a particular application, and to match these to available materials, the inevitable complications of site application may result in less than ideal performance.

Manufacturers of sprayed concrete repair materials now regularly provide a wide range of test results upon which to base an informed selection, although there is still much confusion about which parameters are important for specific applications. *In situ* testing of the applied materials is also fraught with difficulties and uncertainties, particularly with respect to adequate adhesion to the substrate. A wide range of attributes are now routinely tested by the manufacturers of pre-bagged, spray-applied repair materials and provided for the specifier or user on data sheets. The results are generally obtained from cores taken from test panels. Where appropriate, these can be verified with cores taken from test panels sprayed on site under representative conditions. Selecting which aspects are of greatest significance with respect to any one application can be difficult, while comparing the relative performance of alternative materials is difficult because the test methods are generally not standardized. For most applications, the performance attributes of greatest importance, in no particular order, are as follows:

- compressive strength;
- rate of strength gain;
- modulus;
- thermal expansion;
- shrinkage;
- adhesion;

■ gas and vapour transport characteristics;
■ resistivity (particularly for electrochemical applications).

The ultimate strength of these materials is generally far in excess of that required for the repair. It is often more important, therefore, that the rate of strength gain is appropriate for the planned work programme. Traditionally, the high strength of repair mortars went hand in hand with high stiffness. A consequence of this was that the repairs tended to debond when subjected to flexure. Some more recently formulated materials have elastic moduli comparable with 'normal' grades of structural concrete. Control of shrinkage and good adhesion are essential in repair, particularly where relatively thin layers are used, such as cathodic protection overlays. It is likely that a properly applied spray repair material would provide significantly improved resistance to carbon dioxide and chloride ion ingress when compared to the parent material, further enhancing the repair characteristics.

The high density of spray-applied repairs, together with the inclusion of pozzolanic and polymer modifiers, means that such materials usually exhibit relatively high electrical resistivity. In conventional repairs this can help to control the magnitude of corrosion currents, but in cathodic protection applications, which require a flow of current, exceptionally high resistivities may be a disadvantage. Recent wet-sprayed systems have been shown to have much lower resistivities, similar in magnitude to simple sand–cement gunite, and may therefore be more appropriate for use with electrochemical repair techniques. The influence of resistivity on the operation of cathodic protection systems has been discussed elsewhere.[14]

Electro-osmosis
Electro-osmosis has been applied to the movement of moisture through porous materials, most notably masonry, for a considerable time and with varying and generally disappointing results. More recently, an electro-osmosis system has been specifically developed to control moisture levels in reinforced concrete by the application of controlled low-voltage DC pulses.[15] The electronically controlled system is designed to operate at maximum efficiency while avoiding problems of stray-current corrosion to buried steel. Additionally, the design, installation and monitoring of the system are significantly simpler than for existing electrochemical remediation techniques.

The system is capable of reducing moisture levels in concrete to between 60% and 70% RH, and maintaining this level independent of external weather conditions. The technique is equally applicable to new and existing structures, although new concrete should be fully cured before the system is energized.

An additional benefit to the removal of excess free moisture is the associated reduction in dissolved salts, particularly chloride, present within the pore solution of the concrete, with the overall effect of reducing chloride ions to below critical levels for chloride-induced corrosion. The combination of reduced chloride ion concentration and controlled relative humidity can result in the reduction of corrosion rates to low or negligible values. The continuing operation of an appropriately designed and installed system can prevent or control further ingress of moisture and associated dissolved salts, which may be aggressive to either the concrete (e.g. sulphates) or the reinforcement (predominantly chlorides). Additionally, the system is designed to polarize the reinforcement negatively. This offers a degree of cathodic protection, helps to reduce the corrosion risk of embedded steel during the transition period from high to low relative humidity (typically three months), and provides additional protection throughout the life of the installation.

Such a system has been specifically assessed for possible side effects resulting from its operation, such as may be encountered with other remedial techniques. No evidence has been found to indicate significant risks of bond strength reduction, excess alkali generation, hydrogen evolution or stray current corrosion of adjacent discontinuous steel.

Summary

For the majority of degrading structural elements constructed from plain or reinforced concrete, a number of remediation options can be considered:

Do nothing/monitor Such an approach is appropriate for areas that have the potential for corrosion but are presently not actively corroding. Requires commitment.

Simple patch repairs This approach is seldom effective with chloride-induced corrosion, as adjacent areas will typically start to show active corrosion within one to three years (incipient anode behaviour).

Full patch repairs Very effective for dealing with discrete areas of chloride contamination but usually impractical and expensive for highly contaminated concrete.

Patch plus inhibitor In damaged reinforced concrete with sporadic or low-level chloride contamination, the addition of an inhibitor can reduce the risk of incipient anode behaviour. Likely to have reduced life at high chloride levels.

Cathodic protection Long-lasting and reliable but requires specialist design, installation and monitoring. May not be suitable with alkali-reactive aggregates or post-tensioned steel.

Chloride extraction More sensitive to AAR and post-tensioned steel than cathodic protection, less effective at very high chloride levels (e.g. above 2%) and not tolerant of recontamination.

Re-alkalization Can be an attractive and cost-effective solution for carbonated concrete where extensive corrosion of the reinforcement has not yet occurred. Retains original material but may require anti-carbonation coating to ensure longevity.

Electro-osmosis The latest pulsed system is relatively new and only just becoming commercially available. Of particular interest where reinforcement has poor continuity.

References

1   Barneyback, R.S., Jr, and Diamond, S. (1981), 'Expression and analysis of pore fluids from hardened cement pastes and mortars', *Cement and Concrete Research*, **11**, 279–285.

2   Page, C.L., and Treadaway, K.W.J. (1982), 'Aspects of the electro-chemistry of steel in concrete', *Nature*, **297**, (5862), 109–115.

3   Parrott, L.J. (1987), *A Review of Carbonation in Reinforced Concrete*, (Cement and Concrete Association/Building Research Establishment, Department of the Environment), Slough: Cement and Concrete Association.

4   Wood, J.G.M. (1985), 'Methods of control of active corrosion in concrete', *First International Conference on Deterioration and Repair of Reinforced Concrete in the Arabian Gulf*, 139–150.

5   Tuutti, K. (1982), *Corrosion of Steel in Concrete*, Stockholm: Cement and Concrete Institute.

6   Wood, J.G.M., and Johnson, R.A. (1989), 'An engineer's perspective on UK experience with alkali aggregate reaction', *Eighth International Conference on AAR*, Kyoto.

7   Page, C.L., Short, N.R., and Holden, W.R. (1986), 'The influence of different cements on chloride-induced corrosion of reinforcing steel', *Cement and Concrete Research*, **16**, 79–86.

8   Page, C.L., and Lambert, P. (1987), 'Kinetics of oxygen diffusion in hardened cement pastes', *Journal of Materials Science*, **22**, 942–946.

9   Vernon, W.H.J. (1935), 'A laboratory study of the atmospheric corrosion of metals', *Transactions of the Faraday Society*, 31.

10   Cavalier, P.G., and Vassie, P.R. (1981), 'Investigation and repair of reinforcement corrosion in a bridge deck', *Proceedings of the Institution of Civil Engineers*, **70**, 461–480.

11   Wierig, H. (1984), 'Long-time studies on the carbonation of concrete under outdoor exposure', *Proceedings of the RILEM Seminar*, Hannover, 239–249.

12   Lambert, P., and Wood, J.G.M. (1990), 'Improving durability by environmental control', *Fifth International Conference on Durability*, Brighton: RILEM/BRE.

13   Lambert, P. (1995), 'Surface coatings and treatments for the protection of reinforced concrete', *Concrete Durability in the Arabian Gulf*, BSE/Concrete Society, 43–65.

14   Concrete Society (1989), *Technical Report No.36. Cathodic Protection of Reinforced Concrete*, London: The Concrete Society.

15   Lambert, P. (1996), *Evaluation of X-CEL system: Test Programme Report*, Mott MacDonald.

CHAPTER 9

CONSERVING CONCRETE: DEFINING AN APPROPRIATE APPROACH FOR LISTED BUILDINGS

Kevin Davies

In the post-war period, reinforced concrete has probably been more widely used for above-ground buildings and structures than any other construction material. It is generally very durable and versatile, and is favoured by engineers and architects alike for the wide range of construction applications and architectural styles to which it lends itself.

Concrete on its own is unable to withstand tension, so steel is embedded into the structural members to provide the necessary tensile strength. As steel has a similar expansion coefficient to concrete, this results in a useful composite material that can be fabricated on or off site. The range of shapes and styles that can be formed from reinforced concrete is immense.

Unfortunately, however, the theoretical performance standards of reinforced concrete have not been matched by its performance in real life. Problems such as cracking, vibration damage, poor compaction and corrosion of the steel are common. The environment surrounding the building can also produce premature deterioration by altering the condition of the concrete and minimizing the protection afforded by the highly alkaline nature of the concrete to the embedded reinforcement steel. Mechanical abuse and poor drainage are responsible for a number of concrete deterioration problems, ranging from minor discoloration to severe cracking, delamination and spalling.

The deterioration process is now well understood and documented (Figure 9.1), and provided the cause, or causes, of any particular problem is known, steps can be taken to repair the damage and instigate a long-term, commercially and technically correct rehabilitation strategy. Additional care and skill are required when dealing with listed buildings, and it is these aspects that are considered in this paper.

Historical background

Traditionally, it has been the specialist contractor or specialist repair material manufacturer who has spearheaded the repair investigation and selection of rehabilitation materials and techniques. All too often, this has led to inappropriate repairs using the specialist's proprietary process or materials, which – even though they may repair the actual damage – may not have eradicated the cause of the damage. This has led to short-term 'holding' repairs, which are rarely appropriate for listed structures.

It is important to understand what makes a particular building worthy of listed status. What is it that makes it significant and how does conservation apply to such a building? It will almost certainly have special architectural interest; in addition, it may exhibit a special form or features, use a special type of construction or materials, have been built for a special purpose or have some other significance in the history of design. It should be noted that the building may or may not be unique, and it may not even be the best example of that which makes it significant.

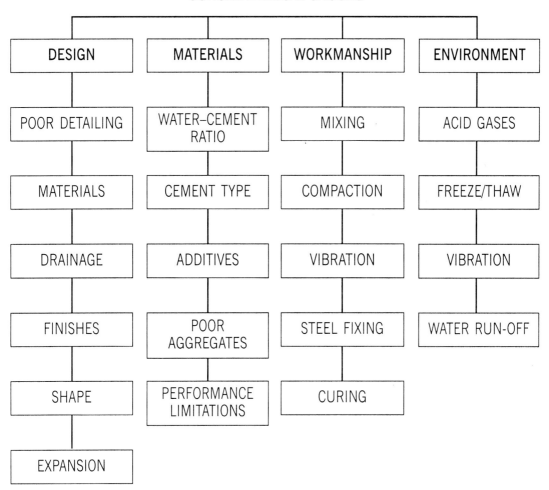

Figure 9.1 Summary chart of causes of concrete decay. (Kevin Davies)

However, once a building has been listed, the question of repair requires special consideration and may become slightly more complicated, and perhaps subject to regulations and legislation.

More and more post-war reinforced concrete buildings are being listed. Many of them were built during the period in which building design codes were least adequate to produce good-quality, durable buildings. It was also the boom period of concrete construction in Britain, and quality control was often poor.

Concrete repair is now a major industry employing thousands of people, yet there are still no unambiguous guidelines available on how to approach the investigation or repair of damaged buildings, whether listed or not.

The appropriate approach to repairs

Before repairs can be carried out correctly and effectively, it is important to understand the problem. It might seem simplistic, but the starting point must be the question: is there in fact a problem? Once it has been resolved that there is indeed a problem, the following should be considered.

Information gathering (historical)

General historical information about the building is always essential for understanding how and why a material is used. It is important to determine changes to the concrete, its environment and its function during its history. Knowing about changes in chloride levels, levels of carbonation and any changes in the chemical and physical characteristics of the concrete will be useful in understanding the pattern of deterioration.

Nature of the problem

Categorizing the problem can make it easier to direct the investigation process appropriately. For example, a problem might fall into one or more of the following categories:

- structural;
- durability;
- moisture;
- drainage;
- safety;
- social;
- cosmetic or aesthetic.

Cause and extent of the problem

There is little point in progressing with repairs without an understanding of what caused the problem in the first place. The extent of the problem will have a significant influence on the repair methods selected.

Likelihood of the problem continuing
Was the damage caused by an irregular occurrence and will it happen again?

Damage obviously caused
Is it repairable? Has it already been repaired previously, and if so, how effective (or otherwise) was the previous repair?

Side effects
Has the damage caused side effects? Could a repair cause side effects, good or bad?

How do you investigate?

Before embarking on an investigation, it is worth considering the various options available. It is most likely that some specialist advice or input is required at some stage, but you have to decide on the level of assistance. The options are:

Carry out your own investigation
This is a good place to start, even if you bring in outside assistance later on. The better your understanding of the problem, the easier you will find it to evaluate the repair options later.

Have outside assistance
There are many specialists who will advise on concrete repair. This advice may be free (as part of proprietary repair materials supply) or supplied on a commercial consultancy basis. Paid-for, independent advice may well be preferable to the 'free' advice of a sales representative. A paid consultancy will usually yield far more useful results than an inspection carried out as part of a free quote, and using an independent specialist ensures that there is no conflict of interest between conservation aims and choosing the best repair method or system.

Farm out the investigation
The whole investigation process and development of repair strategy can be given over to a specialist company or individual. It may also be possible to split the investigation process away from the development of the remedial solutions, since 'free' investigation and advice that leads to the recommendation of proprietary products and materials should be treated with caution (especially since a specialist contractor may hold a licence for only one of the repair methods available).

Whichever route is followed, care must be taken to ensure the competency and experience of the specialist adviser, and it is important to ensure that the specialist is sympathetic to, and understands, conservation principles for listed buildings as well as concrete degradation processes. Such experience and knowledge should be confirmed prior to appointment of the specialist.

What to look for

Once the investigator or investigation team has been appointed, a programme of inspection is required. It is necessary to establish the scope of work and which parts of the building are to be investigated. A thorough physical investigation will be required to quantify the physical damage. Mapping of defects such as spalling, delamination, cracking, depth of friable surface layers, and other defects, will offer information about the nature and extent of the problem. The survey should also help to determine the likely cost of rehabilitating the building. Consideration should initially be given to investigating the following:

Concrete frame
The skeleton of the building, including foundations and roof. Is it sound?

Concrete condition
It is necessary to establish the overall condition of the concrete. Is it discoloured, poorly compacted, cracked, spalled or delaminated, for example?

Corrosion of steel
Is the steel reinforcement corroded or in poor condition? If so, how serious is the problem?

Concrete degradation
Is the problem concrete degradation? If so, this could be caused by one or a combination of the following factors:

- alkali–silica reaction;
- poor quality aggregate;
- poor compaction;
- low cement content;
- high water–cement ratio.

Coating degradation
Is the problem limited to coating degradation, and therefore purely cosmetic?

Inadequate drainage
One of the most common problems. Does water run off in the wrong place, pool or collect in specific locations?

Peripheral components
Is the problem associated with drainage pipes, gutters, balconies, chimneys, fixings, windows, doors, and so forth? Can replacement of these items or revised detailing help? It should be noted that changes that affect the actual appearance of listed buildings might not be acceptable.

Testing: the English Heritage preferred way

Concrete evaluation testing is well documented and, for 'hidden from view' structures and non-listed structures, there is generally no problem in implementing the test procedures. For listed buildings, however, it is important to bear in mind some additional requirements.

Plan the test programme

Too many investigations are attempted without proper planning. This can result in incorrect assessment or, in the worst cases, in damage to the building.

Visual assessment

Visual assessment is a remarkably good investigating tool for accessible areas and is one that causes no distress to the building. Care should be taken when gaining access, e.g. when removing wallcoverings, false ceilings, tiles, floor screeds, and so forth.

Destructive investigation

Destructive testing is frequently required. The types of testing which may be required are likely to include:

- estimate of compressive strength (core samples);
- chloride ion concentration levels and profiling of these (dust samples);
- depth of cover to steel reinforcement (calibrated cover meter survey);
- depth of carbonation (simple, on-site chemical test);
- petrographic examination of core samples for visual inspection and determination of freeze–thaw and alkali–silica reaction (core samples).

Great care must be taken when selecting test sites for coring, drilling, marking or other destructive testing. Sites for taking core samples should be agreed with the architect co-ordinating the project. The test sites should be representative but can generally be selected at discreet, out-of-the-way locations, preferably not on the front elevation. With careful planning, samples can often be taken from rebates and other features without causing severe damage.

Minimize testing

A carefully developed investigation would minimize damage to the structure. In general, only one sample test and a check result would be sufficient to prove degradation causes. Multiple tests can be carried out on one removed core sample, for example.

Reinstate properly

Reinstatement of the investigation holes and so forth requires careful consideration and only approved repair materials should be used. It may be necessary to use lime-based mortars, for instance, rather than modern polymer modified proprietary repair mortars.

Selecting the repair

Once the testing has been completed and the nature and extent of the problem have been established, it is time to consider the repair options available. The level of intervention ranges from doing nothing to demolishing and rebuilding. Figure 9.2 (*pages 136–139*) provides a model for assessing each of the options for a fair-faced concrete building in the short, medium and long term, and is useful for focussing attention on the implications of each option.

Cost estimates for each option can be prepared for the estimated capital, maintenance and operational costs over a twenty-year period – an exercise that is rarely carried out, but is essential to enable repair options to be sensibly weighed up against one another.

The following aspects should be considered:

Technical

- Does the repair provide the most appropriate technical solution?
- Does the repair reinstate the strength of the building?
- Does the repair reinstate the function of the building?
- Does the repair reinstate the durability of the building?
- Is the repair method practical?
- Can maintenance be carried out?

Economic

- Examine the capital cost of the repair, including access scaffolding and so forth.
- Examine the life-cycle cost of the repair.
- Examine the cost of disruption during the repair, such as temporary rehousing.
- Does the repair add value (real or perceived) to the building?

Conservation

- Do the repairs use original building materials and building techniques?
- Is the original design retained after repairs?
- Is the original appearance retained after repairs?
- Can the building be used for its original purpose again after repairs?

Social

- Repairs can create noise and dust pollution. Can these be kept to acceptable levels, and can all appropriate health and safety requirements be met?
- Is temporary rehousing (i.e. of the occupants and contents of the building) or change of use required?
- Will building repairs be perceived to improve the building?

Secondary aspects

- Does the selected repair also solve the problem in the long term? Has the repair removed the cause of the problem, or has it merely addressed the symptoms? Can anything else be done to prevent recurrence?
- In overall terms, has the repair selected remained faithful to the original design and building concepts as intended by the original architect?
- Does the repair satisfy English Heritage and local authority regulations?

Records should be kept on all investigations carried out, with location maps and sketches showing salient points. Details of sample locations and orientation are important in determining crack patterns, failure mechanisms and deterioration causes. They are also invaluable in preparing cost estimates for repair works.

Repair options for reinforced concrete

Several repair strategies are available for reinforced concrete, some traditional and some using modern technology. It is unlikely that any one of the repair options would be sufficient on its own and the most appropriate would probably be a combination of more than one. Figure 9.2 provides summary details on available techniques, along with some of the advantages and disadvantages of each.

Repair Option	Anticipated maintenance-free service life	Advantages
1 No action (do nothing)	Less than five years	▦ cheapest short-term solution – no capital outlay ▦ no access required, no pollution or disruption to site ▦ no conservation problems
2 Traditional repairs with no coating	At five-yearly intervals throughout the service life	▦ cost-effective short-term solution (repairs can be colour and texture matched ▦ minimal scaffolding/access required ▦ minimal ongoing maintenance required ▦ limited disruption to site
3 Traditional repairs with a coating	At five to ten-year intervals throughout the service life	As above
4 Traditional repairs followed by electro-chemical realkalization with no coating	Ten to twenty years	▦ one time fix solution ▦ after application, no further maintenance or monitoring required ▦ minimal alteration to appearance ▦ well-documented and proven technology ▦ can be most cost-effective long-term solution ▦ process re-established corrosion protection properties of the concrete to protect steel reinforcement ▦ minimizes amount of carbonated concrete to be removed
5 Traditional repairs followed by electro-chemical realkalization with a coating	Twenty years	As above ▦ extends maintenance-free life expectancy by retarding ingress ▦ clear sealants will not alter visual appearance significantly ▦ sealants will assist in binding friable surface material to increase durability

Figure 9.2 *Repair of a fair-faced concrete building: balancing remedial options. (Kevin Davies)*

Disadvantages	Level of intervention
■ deterioration will continue at accelerating rate ■ structure becomes unsightly and eventually structurally unsound, service life of structure will be limited ■ unlikely to be the most cost-effective long-term solution	None, but safety checks would be required.
■ will not prevent deterioration in the structure elsewhere ■ corrosion damage continues and further repairs will be required (in say five years) ■ may not provide the most cost-effective long-term solution	Not often if carried out correctly, but adjacent areas would need to be checked.
As above ■ almost all coatings will alter appearance ■ coating will not prevent ongoing corrosion if the carbonation has progressed to reinforcement level or if chloride levels are above threshold levels at reinforcement	As for 2 above, but also at end of coating service life (dependent on type of coating).
■ repair mortar for patching must be compatible with realkalization process (limits manufacturers and products) ■ higher capital costs ■ carbonation and chloride ion ingress will recommence, albeit at a slower rate ■ fairly extensive clean-up operation required to remove materials used in realkalization process ■ some concretes may contain reactive aggregate (AAR), which needs to be determined prior to realkalization	At approximately ten-yearly intervals if carried out correctly.
As above ■ higher capital cost than 1–4	At end of coating service life (dependant on type of coating.

Figure 9.2   continued

Repair Option	Anticipated maintenance-free service life	Advantages
6 Impressed current cathodic protection	Fifteen to twenty years plus, dependent on anode type	▨ minimizes amount of chloride contaminated or carbonated concrete to be removed ▨ provides long-term corrosion protection if operated correctly (service life dependent on anode type) ▨ should prevent further corrosion-related deterioration of the structure
7 Traditional repairs followed by corrosion-inhibiting coating or migrating inhibitors	Unknown (fifteen to twenty years)	▨ clear versions have minimal impact on appearance of structure ▨ extends maintenance-free life by retarding ingress of corrosive ionic species and gases, and at the same time re-establishes corrosion protection properties of the concrete to protect the reinforcement ▨ minimizes the amount of carbonated but still sound concrete to be removed ▨ minimal ongoing maintenance required ▨ coating assists in binding friable surface layer to improve durability ▨ could prove to be the most cost-effective option for some cases

Disadvantages	Level of intervention
<ul><li>higher capital cost</li><li>poor design of ICCP can significantly affect appearance</li><li>disruption to users</li><li>may require significant electrical continuity bonding of steel reinforcement</li><li>requires ongoing maintenance</li><li>requires permanent AC power supply</li><li>requires ongoing monitoring by specialist</li><li>requires specialist design</li><li>repair mortars must be compatible with ICCP system (limits products and manufacturers)</li><li>possible effects of stray current interference with other metallic components must be avoided</li><li>access to internal face of building may be required</li></ul>	Regular monitoring and maintenance. Requires degree of technical expertise.
<ul><li>repair mortar must be compatible with inhibitor (limits manufacturers and products)</li><li>some concretes contain reactive aggregate (AAR), which needs to be determined prior to realkalization</li><li>no long-term data on performance available</li><li>performance claims have not yet been substantiated in practice</li><li>coating may detrimentally affect the re-application of the inhibitor</li></ul>	Routine inspection. Re-application after ten to fifteen years.

CHAPTER 10
THE DEVELOPMENT OF CLAD FRAME CONSTRUCTION AND THE IMPLICATIONS FOR CONSERVATION

Peter Ross

Figure 10.1   The Ritz Hotel, London (Mewès and Davis, 1905). (Peter Ross)

The origins of post-war clad frame construction in Britain – if cladding is defined as a facade that does not take the building's weight – date back to the turn of the century, when the steel frame, originally developed for industrial purposes, was first applied to polite architecture. The frame was hidden behind the facing stonework it supported; nevertheless the stonework was detailed in a style that represented load-bearing masonry. In addition, the London building inspectors still required the thickness of the masonry to conform to the existing Building Acts, not taking into account the structural contribution made by the frame (Figure 10.1). These buildings were not particularly tall, since their height was limited to 100 feet (30.5 metres) by the London Fire Brigade's access requirements.

The true potential of the frame was being exploited in the US. By the first decade of the twentieth century, buildings of twenty storeys and more were common in lower Manhattan. Thus, when Mr Selfridge came over from New York to build his new store in Oxford Street, his engineers brushed aside the 'deemed to satisfy' rules for wall thicknesses, and it could be argued that the Selfridge store is the first true clad frame building of its type in the UK.

Between the wars, the tradition of cladding frames in apparently load-bearing walls continued. To identify the principles by which cladding has come to be defined, we have to look abroad to the work of the Modernists, who argued that if the cladding could be divorced from the structure, then it could be lightweight or even transparent – a principle exhibited in few buildings in the UK. The Boots factory at Nottingham (Sir Owen Williams) and the Daily Express offices in Fleet Street (Ellis and Clarke) (Figure 10.2), both of 1932, are the best-known examples from this era.

1950s – 1970s

The curtain wall

The curtain wall, which combined the principles of visibly non-structural, light cladding with the idea of the grid – repetitive details in both directions – was first exploited in America at Lever House in New York (Skidmore Owings and Merrill, 1952). Although by New York standards it is not a particularly tall building, its height was accentuated by setting the slim tower block over a low podium, and by the use of continuous vertical mullions. The first building in the UK to follow all of these ideas, albeit on a reduced scale, was the former Castrol House in London (Gollins Melvin Ward, 1960) (Figure 10.3, *overleaf*), built originally as offices and recently refurbished as residential accommodation.

These early systems were largely built up on site from small individual elements. Figure 10.4 (*page 143*) shows a cut-away section of

Figure 10.2   The Daily Express offices, London (Ellis and Clarke, 1932). (Peter Ross)

the curtain wall of the Sanderson showrooms in Berners Street, London (Slater and Uren, 1960). The main mullions (1), in galvanized pressed metal, are bolted to cleats (2) attached to the perimeter concrete edge beam (3), with provision for thermal movement. The mullions are linked by short transoms (4), which form a frame for the sash windows (5) and a stove-enamelled glass panel (6) concealing the frame. The pressed aluminium facing mullion (7) conceals the structure and a rainwater pipe, and an internal mullion (8) houses various services. No gaskets or gap-filling sealants are used. When the curtain wall was used for tower blocks, the construction was generally consistent around the entire perimeter, with no differentiation between the north and south facades.

In the meantime, Mies van der Rohe had developed a series of immaculately detailed 'tight skin' facades, exploiting the structural role of the mullions by exposing the outer flanges, which doubled as cradle guides, originally at the Seagram Building in New York (1958). The most direct homage to this Miesian concept in the UK is the Commercial Union Tower, London (Gollins Melvin Ward, 1969). This is a closed facade, with no ventilation: these second-generation curtain walls took the giant step of a commitment to an air-conditioning system for the building as a whole, rather than for a limited number of internal service areas.

Figure 10.3 The former Castrol House in London (Gollins Melvin Ward, 1960), built originally as offices and recently refurbished as residential accommodation. (Peter Ross)

Stone

Not all facades were entirely of glass, and stone was still employed for many commercial projects, using a vocabulary developed from the ashlar facing of the pre-war building tradition. Rectangular stones of uniform thickness were fixed to a backing wall of brick or concrete using metal cleats that engaged in rebates cut into the back face of the stone. At first, the metalwork in work of the highest quality was phosphor bronze; various grades of stainless steel were used on later contracts.

The stylistic influence of Modernism often resulted in large areas of stone cladding unrelieved by any feature. The consequent thermal expansion, especially on south-facing walls, introduced a requirement for 'soft' joints at intervals to restrict cumulative movements. These joints were filled with the newly developed mastic sealants, which came into use from the mid-1960s onwards, initially using materials produced by the petrochemical industry. The early oil-based mastics had a life of ten years or so, but the development of modern polysulphides and silicones has increased service lives to between twenty and thirty years.

Durable stone was expensive, and since it was required only as a facing material, various ways of using thinner slabs were explored. At Angel Court, London (Fitzroy

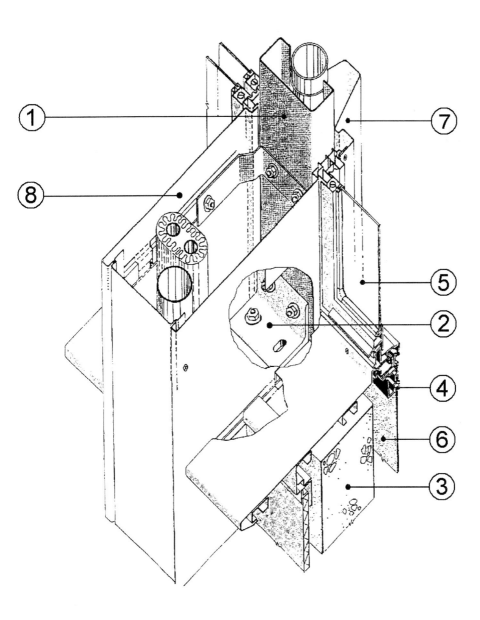

Figure 10.4   Cut-away section of the curtain wall of the Sanderson showroom in Berners Street, London (Slater and Uren, 1960). (1) main mullions; (2) cleats; (3) concrete edge beam; (4) transoms; (5) frame for the sash windows; (6) stove-enamelled glass panel; (7) facing mullion; (8) internal mullion. (Peter Ross)

Robinson, 1977) (Figure 10.5) panels of granite that measured 1.7 by 1.4 metres, but were only 25 mm thick, were bonded to precast concrete backing panels, using stainless steel dowels with thin grommets to allow for differential movements.

Profiled metal sheeting

The classic original metal sheeting was corrugated iron, invented well before the turn of the century. Corrugation gave the relatively thin sheets the stiffness necessary to span up to two metres between purlins, making them eminently suitable for the roofs and walls of industrial buildings. Early corrugated iron was coated with bitumen paint; later, the development of the hot dipped galvanizing process extended the life of the material considerably. The introduction of a range of profiles and factory-applied paint improved the status of the material in the post-war period, when it has been used as an economical covering for a variety of commercial premises, such as factories, warehouses and retail outlets.

Figure 10.5   Angel Court, London (Fitzroy Robinson, 1977). (Peter Ross)

Concrete, GRC and GRP

The use of *in situ* fair-faced concrete, much admired by architects as an 'honest' expression of structure, was in practice a demanding technique, and it was difficult for contractors to produce satisfactory results. One solution for cladding applications was the fabrication of precast panels, which allowed factory control of the finishes, although it then became necessary to develop details for sealing the perimeter joints. The individual panels were inevitably heavy, since the panel thickness was governed by the cover to the steel reinforcement. The cover – and hence the weight – could be reduced if stainless steel reinforcement was used, but this increased the production costs.

In the 1960s, Pilkington experimented with glass-fibre reinforced concrete (GRC). Here, the reinforcement consisted of chopped strands of glass fibre, which controlled cracking and at the same time gave the concrete a modest tensile strength. This allowed the fabrication of thinner, lighter panels with no risk of corrosion. However, concrete is a poor insulator, and so fabricators went on to develop sandwich panels, incorporating a central leaf of insulation.

A technique for the construction of truly lightweight panels, using glass-reinforced polyesters (GRP), came originally from the boat-building industry. The panel profile was formed as an open mould, which was lined by hand with glass-fibre mats encapsulated in a resin matrix applied by brush or roller in layers to build up a thickness of 6 mm or so. Larger panels incorporated a metal backing frame, to give the necessary rigidity and to provide fixing points.

The problems of the 1970s

By the end of the 1960s, however, some elements of Modernist construction were performing poorly. Much fair-face concrete construction (a technique conceived in the sun and warmth of a Mediterranean climate) was looking dirty and rust-stained, and some of the newer lightweight materials were not proving durable. In addition, the low thermal insulation values of many building envelopes (which were allowed by the bylaws of the time) made some interiors uncomfortable, and others prone to condensation.

Moreover, events in the Middle East, culminating in the 'winter of discontent' in 1973–4, meant that the cost of the energy necessary to heat these lightly insulated buildings rose significantly. Thus arose the public disaffection for 'modern architecture', and a search for alternative vocabularies of style and form. In response to concern about energy costs, the Building Regulations, which had up to this time set down thermal transmittance limits only for domestic construction, were from 1976 broadened to include all new building, with successively lower limits.

1980 to the present

The curtain wall

Considerable developments in curtain wall construction were made in the 1980s. By now, most curtain walling consisted of sophisticated factory-made panels, incorporating double glazing and panels of insulation to reduce thermal transmittance, which were supplied throughout Europe by specialist firms. Some designers experimented with external shading, which cut internal solar gain in summer, and which doubled as access for window cleaning.

Stone cladding

The 1980s also saw an increase in the use of stone facing, which was sometimes prefabricated into composite panels incorporating insulation into the overall build-up. The joints were generally filled with mastic. As with curtain walling, internationalization of the industry led to the use of more stone from outside the UK, with sandstones now often preferred to the granites favoured in the 1960s and 1970s. Sealing all the joints with mastic was both expensive and a future maintenance liability for the owner; and so, in the late 1980s, many designers abandoned mastic in favour of open joints. The cladding itself was then regarded as a rain screen, allowing a small amount of water to penetrate the joints to the zone of the fixings, which was designed as a drained cavity. The fixings themselves, which were inaccessible for maintenance, were generally of stainless steel.

Modernism and glass

Modernism as a style survived, often associated with high tech architecture, in which the mechanism of the construction was revealed rather than concealed. The problems of sealing and jointing glass panels were made easier by the use of EPDM (ethylene propylene terpolymer) gaskets, which could be formed to a great variety of profiles, and which, unlike natural rubber, maintained their flexibility when exposed to light.

Glass was always a major component of curtain walling systems, but from the 1970s onwards it began to be used as a structural component in some high tech facades. Glass 'blades' were used to stabilize large floor-to-ceiling glass panes in the Sainsbury Centre at the University of East Anglia (Sir Norman Foster, 1977) (Figures 10.6 and 10.7). This technique had already been used by Foster at the Willis Faber Dumas (now Willis Faber Carroon) building in Ipswich in 1974 (Figure 10.8), where each glass panel was hung from the one above, surrounding the building with a true 'curtain' wall.

RFR, based in Paris, designed a series of glazed enclosures in which the individual glass panels became the compression elements of a finished support framing system. The tension elements were formed from stainless steel rods and cables with connection designs drawn from the vocabulary of yacht rigging. Examples in the UK include the entrance screens at Liverpool Street Station.

Further developments in glass included coatings to improve thermal resistance, and the so-called 'smart' facades of either photochromic glass, which automatically responds to external

Figure 10.6   Sainsbury Centre exterior, University of East Anglia (Sir Norman Foster, 1977). (Peter Ross)

*Figure 10.7   Sainsbury Centre interior, University of East Anglia (Sir Norman Foster, 1977).
(Peter Ross)*

*Figure 10.8   Willis Faber Dumas (now Willis Faber Carroon) building, Ipswich (Sir Norman
Foster, 1974). (Peter Ross)*

lighting levels (in the manner of sunglasses) or electrochromic glass, whose opacity can be varied at will. Whether these materials will form a genuine development of facade design, or remain expensive toys, remains to be seen.

Metal and composite panels

The need to provide increased thermal resistance encouraged the incorporation of insulation into facade construction generally. Initially it was installed as a simple backing material to profiled sheeting, and later used to make composite panels. A slab of insulation, such as polystyrene or glass fibre, was sandwiched between an aluminium facing sheet and a steel backing sheet. The composite nature of the assembly allowed the panel to resist wind loading while supported only around the perimeter, using fixing cleats attached to a backing frame. The joints between the panels were generally sealed with gaskets.

Additionally, at the Sainsbury Centre, Foster introduced the idea of flexibility – the solid and glazed panels, of identical shapes, could be interchanged, although a client might not, in practice, take advantage of such a facility.

Maintenance and conservation issues

The large majority of the pre-war building stock was of traditional construction – brick walls with pitched slated or tiled roofs – which had developed over some three hundred years. This had resulted in a vocabulary of construction that was reasonably durable and could be repaired when necessary as part of a maintenance regime. In the post-war period, new materials and new methods of construction were introduced without an evaluation in every case of their performance capabilities, particularly in relation to durability. The durability of a particular element is difficult to predict, and tests designed to accelerate an effect such as weathering are not always reliable. It is not surprising, therefore, that some elements of innovatory external cladding were performing poorly by the 1970s.

Assessment of the condition of the cladding of individual buildings is often made more difficult because critical elements, such as fixings, are concealed. Even though much of this work was only carried out some thirty years ago, many clients have not retained drawings, and further searches may have to be made for material from the archives of the designers or the fabricators involved, which may or may not be available. For this reason, some opening-up is generally necessary to determine the form as well as the condition of the concealed elements.

The curtain wall

The curtain walls of the early post-war years are now over forty years old, and most owners have now to consider the issues of maintenance and repair. While the performance of individual buildings obviously depends upon the quality of the original construction, the principal factors that will in general determine the performance are:

- the durability of the metal components, sealants or gaskets;
- any maintenance requirements of the finishes;

- the effects of thermal cycling;
- the method of sealing joints;
- the feasibility of individual component replacement;
- maintenance of any window furniture;
- provision for access.

The internal environment may also be adversely affected by:

- relatively high thermal transmittance;
- relatively low thermal storage capacity;
- solar gain on southern elevations;
- any wind or rain penetration in the upper levels.

Generally speaking, 'traditional' construction can often be repaired as necessary, but this approach is not so easily applied to the curtain wall. Any environmental problems of the curtain are similarly difficult to address piecemeal. In addition, curtains were fixed to some of our first 'tall' buildings, without necessarily a full appreciation of the effects of wind and rain at height. It is not surprising that replacement, rather than conservation and repair, has to date been the preferred option.

Concrete/GRC/GRP

The sea change in architectural thinking that took place in the later 1970s meant that exposed concrete, and materials that looked like it, fell from favour. The problems of *in situ* concrete finishes are familiar, and related in part to a tendency to stain and weather badly. The principal problem, however, was the corrosion of inadequately protected reinforcement and the surface spalling that resulted from this.

GRC was not susceptible to these corrosion problems, and in general the early single-leaved panels have performed reasonably well. GRC does, however, have a fairly high coefficient of thermal expansion, which results in induced stresses in sandwich panels under thermal cycling. These stresses could in turn cause cracking, which although not serious enough to affect the integrity of the panels, damages their appearance.

The performance of early GRP panels has been variable, since they were based on a variety of material formulations and designs before a consensus of practice had been achieved.

All these materials are essentially self-finished, and there is no effective remedial work that does not involve some form of over-coating, such as a paint treatment.

Profiled steel sheeting

Although the different proprietary products vary in their detailed design, most profiled steel sheeting is made from sheet steel around 1 mm thick rolled to profile after galvanizing, and then coated with a PVC paint applied by roller. Some early production runs gave problems of fading and paint delamination, but the technology of formulation and application improved significantly over the thirty years or so that the material has been in production. Its performance is now generally reliable – given that it is a relatively cheap cladding, with a medium-term life expectancy.

Eventually performance is affected mainly by corrosion at cut ends and around fixing points. While it is possible to carry out remedial painting on site, most owners would eventually replace the sheets from profiles in current production.

Conclusion

As I have shown, many of the forms of cladding introduced in the post-war period were non-traditional. New and untried, they brought with them problems of durability that could not always be solved according to conventional conservation principles, which were conceived and developed in relation to the traditional materials – solid masonry, brick, render and timber. This dilemma is most obvious in the case of the curtain wall, where we may have to choose between the original fabric drastically modified, or new fabric as a replication (or as near as can be achieved) of the old – the choice between substance and style.

Of course, this discussion only becomes relevant if a consensus is reached with regard to the architectural interest of a particular building, and it may be argued that, at least for buildings constructed using the humbler materials, conservation issues are not likely to arise. But as the listing categories are broadened to contemporary building types, and interest in post-war architecture grows (witness, for example, the National Trust's purchase of Sir Paul McCartney's Liverpool home), the conservation debate is likely to centre increasingly on modern, rather than traditional, materials.

CHAPTER 11

THE GLASS AND METAL CURTAIN WALL: HISTORY, DIAGNOSTICS AND TREATMENT

Stephen J. Kelley

History

The curtain wall fulfils one of the most demanding roles in building construction. Not only does it provide the primary image for the building, but it also performs the multiple functions required of an exterior skin – forming a protective enclosure, keeping out the outside environment and maintaining the inside environment – in an efficient, economical manner. The beginnings of the curtain wall can be traced back to numerous nineteenth and early twentieth-century sources. Its development was governed by technology, economics, and aesthetics. Technology was dependent upon the evolution of the skeletal frame, the development of new building materials and processes, and the invention of adequate fireproofing and insulation systems. Economy dictated that the quantity and weight of materials used be minimized, that more prefabrication occur, and that construction become standardized. Aesthetics called for transparency, brought about by ever-greater expanses of glass. These factors led to the sleek, glass and aluminium skins that cloak the buildings of our era.

In the United States, curtain wall development became intertwined with that of the skyscraper. Skyscrapers would not have been technically feasible without the curtain wall. And it was through the skyscraper that the curtain wall achieved its greatest realization.

Antecedents

London's Great Exhibition building of 1851, the Crystal Palace, is identified by Pevsner as the 'touchstone' of those technical achievements that point forward to our own era. It was an example on a very large scale of the aesthetic of a transparent skin encasing a wholly visible frame. It was also an early illustration of the use of mass production, having been designed with modular sections of cast iron and glass.[1] Only by means of prefabrication and the use of construction techniques using dry materials (glass and metal) rather than wet materials (mortar) could a building of such size be erected in the short period of four months.[2] The Crystal Palace also exhibited the future trends in manufacturing and construction, in which operations previously performed on site would be transferred to the factory[3] and the machine would supplant work by hand.[4] Like the Crystal Palace, later glass-walled exhibition buildings were not permanent

Figure 11.1 An archetype of the Chicago School can be found in the rigid steel frame Reliance Building (D.H. Burnham, 1895), the first skyscraper to use terracotta exclusively as a cladding. The Reliance Building curtain wall clearly expresses the underlying structure and provides a maximum of natural lighting. The terracotta units of the curtain wall are connected to a gridwork of cast-iron mullions, lintels and sills which span between levels. (Stephen J. Kelley)

structures, and the glass curtain walls they employed would not gain general acceptance until the middle of the twentieth century.

The Crystal Place in New York (Cartensen and Gildemeister, 1853) was also an impressive demonstration of the versatility of this glass building form. The structure was not fireproof, and in October 1858 it burned to the ground in less than an hour, illustrating the necessity for adequate fireproofing systems with glass and metal curtain walls.

The first curtain walls

The first curtain wall structures were of brick and stone masonry rather than iron and glass. Chicago architect William LeBaron Jenney was an innovator of the application of this type of curtain wall to the iron frame. The Home Insurance Building (1884–5), exhibited the essentials of a fully developed curtain wall on its main facades. Spandrel beams supported the exterior walls at the fourth, sixth, ninth, and above the tenth levels. These loads were transferred to stone pier footings via the metal frame without load-bearing masonry walls.[5] Jenney trained many of the architects – including Louis Sullivan, William Holabird, Martin Roche, and Daniel Burnham – who designed Chicago's early skyscrapers and perfected the masonry curtain wall (Figure 11.1).

In the same year, a cap of the semiprecious metal aluminium was cast for the Washington Monument by Frismuth of Philadelphia. The cap was such a novelty that it was exhibited at Tiffany's in New York, before it was set in place. Five years later, Charles Martin Hall discovered a process by which aluminium could be made on a commercial scale. The electrolytic process, still in use today, drastically reduced the price of aluminium, and would eventually revolutionize curtain wall construction.[6]

In New York City, which became the centre of skyscraper development by 1900, the masonry curtain wall concept became well established as skyscraper heights increased dramatically. The once impressive twenty-storey buildings of Chicago were overshadowed by buildings of 300 feet (91.4 metres), then 600 feet (182.8 metres), and finally, with the Woolworth Building (Cass Gilbert, 1913) 792 feet (241.4 metres).

By the turn of the century, however, architects were exploring the aesthetic possibilities of glass and metal on building facades. An example was Victor Horta's Maison du Peuple in Brussels (1896, demolished), where the metal skeleton was enclosed only by glass or thin panels held in iron frames.[7] Another was Bernhard Sehring's Tietz Department Store in Berlin (1898, demolished), which featured a facade of glass with thin iron mullions and rails.[8] The Boley Building in Kansas City (Louis Curtis, 1909) incorporated a transparent glass wall enclosing an entire structure (Figure 11.2).[9]

Figure 11.2   The Boley Building in Kansas City was designed by Louis Curtis and constructed in 1909. A handful of other glass-walled buildings in the US had explored the transparent glass wall enclosing the structure, but this lead was largely ignored by architects of the period. (Stephen J. Kelley)

The Modern Movement and the curtain wall

The First World War administered a fatal blow to the handicraft movement. The machine was to become the basis of a new architecture. During the war, Hugo Junkers produced some of the first practical all-metal aeroplanes from Germany. By 1917, he was using an aluminium alloy to reduce the weight of the aircraft. Aircraft built with aluminium thereafter came into widespread use.[10] The location of the Junkers factory in Dessau is one of the reasons that the new Bauhaus school would also be constructed there.

The German architects Walter Gropius and Adolph Meyer were commissioned to build the Faguswerke Factory (Alfeld-an-der-Leine, 1911), regarded as one of the founding monuments of the Modern Movement. At this factory, each level is indicated by solid spandrel panels that are installed like the glass above and below them, a treatment echoed in the curtain walls of post-World War II high-rise buildings.[11]

The theme of the curtain wall of the Faguswerke Factory was furthered by the construction of the Bauhaus School (Gropius, 1925), with a studio featuring an impressive glass-and-steel curtain wall.[12] At the same period, Ludwig Mies van der Rohe, who followed Gropius as head of the Bauhaus School, prepared a series of unrealized projects in which the most famous, enveloped totally in glass, became known simply as 'The Glass Skyscraper'.

The period following World War I witnessed the widespread use of aluminium in cast, sheet, and extruded form for a variety of architectural purposes. Aluminium, popular because of its colour but not yet considered economical, was used for window sashes, trim, and signage.[13] Simultaneous with the first commercial use of anodized aluminium in the 1920s was the use of anodized coatings.[14]

Improvements in glass manufacturing made it possible to produce larger panes of glass. The Fourcault process, developed in Belgium in 1905, was the basis for the first machine-drawn plate glass production in 1914.[15] In 1917, Colburn in the US invented another drawing method that became known as the Libbey-Owens process. The advantages of both of these processes were combined in a rapid new glassmaking technology known in the US as the Pittsburgh process.[16]

The Modern Movement, known in the United States as the 'International Style,' was formally introduced to American architects in 1932 and created an immediate sensation.[17] Due to the economic constraints of the Great Depression, speed was necessary in design and erection. The International Style was characterized by the elimination of costly and time-consuming decorative features on the facade, an aesthetic realized on such buildings as the New York Daily News (Hood and Howells, 1930), the McGraw-Hill (Hood and Fouilhoux, 1932) and the Philadelphia Savings Fund Society buildings (Howe and Lescase, 1931). Curtain wall construction, however, continued to utilize masonry panel and metal frame techniques that had been developed by the turn of the century,[18] and prefabrication was not yet extensively used.[19]

One of the architects of the Empire State Building (New York City, 1931) wrote of the masonry curtain wall:

Tradition has clung to the heritage of thick masonry walls. We inherited masonry walls and seem unable to outgrow our inheritance. The idea that masonry is the

*only form of permanent construction was so deeply rooted that practically all build-
ing codes made masonry walls mandatory ... The covering of the observation tower
... accomplished by a combination of aluminium, chrome-steel and glass, was
designed and fabricated into forms entirely free from masonry influences. The extension of similar treatment to embrace all of the inclosing walls of a tall building is
quite conceivable and, if backed with insulating materials to reduce heat loss and
properly finished on the interior, will result in a light wall, readily made weather
tight, easy to fabricate and erect and requiring practically no maintenance.*[20]

Acceptance of the glass and metal curtain wall

New technologies resulting from World War II had a great influence on the acceptance of the
glass and metal curtain wall and the realization of a machine-made building envelope.
Lightweight, workable, and resistant to corrosion, aluminium had become the metal of choice
for curtain walls, and its use would outstrip that of other durable metals. Advances during World
War II brought about new processes and techniques for fabricating and working aluminium, and
placed unprecedented quantities of the material at the disposal of designers, and at an economical price.[21] Extruded metal components were suitable for standardization and could be prefabricated for delivery to the site. This was important because labour costs had now become a
significant part of construction costs. The glass and metal curtain wall further reduced building
weight,[22] and installation was less limited by cold temperatures, which prohibited erection of
'wet' walls of brick and mortar. Developing in this environment, the curtain wall had finally
become almost entirely machine-made.[23]

In 1959 Pilkington Glass introduced their revolutionary float method for the manufacture of
plate glass. Glass made by this process combines the high surface finish of sheet glass with the
flatness and lack of distortion of plate glass, and other existing processes soon became obsolete.[24] In the 1950s, heat-absorbent or tinted glass was introduced into the building market.
Though green was initially the only colour possible in transparent optical glass, by the 1960s
other colours were also becoming available.[25]

The new curtain walls experienced greater movement, and that movement was restricted to
fewer joints that were spread further apart. Traditional oil and resin-based caulking compounds
were the only joint sealants available before the war, and they did not provide the flexibility
required. War technology[26] spawned a new family of elastomeric sealants – polysulphides, solvent acrylics, urethanes and silicones – that would fulfil this role. Polysulphides were the first
elastomerics to be used for curtain wall construction, in the early 1950s. Their use to seal the
curtain wall of the Lever House in 1954 signalled their widespread acceptance. Silicone sealants
were introduced in the 1960s and urethane sealants in the 1970s.[27]

Technical guidance in the use of glass and metal curtain walls for 1950s designers was
limited.[28] The ideal curtain wall was described as 2–5 inches (5–13 cm) thick, self-insulating,
able to withstand high winds, weatherproof on the outer surface, vapour-proof on the inner surface, ventilated and drained for control of internal moisture, designed for expansion and contrac-
tion of the building, easily removable for repair, sound deadening, adaptable to all types of

building frames, installed from the inside without scaffolding, easy to fabricate, ship, and handle, attractive, maintenance-free, and moderate in cost. Furthermore, it would last 40 to 100 years.[29]

The approach to curtain wall design that evolved was to make the joints as weathertight as possible, then provide positive means for conducting any water leakage out of the wall through an internal drainage system. At first, the use of caulking compounds, which have become indispensable for sealing joints in curtain walls, was frowned upon. They held little promise because they 'fail due to expansion/contraction and will require constant maintenance'. It was envisioned that rubber gasket systems would fulfil this role.[30]

Figure 11.3 *The Lever House in New York stands today as a monument to the American Modern Movement. The curtain wall treatment was experimental at this date. Consequently the mixture of metals used (stainless and mild steels) led to problems with chronic glass breakage. The proposed recladding will replicate profiles and materials as originally specified. Ferrous metal glazing channels will, however, be replaced with aluminium. (Stephen J. Kelley)*

Large-scale commercial adoption of building air conditioning profoundly influenced the development of glass and metal curtain walls, which now made up the entire envelope, not just a portion. Air conditioning initially led to curtain walls which were not provided with operable windows for natural ventilation. Architects of the 1950s had little concern for energy conservation. It was left to mechanical engineers to ensure the comfort of the occupants.[31]

One of the first post-war buildings in the US to be constructed with a glass curtain wall was the Equitable Building (Pietro Belluschi, 1948) in Portland, Oregon. Belluschi was able to take advantage of leftover aluminium stockpiled for World War II, and to use assembly techniques derived from West Coast aeroplane plants.[32] The Equitable Building was constructed with cladding panels made from rolled sheets of aluminium, and glazing frames of extruded shapes. Insulated glass units were used for the glazing – one of the first commercial uses of this product.[33]

The 860–880 Lake Shore Drive buildings in Chicago (Mies van der Rohe, 1949–51) were among the first residential buildings in the US to be sheathed entirely in glass, and were the realization of Mies' earlier proposal for a glass skyscraper. The steel, aluminium, and glass skin was assembled on the buildings' roofs in two-storey units, and then lowered into place on the facade.[34] Buildings following this distinctive 'glass box' aesthetic subsequently began to appear in many cities.

The United Nations Secretariat Building (Harrison and Abramovitz, 1950) was conceived as a pure sculptural form – a narrow tower slab set so that its long walls of glass faced east and west, and its shorter walls of white marble faced north and south. The glass walls were composed of an aluminium mullion and rail grid which captured green-tinted glass.[35] The lower portion of the curtain wall at each level was backed up by a concrete block masonry to provide fire protection.[36] The Secretariat Building was a thermal failure, its all-glass facades offering little protection from the harsh rising and setting sun. Designers learned to consider the orientation of buildings relative to the path of the sun, and to moderate the size of windows in order to control heat gain.[37]

At the Lever House (Skidmore, Owings & Merrill, 1952), the curtain wall has an interior frame of mild steel clad with stainless steel (Figure 11.3). Its simple appearance 'belies its complex internal construction which was cobbled together from off-the-shelf parts'.[38] The curtain wall, like that of the Secretariat building, was backed at each floor by a knee wall of concrete block to provide the fire protection that code officials felt was not provided by the curtain wall itself.[39]

Other durable metals were also utilized in the 1950s. New York's House of Seagram (Mies Van der Rohe, 1957–8) was constructed with a curtain wall of bronze-tinted glass and metal grid of bronze. Frank Lloyd Wright's Price Tower in Bartlesville, Oklahoma (1955) is a mixed-use skyscraper with a curtain wall of copper and precast concrete units.[40]

An alternative response to the all-glass curtain wall, the Alcoa Building in Pittsburgh (Harrison, 1952), used single storey-high panels of aluminium penetrated by relatively small windows (Figure 11.4, *overleaf*). The windows were set in aluminium frames and sealed with rubber gaskets. Aluminium panels were formed with a pressed pattern to add rigidity, create relief, and produce scale.[41] Instead of using concrete block behind the curtain wall, perlite insulation was sprayed on aluminium lath to provide fireproofing. This curtain wall style became quite popular during the mid-1960s.

While the potential of the machine-made glass and metal curtain wall was first being exploited, purveyors of more traditional cladding systems could not compete economically. In the face of competition, the adaptation of precast concrete, masonry, and thin stone veneers to the new curtain wall vocabulary – lightness, prefabrication, and standardization – began to develop in the 1960s.

New technologies in the past thirty years have created the economy of using less material and new materials to achieve better thermal standards and cost-effective construction. By the 1960s, reflective coatings of thin metal applied to glass became available to the construction industry. At first only silver was available, but the colour palette would eventually include gold, bronze, copper, pewter, grey and blue.[42] Thermal efficiency became important in building construction after the energy crisis of the 1970s. A 1980s application is the coating of glass with clear low-emissivity (low-e) films that are used to improve the energy efficiency and performance of buildings.[43] The 'rain screen principle' to prevent water penetration through building envelopes was first published by the Norwegians in 1962 and a year later in Canada. It was not until the 1970s that this principle was first applied to

Figure 11.4 The Alcoa Building spawned numerous curtain wall buildings similar to the one in this illustration, that were unitized panels and not made primarily of vision or spandrel glass. These 'unit systems' are composed of panels that are assembled and glazed in the factory prior to installation in the field. The units are then stacked together to form the mullions and rails. (Stephen J. Kelley)

curtain walls. Structural silicone glazing, which has been responsible for the large expanses of mullionless glass, began to appear on building curtain walls toward the end of the 1960s.

Diagnostic techniques

Investigating curtain wall problems requires techniques that may range from basic to sophisticated. Basic techniques often help to determine the necessary sophisticated techniques to complete the diagnosis. The following is a brief description of diagnostic techniques.

Document review

The architectural, structural and shop drawings, and the specifications, if available, should all be reviewed to understand the original intent of the curtain wall. Drawings and specifications can shed light on the relationship of the curtain wall to the structural system, the presence and location of flashings, and hidden conditions within the wall.

Occupant survey

In a large building, the survey may take the form of a questionnaire to which the building's occupants are asked to respond. Data received from such a survey will be qualitative rather than quantitative but can provide useful information about water and air leakage.

Visual inspection

The inspection should determine whether the curtain wall construction matches the original design documents. It can determine the condition of all the parts that make up the curtain wall, including glazing, frame material, material finishes, hardware and sealant joints. Locations of damage or suspected water leakage can be viewed.

Curtain wall disassembly

Disassembly of components and adjacent construction can reveal concealed conditions. Trim, glazing stops, glass and hardware can be removed in order to expose connections and flashings. Inspection openings in adjacent walls are typically performed in areas where interior finishes have already been damaged by water leakage, necessitating their repair.

Field testing

If water and air leakage are discovered during the inspection or survey, field testing is a useful tool to locate the causes. It is also helpful for measuring the effectiveness of repairs. Testing more than one area is recommended in order to obtain representative behaviour. Structural testing can also be performed in the field. Based on the findings of the investigation, different options may be available to repair excessive air infiltration or water penetration, as described below.

Laboratory testing

Laboratory testing is performed to verify certain attributes of the curtain wall system and develop remedial measures to improve the system. Typically air infiltration, water penetration, and structural testing are performed. Thermal performance testing to measure insulating performance and resistance to condensation can also be implemented.[44] Though laboratory testing is useful, it should not be considered as the final word on system performance.

Common problems

Water penetration

The prevention of water leakage, which is the source of the most common problems associated with curtain walls, relies upon either the elimination of leakage into the wall or the control of water flow through the wall. Drainage strategies developed to achieve a watertight wall include interior drainage systems,[45] pressure equalized systems[46] and barrier walls.[47] All successful treatments rely upon understanding the type of wall system and drainage strategy, as well as the various forces acting on and attempting to drive water through the wall. Wind, capillary action and gravity are but a few of the forces that must be accommodated. Proposed treatments must ultimately handle these forces successfully. The following are some of the more common causes of water penetration.

Incorrect design

Interior gutters and glazing pockets may not be designed with enough features to accommodate water that penetrates the exterior wall and to direct it back to the exterior. Inadequate design sometimes does not accommodate interior water flow or is inadequate to resist the wind-induced pressures accompanying the water.

Incorrect installation

Drainage systems rely upon internal gutters or flashings to achieve watertightness. An interior drainage system can not perform adequately unless it is properly sealed. End dams created where horizontal and vertical members intersect, discontinuities at splices, and penetrations for connections are common sources of water penetration.

Glazing leaks

Glazing joints between the metal frame and glass or other inserted panel are common sources of water leakage into a curtain wall system. In dry glazing systems, glazing gaskets, if installed improperly, will creep away from the corners of the glass or panel over time and allow water to reach the glazing pocket. Unless the glazing pocket is designed to control the resulting volume of water, leakage can occur.

Sealant failures

When modern elastomeric sealants, such as silicone or urethane, are properly installed and the joints are designed to be compatible with the sealants, an effective seal can be obtained. Failure of sealants, whether cohesive or adhesive, can create many problems, especially since sealant joints are the final barrier to weather penetration. Sealants should also be designed so they can be maintained or replaced, and to prevent the contamination of adjoining surfaces.

Weatherstripping

Weatherstripping is used in operable windows within curtain wall systems as a means of sealing the window vent to the frame when in a closed position. Weatherstripping is commonly the first component of a vent to wear out and should be designed to be replaceable. Weatherstripping can also become permanently set, shrink away from the corners, or become detached.

Incorrect repairs

Previous repairs that seal drainage holes and other joints that were originally provided to allow leaked water to drain from the interior of the curtain wall system can exacerbate leakage problems. When this occurs, leaked water will find another pathway, perhaps into the building rather than through the plugged internal drainage system.

Some other common problems

Air leakage and thermal discomfort

One of the main causes of thermal discomfort with curtain wall systems is air infiltration, which causes draughts. Air leakage can occur around operable windows, through stack joints at mullions, at defective sealant joints, and in any place where water leakage can also occur. Though the exchange of air is needed in any building, air infiltration must be controlled.

Condensation

Condensation occurs on curtain wall systems when climatic conditions are such that water vapour turns to liquid or ice on the interior surface.[48] Older curtain wall systems were normally designed with an exposed gutter at the inside base of the curtain wall at each level to collect the condensate run-off that was then expected to evaporate. Excessive condensation may indicate a poor thermal design or areas of excessive air infiltration.

Material failures

Aluminium forms a tough, protective coating of aluminium oxide as it weathers. This coating arrests further oxidation of the aluminium surface.[49] Older aluminium curtain walls dating from the 1950s or earlier may not have any protective coating or treatment on the aluminium surface. In these cases, pitting of the frame may occur as the aluminium oxidizes in an uneven fashion. There is no gentle method of treating this unsightly oxidation; however, pitting of the frame does not typically indicate a structural problem.

Aluminium is a highly anodic metal. It can deteriorate through electrolytic action when in contact with nobler metals such as lead, copper, or mild steel in the presence of water. Staining, excessive oxidation, or frame failure can result if this phenomenon is not accommodated in frame or connection design.

A difficulty with curtain walls composed of mild steel is the tendency of ferrous metals to corrode. Corrosion of the steel frame over time can cause glass breakage, loss of use of operable vents, and eventual failure of the structural frame. Steel curtain wall systems can last a long time, but only if they are frequently maintained.

Other metals, such as copper, stainless steel and bronze, have also been used for curtain walls. Like aluminium, these metals are extremely durable as they weather and may cause only problems with staining as they develop a patina.

Peeling or chalking paint coatings on aluminium or steel can cause chronic maintenance problems. Causes of paint failure include improperly selected paint coatings or poor preparation of the surfaces to be painted. Metal surfaces are best painted in the factory, where all the variables for a successful paint coating can be controlled. Repair of painted metal surfaces in the field must be carefully monitored to approximate these factory controls.

Impurities in the manufacture of glass have resulted in glass failures. Glass that is heat tempered can spontaneously break, due to nickel sulphide inclusions that expand within the glass some time after fabrication. Glass can also break when struck by projectiles such as roof gravel or larger building materials during high winds.

Glass surfaces can become damaged when they come into contact with chemicals that are used to treat other parts of the building facade. Glass coatings such as low emissivity and reflective treatments can become splotchy or discoloured, or begin to peel. Glass coatings should be studied to verify compatibility with all components of the glazing system, and measures should be taken to control potentially damaging glass-cleaning operations.

Insulating glass units can fail if excessive moisture collects between the two sheets of glass. Insulating glass units are designed with a hermetic edge seal to prevent moisture entering the unit. However, the edge seal can break down, especially if the unit is subjected to standing water.

Figure 11.5   Overcladding: the original curtain wall system is left in place behind a new curtain wall system. In this example, once the new curtain wall is installed, elements of the old curtain wall are selectively removed and the interior is refinished to the new wall. Those portions of the original curtain that remain are abandoned within the finished wall assembly.
(Stephen J. Kelley)

Panel systems made of composite materials – for example, an insulating material sandwiched between aluminium or porcelain-coated steel – are also a source of material failure. Some insulating materials are volumetrically unstable in the presence of moisture, and permanent distortion of the panels can result from water leakage.

Structural failure

Permanent distortion of the curtain wall system due to wind is rare, though curtain wall distortion has occurred as a result of earthquakes. A more common type of structural failure occurs from loss of structural integrity of the connections between curtain wall components or the curtain wall and the building frame. Areas of the building that receive higher wind loads, such as at corners or at the tops of skyscrapers, are more prone to curtain wall connection failure.

Treatment

Repair options range from temporary stabilization to a very intrusive recladding project. The options are discussed below.

'Band-aid' repairs

A 'band-aid' can be defined as a short-term solution to water leakage on a curtain wall. Band-aids entail the introduction of sealant to the exterior of the curtain wall to retard water leakage or air infiltration. Sealant can be introduced to all metal-to-metal joints, to the perimeter of window walls where they meet stone or masonry, or at glazing joints.

Selective reconstruction

In a selective reconstruction, only those members of the curtain wall that are defective are removed and replaced with members that are identical or similar. Examples would be the selective replacement of corroded portions of steel frames, reglazing of existing frames, or the selective replacement of spandrel glass.

Overcladding

In overcladding repairs, the original curtain wall system is left in place and is covered with a new curtain wall system (Figure 11.5). The old curtain wall system can become part of the waterproofing for the new curtain wall, or it can be abandoned altogether behind the new wall. Overcladding will normally have an impact on the appearance of the building. The increased load of the new curtain wall on the existing structure must be taken into account. It is also important that the connections for the new curtain wall adequately transfer all loads to the building frame.

Recladding

The recladding option has become quite popular for the repair of 1950s skyscrapers. It entails complete replacement of the original curtain wall. It is a popular option because it allows the building owner to update the image of the building completely, as well as install a state-of-the-art curtain wall that will perform better than the original curtain walls. This option, however, is bound to become more controversial as our early post-war buildings become listed (or, in the US, landmarked).

Conclusion

Though the tenets of the Modern Movement no longer hold sway over building design, the appearance and details of the curtain wall will remain forever influenced by the machine-made aesthetic that captivated the early Modernists. Curtain wall technology will continue to evolve, resulting in curtain walls that are lighter and more economical. New materials will be introduced and used in conjunction with each other. This ever-increasing sophistication, however, will present new challenges in the repair and preservation of curtain walls as the present-day buildings that they enclose become our children's heritage.

A look at the technology of today's curtain wall makes the words of D. H. Burnham, written a century ago, prophetic:

> The design of a metal frame for a great building involves much more than a mere burying of steel in masonry; indeed the latter process may not long remain an essential part of first class structures. The day may come when brick, stone, terra cotta and granite will not be used, and yet the principle first employed in the Home Insurance Building of Chicago will remain.

References

1   Richards, J.M. (1962), *An Introduction to Modern Architecture*, Baltimore, Maryland: Penguin Books, 66–67.

2   Pevsner, N. (1974), *Pioneers of Modern Design*, Harmondsworth and Baltimore, Maryland: Penguin Books, 133.

3   Williams, T.I. (1978), *A History of Technology*, Oxford: Clarendon Press, 937–938.

4   Hamlin, T. (ed) (1952), *Forms and Functions of Twentieth-Century Architecture, Volume IV*, New York: Columbia University Press, 462.

5   Upjohn, E.M. (1935), 'Buffington and the skyscraper,' *The Art Bulletin*, **17**, (1), (March), 53.

6   Brown, H. (1948), *Aluminum and Its Applications*, New York: Pitman, 3 and 11–12. The same electrolytic process was discovered simultaneously in France by Paul L.T. Heroult and is thus called the Hall–Heroult process.

7   Hitchcock, H.-R. (1977), *Architecture: Nineteenth and Twentieth Centuries*, New York: Penguin Books, 394.

8   Pevsner, N. (1986), *The Sources of Modern Architecture and Design*, London: Thames and Hudson, 96.

9   Burchard, J., and Bush-Brown, A. (1966), *The Architecture of America. A Social and Cultural History*, Boston: Little, Brown and Co., 346.

10   Williams, T.I. (1978), *A History of Technology*, Oxford: Clarendon Press, 88.

11   Hitchcock, H.-R. (1977), *op.cit.*, 491.

12   *Ibid.*, 449.

13   Fistere, J.C. (1931), 'Use of White Metals,' *Architectural Forum*, **55**, (August), 232–240.

14   Van Horn, K.R. (ed) (1967), *Aluminum, Vol. III. Fabrication and Finishing*, Metals Park, Ohio: American Society for Metals, 660.

15   Also known as the machine-cylinder method, the process formed a cylinder of glass using compressed air. The cylinder was then split, flattened, and annealed.

16   Most plate glass was drawn in continuous sheets directly from a melting tank using these processes. Pulker, H.K. (1984), *Coatings on Glass*, New York: Elsevier Science Publishing Company, 2.

17   The exhibition on the International Style opened at the Museum of Modern Art on 10 February 1932, in the middle of the Great Depression, to a profession that was 85% unemployed. Fitch, J.M. (1966), *American Building and the Historical Forces that Shaped It*, Boston: Houghton Mifflin Company, 247–248.

18   Richards, J.M. (1962), *op. cit.*, 71–72.

19   Burchard, J., and Bush-Brown, A. (1966), *op. cit.*, 330.

20   Dowswell, H.R. (1931), 'Walls, Floors and Partitions in the Tall Building', *Engineering News-Record*, (19 February), 319 and 321.

21   Hamlin, T. (ed) (1952), *op. cit.*, 165. During the Second World War, more than 200 extrusion presses produced aluminium shapes and tube. After the war, with the introduction of press heat treatable intermediate-strength alloys having good extrudability, the aluminium extrusion industry entered a period of rapid growth. Van Horn, K.R. (ed) (1967), *op. cit.*, 81.

22   Pre-war masonry curtain walls could weigh up to 175 pounds per square foot. The new glass and metal curtain walls were designed to weigh about 5–15 pounds per square foot. Building structures and their foundations could be more economical since they would be designed to support a lesser load. 'The Trend to Building with Metal Curtain Walls,' *Engineering News-Record*, (20 October 1955).

23   Goldberger, P. (1989), *The Skyscraper*, New York: Alfred A. Knopf, 103–105.

24 Float glass is formed by laying molten glass upon a bed of molten metal upon which it floats. Glass formed in this way can be fabricated in continuous sheets that are then cut as part of the fabrication process. Persson, R. (1969), *Flat Glass Technology*, New York: Plenum Press, 4.

25 The colour and heat absorbing qualities were achieved by increasing the iron content in the glass batch. Grey coloured glass was introduced in the 1960s, bronze in the 1970s, and blue in the 1980s. Griffiths, H. (1987) 'Colors of the City', *The Construction Specifier*, (August), 100.

26 Butyl sealants were developed in the 1930s as part of the production synthetic rubber process. Urethanes were also developed in tandem with synthetic rubber during World War II. Panek, J.R., and Cook, J. P. (1984), *Construction Sealants and Adhesives*, (2nd edn), New York: John Wiley and Sons, 130 and 144.

27 Panek, J.R., and Cook, J.P. (1984), *op. cit.*, 106–7, 120–1, 130–1, 138.

28 American Architectural Manufacturers Association (1979), *Aluminum Curtain Walls, Volume 5*, Chicago: American Architectural Manufacturers Association, 8.

29 Building Research Institute (1955), 'Metal Curtain Walls,' *Proceedings of the Building Research Institute*, Washington, DC: National Academy of Sciences – National Research Council.

30 Callender, J.H. (1955), 'The Design of Metal Curtain Walls,' *Proceedings of the Building Research Institute*, Washington, DC: National Academy of Sciences – National Research Council, 79–97.

31 Wright, H. (1955), 'What Next for the Window Wall?' *Architectural Forum*, (July).

32 In 1943, during the planning stages for the Equitable Building, Belluschi stated, 'Our assumptions were affected by the peculiar circumstances found in our Northwest region – cheap power and a tremendous expanded production of light metal for war use, which beg utilization after the emergency.' *Architectural Forum*, (May).

33 Anon. (1989), 'Icons of Modernism or Machine-age Dinosaurs?', *Architectural Record*, (June), 145. Insulated glass units had first been developed in the 1920s.

34 Carter, P. (1974), *Mies van der Rohe at Work*, New York: Praeger Publishers, 46.

35 Tinted glass, available before the war, would now come into widespread use in commercial architecture. Burchard, J., and Bush-Brown, A. (1966), *op. cit.*, 473.

36 Anon. (1955), 'The trend to building with metal curtain walls', *Engineering News-Record*, (20 October).

37 Wright, H. (1955), 'What Next for the Window Wall?' *Architectural Forum*, (July).

38 Anon. (1989), 'Icons of Modernism or Machine-age Dinosaurs?' *Architectural Record*, (June), 142.

39 Williams, T.I. (1978), *A History of Technology, Volume II*, Oxford: Clarendon Press, 943-4.

40 The Price Tower was the realization of the St Mark's Tower project that Wright had designed for Manhattan in 1929.

41 Burchard, J., and Bush-Brown, A. (1966), *op. cit.*, 473.

42 Early reflective glass relied upon a chemical spray deposition process, much like that used for mirrors. In the 1960s, the electron beam evaporation system was introduced which rendered a more durable coating and allowed the process to be performed at the glass factory rather than by the fabricator In the late 1970s, spatter coating made the previous processes obsolete. Griffins, H. (1987), 'Colors of the City', *The Construction Specifier*, (August), 105–107.

43 Pulker, H.K. (1984), *Coatings on Glass*, New York: Elsevier Science Publishing, 5.

44 At present, the insulating performance and condensation resistance of a curtain wall system can not be determined by field testing due to the complexity and size of equipment that is required to perform such testing.

45 A drainage or weeped system employs two lines of defence against water penetration. The first line provides a wall that can endure the various movements to which a curtain wall is exposed and still remain relatively watertight. The second line is a series of internal gutters and drainage holes designed to catch and collect any water which does bypass the exterior plane of the wall and direct that water back to the exterior.

46 Pressure equalized curtain walls rely upon the inclusion of an interior air space formed between an inner and outer wall of the curtain wall. The outer wall or rain screen is designed to shed most of the water but is not airtight. The inner wall is airtight and watertight, and is designed to withstand pressure induced by wind. The pressure within the interior air space between these walls equalizes to the outside pressure and prevents the build-up of pressure across the outer wall.

47 A curtain wall that relies upon the elimination of all voids and discontinuities on the exterior plane of the wall to control water penetration is referred to as a 'barrier system'. A barrier system is entirely dependent upon the barrier formed by the sealing of the exterior face. This system contains no drainage wall features or other techniques to improve its watertightness.

48 The type of condensation that occurs in hot weather on the exterior side of a vapour barrier of an environmentally controlled building is not normally of concern with a glass and metal curtain wall. Water and frost can form, however, on the interior side of a curtain wall in extremely cold weather when the interior faces of curtain wall members become cold enough to bring water vapour out of warm and moisture-bearing inside air. This type of condensation can be damaging to interior surfaces.

49 Aluminium anodizing, a popular aluminium surface treatment, is a factory-controlled homogeneous formation of aluminium oxide that is created integrally with or without a colourant to achieve colours from clear (silver), gold, and the range of light bronze to black.

PART THREE

CASE
STUDIES

CHAPTER 12

THE LANSBURY ESTATE, KEELING HOUSE AND BALFRON TOWER: CONSERVATION ISSUES AND THE ARCHITECTURE OF SOCIAL INTENT

Martin O'Rourke

The wave of optimism that characterized the post-war period of fifty years ago is difficult to appreciate in our more guarded and cynical times. It was an era when market forces and spending limits counted for less than social cohesion and better living standards for all. Imaginative architectural ideas were enthusiastically harnessed to the task of rehousing the working class of East London, who had endured generations of slum conditions and the trauma of the Blitz, when up to one in six Londoners were made homeless. The response to this great social need was a wave of public investment and confident new architecture.

Dealing with the legacy

Many East London estates and building groups survive from the post-war period, the best serving as inspirational beacons against which to test our own feeble attempts at a robust celebration of urbanism.

Current preoccupations in town planning urge us to concentrate new development on brownfield sites and restrict new building in the Green Belt. It is therefore especially relevant to revisit earlier modern attempts to reshape the city with high-density urbanism, based on an egalitarian architectural programme employing twentieth-century aesthetic forms. Can we regain a faith in recasting the city in exciting but humane forms?

When considering post-war historic buildings, we need to judge architectural quality and value from a new perspective. Traditional conservation attitudes tend to revolve around buildings from a past age, shaped by forces that are safely remote from us. An archaeological approach to building fabric and artistic intent is used to establish relative value. We need to incorporate modern philosophical and architectural ideas into the value systems we use to judge post-war buildings. We must recognize the values and achievements of our own culture. The reluctance to do this explains why historic modern architecture still struggles for wider acceptance in the conservation world.

Serious conservation of post-war buildings must involve an understanding of how building processes shaped the architecture. Much of the modern aesthetic was forged from industrial techniques. We need a sophisticated repertoire of diagnostic methods and repair techniques peculiar to the problems of ageing concrete and steel. The variety of products and advisers is growing as more modern buildings are listed, but a system of values and ethics for the repair of such buildings is barely established.

A brief review of some cases involving post-war buildings may be useful in highlighting conservation problems, and showing how the historic building interest can be a positive tool of regeneration.

Live Architecture: the Lansbury estate

This estate encapsulated the post-war willingness to believe that good planning and architecture could improve people's lives. It was the Live Architecture exhibition of the 1951 Festival of Britain, and the most enduring manifestation of that celebration of post-war hope. The 1943 County of London Plan sought to recognize the urgent housing need of the East End by dividing Stepney, Poplar and Bow into neighbourhoods, each accommodating the housing and community needs of the local inhabitants.

One of the Poplar neighbourhoods was named Lansbury, after the local socialist hero George Lansbury. The area was composed of 124 acres between the East India Dock Road, the Limehouse Cut waterway and the railway. It was intended to house 9,500 people. For the purposes of the Festival of Britain, a representative 30-acre section of the neighbourhood was built. The London

Figure 12.1   Market Square Shops, Lansbury Estate, Tower Hamlets, designed by Frederick Gibberd for the Festival of Britain Live Architecture exhibition in 1951. (English Heritage)

County Council (LCC) was the strategic planning authority for the scheme, and the Council's own Housing Department designed the medium-rise flats at the west end of the site. But Lansbury's most convincing attribute is a real sense of place, derived from a strong neighbourhood plan coupled with the introduction of building designs that combined variety with a common vernacular. The most notable and satisfactory building groups are the Crisp Street market square, clock tower and shops by Frederick Gibberd, the houses and flats by Geoffrey Jellicoe and the landmark community buildings, such as the Ricardo Street School by Yorke Rosenberg and Mardell, the concrete Trinity Church by Handisyde and Stark, and the more traditional Roman Catholic church by Adrian Scott. These buildings are linked together by a network of streets, alleys, landscape and paving (Figures 12.1 and 12.2).

Lansbury is essentially humane in scale, utilizing modern Anglo-Scandinavian design with some touches of neo-Georgian. It is imbued with a very English sense of the domestic landscaped street scene and, as such, represents a rehearsal for the later postwar New Towns. It is a more spacious reinterpretation of the previous relentless terraced house townscape and is mercifully free of the giant leap in scale of later public housing or the reactionary excesses of the recent postmodern domestic style. In concept and design it has much to teach us about how to make successful, modest living places. It is still a well-loved estate, but changes in attitudes, building ownership and funding threaten to destroy the subtle charms of Lansbury.

The regeneration of Lansbury

Lansbury is not a museum but a living community and after more than forty years of use, it needs refurbishment and improvement. Many unfortunate alterations, such as alien types of cladding and window replacement, have damaged the estate's special interest.

Tower Hamlets Council has secured £19 million from the Government's Estates Regeneration Challenge Fund (ERCF) for the housing stock of Poplar; £13.3 million of this funding is allocated to Lansbury. This is the most significant and comprehensive funding package for Lansbury since the estate was built.

Figure 12.2   The clock tower, which provides a focal point in the shopping precinct of the Lansbury Estate. (English Heritage)

These funds were secured on the basis of the need for repair and improvement, and do not include any particular element for restoration or sensitive repair. In order to recognize the conservation interest, a conservation area has been designated by Tower Hamlets with the support of English Heritage. The boundary of the conservation area follows the original Live Architecture boundary. Key buildings, such as churches, the Ricardo Street School and Gibberd's shopping parade and clock tower have been listed. The ERCF regeneration budget of £13.3 million can now be utilized with the conservation of Lansbury as one of the key criteria for specifying works. An application has also been made to the Heritage Lottery Fund (HLF) for the £1 million needed for extra costs engendered by specifying non-standard paving, street furniture and architectural details to safeguard Lansbury's character.

Lansbury has a regeneration project that recognizes the special interest of the area. More funding can be attracted via the HLF, and the whole scheme benefits from the respect that is being given to Lansbury's unique sense of place, encouraging local people to value their own neighbourhood. The aim of the future must be to maintain the conservation and repair works achieved by the regeneration scheme, and to resist the piecemeal destruction of original details by misguided owner-occupiers.

Keeling House, Claredale Street, Bethnal Green: working-class streets in the sky

Keeling House was designed by Denys Lasdun in 1955 for Bethnal Green Borough Council. It is a fifteen-storey reinforced concrete building composed of a cluster of four towers, each with fourteen maisonettes and two bedsit flats, around a stair and lift core. The novel and highly sculptural effect of the angled towers means that each flat has a private balcony access with dramatic views, but also the opportunity for neighbours to chat from balcony to balcony between the towers. By breaking up the more usual slab block into a cluster of four, Lasdun managed to make a large building out of a series of more domestic-scale components. The geometry of the cluster towers makes a walk up the central stair a dramatic experience, full of unexpected views and angles through the massing of the architectural components (Figure 12.3).

Denys Lasdun felt, with some justification, that this building was a vertical reinterpretation of the cockney street. Although this idea could never be wholly achieved, Keeling House was genuinely popular with tenants, and the domestic scale produced by the cluster tower design is still refreshingly humane as well as architecturally exciting. Keeling House is listed grade II*, the first modern block to be so recognized, and it is a powerful and moving architectural experience.

In 1993, a Dangerous Structures Notice was served due to falling concrete caused by the decay of the steel reinforcement within the structure, and the building was abandoned. The question for Tower Hamlets Council was, should they repair and renovate Keeling House or demolish the building and reuse the land to build houses? Current thinking in housing departments does not favour novel 1950s architectural experiments and, without the spur of a grade II* listing, it seems highly likely that the Council would have demolished Keeling House, whose repair costs would in any event exceed normal local authority yardsticks. This fate seems to be confirmed for the maisonette blocks nearby, also by Lasdun but not listed.

By 1995, the Peabody Trust, one of the most enlightened patrons in the social housing field, had offered to take Keeling House from Tower Hamlets for £1, if an application to the HLF for the lion's share of £10 million was successful. Peabody would renovate Keeling House and set rents slightly higher than usual to provide for the future maintenance of the building. The HLF bid was unsuccessful, mainly due to the high costs of the scheme. Once again, Keeling House was threatened with demolition.

In mid-1998, Tower Hamlets Council advertised Keeling House for sale, and at the time of writing, a number of potential buyers have been shortlisted as suitable candidates to take over the building. It is unlikely that Keeling House will be renovated as affordable housing. High building costs will dictate profitable sales and the possibility of HLF funding is now much reduced.

Only a few years after Lasdun designed Keeling House, he designed a block of flats at 26 St James's Place, one of the most expensive addresses in London. The St James's block of private flats is an elegant composition of horizontally stratified, double-height apartments. The building is fully occupied and well maintained, and appears to be in good condition. Why should the fates of two Lasdun buildings built within a few years of each other be so different? The answer lies in different standards of construction and the level of subsequent maintenance. While 26 St James's Place has been appropriately cared for over the past forty years, Keeling House has been neglected by a cash-strapped housing department and has been subjected to misguided short-term methods of repair.

The current efforts to market Keeling House are likely to result in the building entering the private housing sector as an icon for a design-conscious public. It is regrettable that a fine example of modern social architecture built as affordable housing should no longer provide for its original need.

Figure 12.3   Keeling House, Claredale Street, Tower Hamlets, designed by Denys Lasdun in 1955. (English Heritage)

Balfron Tower: a heroic landscape

Heading east from the domestic scale of Lansbury, we come to a different architectural world, the Brownfield estate. Most of the estate is made up of unremarkable LCC and Poplar Council four-storey maisonettes. In St Leonards Road, however, is Balfron Tower, part of a housing development designed by Ernö Goldfinger, begun for the LCC in 1963. Balfron Tower is a boldly modelled concrete tower block containing ten maisonettes and 136 flats. It is a major landmark and shows Goldfinger's mastery of concrete, which he gained in the 1920s with Auguste Perret in Paris. Balfron Tower is also notable for the clever device of having a separate lift and stair tower, linked at every third floor to the main block. This device reduced the need for corridors, thereby permitting more spacious flats, and providing a dramatic architectural articulation of the building form (Figure 12.4). Balfron Tower is complemented by a subsidiary group of buildings including flats for the elderly, a shop, community centre and underground car parking. The development was carried on to Goldfinger's design in a more softly spoken idiom over the next ten years in further smaller blocks beyond the adjacent Carradale House.

Balfron Tower and its attendant building group constitute a major achievement of full-blooded modern architecture in the post-war period. It demonstrates that a social housing programme can be achieved with dramatic and high-quality architecture.

Meeting new needs

Balfron Tower sits close by the Blackwall Tunnel Approach, a major traffic artery. The recent road-widening scheme has brought

Figure 12.4   Balfron Tower, St Leonard's Road, Tower Hamlets, designed by Ernö Goldfinger for the LCC in 1963. (English Heritage)

increased traffic volume closer to the building, creating a need to soundproof and upgrade the windows. The occupants of the flats objected to the installation of secondary glazing, as great disruption would have been caused to internal fittings and all work would have been carried out inside each flat.

It was decided that replacement windows were the only practical solution. Because the budget was tight, a standard UPVC window was selected. It was at this point that Balfron Tower was spot-listed to ensure that the question of an architecturally sensitive solution could be fully addressed.

The question of new windows for Balfron Tower raises many points that are peculiar to the control of change in post-war social housing. The spot-listing meant that works that had already begun had to be interrupted. The standard windows destined to replace the originals before the spot-listing did not match the geometry of the Goldfinger windows; they also had 'storm window' casements set proud of the surrounding frame, unlike the original flush-fitting window and frame detail. Alternative timber products proved to be prohibitively expensive and were, in any case, further from Goldfinger's original design due to a thicker section of the timber frames. A more suitable window design had to be sourced – one that was quickly available, would con- form to current safety and performance standards, and was affordable. In the event, a French UPVC section was found that allowed a very close match with the original window section and geometry, and satisfied all the other requirements. The French UPVC windows were, therefore, chosen as the best solution that could be achieved given the tight constraints of time, resources and performance.

The windows at Balfron Tower raise a more general issue for large post-war social housing complexes. As these buildings are now thirty to forty years old, the question of replacing doors, windows or even external cladding will become more pressing. A balance must be struck between respecting the historic architecture and finding appropriate solutions to performance upgrading for thermal, acoustic or safety purposes.

The future of Balfron Tower

Most post-war public housing developments have suffered from inadequate or sporadic maintenance, due to tight funding restrictions on housing authorities. With the lack of a consistent, adequately funded maintenance and repair regime, urgent repairs can sometimes be underfunded and ill-advised.

Balfron Tower and its surroundings now need a comprehensive scheme of repair, landscaping and improvement. With the listing of the building, Tower Hamlets have recognized the need for special care to protect and enhance Balfron Tower. In consultation with English Heritage, the Council are considering the possibility of designating a conservation area around the whole group of Goldfinger buildings. Proposals are also being considered for an improved automatic entry system and the restoration of the public areas, including the distinctive marble and mosaic finishes that are characteristic of Goldfinger's work.

Like the people of Lansbury, the inhabitants of Balfron Tower are protective of their building and frustrated by many years of inadequate funding. The listing of the building and the inclusion of the whole group within a conservation area will assist Tower Hamlets Council, in co-operation with English Heritage, to harness regeneration resources in a sensitive manner.

Conservation and regeneration:
a richer future for the social heritage

The listing of post-war public social housing has brought into focus the fundamental issues of what should be preserved and how best to achieve this. It is essential that the world of conservation learn the skills of the housing manager and understand the difficult choices imposed by limited funding. The accolade of listing can, however, support local people's sense of value in their own environment and encourage high aspirations for repair and improvement.

The Government is committed to the regeneration of more than 2,000 deprived areas: major funding will be committed to housing repair, environmental improvement and other, wider social concerns. At the time of writing, a reshaped Single Regeneration Budget has already been given £3 billion to target 50 areas with populations of around 20,000. There has also been a release of £3.6 billion from council house sales to fund further housing repair.

Many of the chosen areas may include buildings that are either listed or deserve to be considered for conservation area designation. A partnership between local bodies, housing departments, conservation officers and English Heritage can ensure that the substantial funds available will be used not merely to repair buildings, but to respect and restore real architectural quality and the special sense of place that often exists, masked by neglect and low resources. Previous attempts at estate regeneration in the public sector have often been criticized for being only skin deep and not addressing the causes of decay. Repairs and changes that do not respect the positive characteristics of buildings and places can often lead to a new spiral of decay.

The substantial new government funding is a spectacular opportunity to recover post-war optimism, rediscover the hidden riches of modern social architecture and enhance the lives of some of the most deprived people in our cities.

CHAPTER 13
A FUTURE FOR PARK HILL
Andrew Beard

The Park Hill estate in Sheffield is arguably the most influential flat development in post-war Britain in terms of its design. This paper describes the proposals developed by Sheffield Design and Property for the refurbishment and conservation of the estate. It describes the background to Park Hill and how it came to be built, and notes that it is just one part of a larger area that has undergone major regeneration in the past decade. It looks at the Council's response to the proposal by English Heritage to list the estate grade II*, and then describes in some detail the investigations carried out in preparation for a major refurbishment and conservation scheme. I would like to acknowledge all the work put into this project by my colleagues Steve Collins and Ian Peck of Sheffield Design and Property, and Nicola Ashurst of the Adriel Consultancy. In particular, I wish to pay tribute to all the staff of the City Council's Housing Department, whose commitment and enthusiasm have been so vital to the project.

The origins of Park Hill

Park Hill is a direct response to the appalling housing conditions in Sheffield that were so well described by George Orwell in *The Road to Wigan Pier*. However, the slum clearance programmes of the 1930s, which had begun to tackle the back-to-back housing courts of the Park area of the city, were abruptly halted by the Second World War. Post-war shortages prevented any thoughts of renewed slum clearance until 1953, and by then the housing crisis was so severe that the Council and its architects immediately sought a solution in mass production of housing. Their precedents were inevitably Corbusier's Unité d'Habitation in Marseilles, and the Smithson's Golden Lane housing competition design.

Thus it was in the mid-1950s that two young architects, Jack Lynn and Ivor Smith, working for Lewis Womersley, the Sheffield City Architect, conceived the massive concrete structure known as the Park Hill estate (Figure 13.1, *overleaf*).[1] Built between 1957 and 1960, it provided 995 flats and maisonettes in a series of linked blocks ranging from four to fourteen storeys in height with three metre-wide access decks, or rows, at every third floor providing access to the front doors of all the flats and maisonettes.

Figure 13.1   Park Hill flats, Sheffield. (Andrew Beard)

The structure was to be an exposed concrete frame, with brick and aluminium window infill panels. Rigid concrete H-walls along the spine housed the staircases and service ducts. Household waste was disposed of down an enlarged kitchen sink waste-pipe and transferred to a central waste station by suction: the so-called Garchey system. Heating (to living areas only) was provided from a central boiler house.

Park Hill was much more than just a block of flats. It was conceived as a complete community, with shops at ground level, a community centre, several public houses and a laundry. There was a nursery school, a new primary school next to the estate, and generous landscaped areas with children's playgrounds between the blocks. The inner city analogy continued with the decks, intended to replicate the urban street, where residents would interact socially, and as a consequence nicknamed 'streets in the sky'. Large goods lifts served every level, so that milk floats and other small delivery vehicles could be driven up to each front door.

The scheme attracted enormous interest, and its influence on housing design worldwide was immense. From inception to the present day, its history has been well charted and documented, which adds to its historical interest. Even as late as 1985, I recall showing a party of admiring Chinese government officials around Park Hill, and no doubt there are still variations on its theme being constructed in the People's Republic. However, by this time the whole of the Park hillside, with around 3,000 dwellings, was an area in a rapid downward spiral – the classic 'sink' estate.

The Council's Director of Housing recognized the need for drastic action, and over the next ten years over £50 million was injected into the area, with a programme of new-build council housing at Bard Street, refurbishment of Hyde Park Walk and Terrace, partial demolition and refurbishment at Hyde Park and, most recently, housing built for sale. The decline has been largely reversed, but while Park Hill still has a good proportion of long-established residents (half the residents have been there for more than five years), there is rapid turnover of newer tenancies and demand for flats only just reaches supply. Park Hill itself remains largely unaltered since its construction nearly forty years ago, and it is now in urgent need of new investment. In particular, the flats have their original 1950s kitchens and bathrooms, which are now looking very shabby and are far from appealing to prospective tenants.

The proposal to list Park Hill as a grade II* building a couple of years ago therefore created a major challenge for the City Council. If the estate was to have a future, its waning popularity with tenants would need to be reversed. The flat interiors would need major improvements, and the external envelope would need sensitive restoration commensurate with its historic status. The Council (working with English Heritage) therefore initiated a survey of tenants' opinions, which elicited some 90 replies and an even split between those in favour of retaining the estate and those in favour of demolition. At this point, Sheffield Design and Property, the Council's in-house design consultancy, was commissioned to carry out a detailed feasibility study of the works needed to Park Hill, and potential sources of funding.

A preliminary investigation of essential areas of work indicated the need for window replacement, concrete repairs and balustrade replacement, partial re-roofing, and kitchen and bathroom refurbishment. The Garchey waste disposal system, worn out and no longer suitable to cope with modern household waste, was also to be removed. The initial cost estimate was around £20 million, not unreasonable at £20,000 per flat, considering that this was the first major upgrade for forty years. While it was recognized that the internal refurbishment of the flats would have to be funded by the City Council, the Heritage Lottery Fund (HLF) was approached to discuss the possibility of a major grant towards the external repair and conservation works. The HLF encouraged the City Council to make an application for what it calls the 'conservation deficit', equivalent to the additional cost of carrying out repairs in a manner sympathetic to the original appearance of the building. Work on submission of a bid is now well advanced. The HLF encouraged us to carry out as much investigation work in advance of the bid as possible, in order that detailed work specifications and accurate costs could be submitted. This case study looks at the investigations carried out to date, and these will subsequently support the lottery bid.

Brickwork and concrete cleaning

The advice of English Heritage was sought at an early date, and extensive advice was offered by Susan Macdonald. We were steered in the direction of specialist advisers on brickwork and concrete cleaning and repair. The first investigation was carried out by Nicola Ashurst of Adriel Consultancy, and involved cleaning trials and preparation of a specification for the exterior brick and concrete cleaning.

One of the interesting features of the design of Park Hill is the changing colour of the brickwork for each group of three floors above and below an access row. The lowest band is purple, rising through orange and yellow ochre to a light buff. This is both an interesting device for articulating the section of the blocks, and a way of emphasizing the height of the taller eleva-tions; but the years of dirt, particularly on the exposed west-facing city-centre side of the blocks overlooking the railway line, have dulled the effect. Nicola Ashurst also discovered evidence of a tan-coloured stain, which suggested that the concrete frame had at some time been coloured. There are, indeed, coloured streaks on the concrete in several locations, and it is tempting to believe that the concrete was originally painted or stained to blend it with the brick colours. However, chemical tests into the composition of this colouring have been carried out and shown that it is not any kind of paint. Further tests are now being carried out, but Jack Lynn, the pro-ject architect, has confirmed that the original specification was fair-faced concrete with no decorative finish. In fact, the extent of these coloured streaks is quite limited, and any decision on what action to take will depend on the outcome of the latest tests.

It also appears that a water repellent has been applied to the concrete at some stage since construction, actually over the initial soiling. This has been found to have a slight adverse effect on the cleaning works.

The surfaces of the structural concrete frame are very varied in texture, with strong board patterns in many areas, and these features were found to be very fragile. The brickwork panels were also found to be very sensitive to impact from abrasive cleaning or pressure water washing.

Figure 13.2   Brickwork cleaning trial on purple brickwork panel. (Andrew Beard)

It was therefore decided to seek a non-abrasive cleaning method that was effective on both the brickwork and the concrete. A range of chemicals was therefore used in various combinations.

The first trials, on purple brickwork (Figure 13.2), tested the effects of four different treatments as follows:

- mild alkaline detergent and low-pressure water rinsing on brickwork;
- thixotropic alkaline cleaner followed by neutralization on the concrete;
- thixotropic alkaline cleaner followed by very dilute HF-based cleaner on brickwork;
- thixotropic alkaline cleaner followed by acetic acid-based neutralization on brickwork.

From this, it has been concluded that two applications of alkaline/acetic acid will be necessary on the concrete, and the thixotropic alkaline cleaner followed by acetic acid-based neutralization was the most successful process, with low-pressure water rinsing. The use of the correct pressure washing is seen as critical in order to achieve maximum cleaning with minimal damage. The second trial used the same techniques on buff and red coloured brickwork, and was equally successful.

Among the positive aspects of this specification are that it uses relatively environmentally friendly chemicals and is reasonably quick to complete, thus mimimizing the risk to residents. However, the next stage will be to discuss the proposed specification with the Council's safety officers in relation to resident and operative safety. The one disadvantage of the process is that the concrete is only about 95% cleaned, acceptable from an aesthetic viewpoint, but possibly incompatible with the preparation required for concrete repairs.

Concrete repairs

Investigations into the concrete repairs were carried out by Ian Peck, of the Council's in-house structural engineers, with advice from Kevin Davies of Rowan Technologies Ltd. The extent of spalling concrete varies a great deal across the estate. The balcony and deck balustrades are the worst-affected areas, with a large proportion of the slender baluster shafts seriously damaged. The structural frame is very good in parts, whilst other areas have extensive exposed reinforcement where the concrete has spalled.

The investigation of the structural concrete had three stages. The first was an examination of the historical records of structural problems. Because the estate was designed in-house, and has been regularly inspected by the Council's engineers, the extensive records provide a valuable insight into problems that have developed. Abseilers inspect the concrete at regular intervals and use hammers to remove unsafe pieces to prevent them from falling. These records indicate that there have been no problems of structural movement, alkali–silica reactions or sulphate attacks. However, the random and gradual spalling of concrete has been regularly charted.

The second stage of the study was a physical and diagnostic investigation of the concrete in a pilot study area (Figure 13.3, *overleaf*). A complete physical inspection was carried out of both sides of one five-storey block at the south end of the estate, together with diagnostic testing of concrete samples. The inspection indicated that the spalling is due to corroding mild steel reinforcement, and it was generally worse on the highway elevation, suggesting a possible link with environmental factors. There are also areas where the reinforcement is visible on the

Figure 13.3 Pilot area for study of concrete condition at south end of estate. (Andrew Beard)

Figure 13.4 Spalling concrete on balcony balustrade panel. (Andrew Beard)

finished concrete surface, suggesting that it has been poorly placed. The concrete balustrade units showed particular signs of cracking and deterioration, assumed to be the effect of carbonation on the slender baluster shafts and displaced reinforcement during casting (Figure 13.4).

The diagnostic survey involved thirty concrete samples, taken from various locations on each elevation. These showed an absence of chlorides, and varying degrees of carbonation, up to a maximum of 100% and to an average depth of 20 mm.

The third part of the investigation was a series of remedial action trials carried out in conjunction with Sika Ltd and Dew Pitchmastic Ltd. The repairs included a series of different surface treatments, none of which was wholly successful. There are clearly issues of colour and texture still to be resolved, but valuable insights into the most appropriate specification have been obtained.

The test site used for the concrete repairs is also at the south end of the estate, where there is a row of free-standing concrete columns forming a colonnade to the ground floor of a block. The preparation consisted of grit-blasting the faces of the columns and beams and then breaking out the spalling and damaged concrete. Five different finishing treatments were tried, and all commenced with application of a rust inhibitor to the exposed reinforcement, application of a priming/bonding bridge and then repair with a proprietary mortar. The different finish treatments are shown on Figure 13.5. Reading from left to right:

- Panel one simply had between three and five coats of corrosion inhibitor applied. It was found that the visual effect is almost non-existent.
- The second panel had cosmetic mortar applied, using the dust and aggregate saved from the break-out process. This was followed by two coloured finishing coats, which (apart from the colour mismatch) has obliterated the original surface texture.

Figure 13.5   Test site for concrete repairs. (Andrew Beard)

- The third panel appears to be the most promising, and consists of an aquaprimer over the concrete repair, followed by an elastomeric finish to maintain the board texture. This is different from the mineral paint recommended by Nicola Ashurst, and further trials with both materials and different colours are still required.
- The fourth panel has a levelling mortar applied, followed by a coloured render type of finish. This has given a smooth finish that destroys all the textural features.
- The final (fifth) panel, partially shown in figure 13.5, has a cosmetic mortar applied using the dust and aggregate saved from the break-out process, and then a corrosion inhibitor has been applied to half of the panel. Again, this demonstrates the minimal visual effect of the corrosion inhibitor.

Apart from repair, it will be necessary to protect the remaining original concrete for as long as possible to minimize further deterioration. The two approaches considered were stabilization of the environment within the concrete to neutralize the contamination process, and the application of a barrier to exclude further contamination. Because of the extent of contamination so far, a barrier in isolation is impractical. For stabilization, either impregnating corrosion inhibitors or re-alkalization can be considered.

The clear corrosion inhibitor by Sika used on two of the trial panels was found to cause very little alteration to the appearance of the concrete. In theory, this inhibitor is maintenance-free, and it works by retarding the ingress of further deleterious elements, and re-establishing the corrosion protection properties of the concrete around the mild steel reinforcement. However, it is a relatively new technology with no long-term track record.

Re-alkalization is an electro-chemical process that re-establishes the corrosion protection properties of the concrete. It is also has a minimal effect on the visual appearance of the existing structure. Although the process is labour and equipment intensive, only areas susceptible to further deterioration need to be treated. These can be identified by a full survey of carbonation and reinforcement depths. Consequently, initial indications are that, in the case of the Park Hill complex, the two processes are similar in cost.

Finally, turning to the balustrades, it is considered that complete replacement of top rails, as well as the balusters, is the most appropriate solution. In the past, economical alternatives to 'like-for-like' replacement were considered, including a steel replica made from rolled hollow sections, and lightweight modern designs. The modern panels have been made from steel plate with perforations to create a pattern, but these are obviously visually inappropriate in view of the buildings' listed status. The steel replica version proved to be extremely heavy and difficult to manoeuvre into place. Investigations have now been carried out into procuring replacement precast units to match the existing panels and quotations obtained from potential fabricators. If funding permits, these will be cast with stainless steel reinforcement.

To date, the Council has invested approximately £13,500 in these investigations. Have they been worthwhile? There is no doubt they will enable a very thorough Heritage Lottery Bid to be submitted with accurate specifications and costs. Our latest estimate indicates that £15 million will have to be spent on works to the external envelope of the flats. The largest components will be window replacement at £4.5 million, concrete repairs at £4.2 million, and balustrade replacement at £2 million. This is in addition to the £3 million being spent on upgrading the flat interiors.

The early discussions with English Heritage have also been very useful, and it is to be hoped that they will help to smooth the way for the Lottery bid and any subsequent listed building application. Above all, the Council, as owners of the building, now have a much clearer idea of their likely liabilities for the conservation of the estate now that listed building status has been confirmed.

However, the bottom line in securing this immensely important housing estate as part of the country's architectural and historical heritage is to ensure that it remains popular with the 1,000 households who live there. The Housing Department have therefore commissioned a major consultation project with Park Hill residents on the future of the estate. It will explore vital issues such as how to address the high turnover of flats at the lower end of the estate, how to manage nuisance and vandalism, how to improve day-to-day housing management, and whether current and future investment is being carried out in accordance with tenants' wishes and priorities. It is only when all these social issues have been successfully resolved, alongside all the technical conservation matters, that a secure future for Park Hill will have been found.

The future of Park Hill – June 2000 update

The Housing Department of Sheffield City Council has continued to put a lot of work into developing a Heritage Lottery Fund bid for the restoration of the exterior of the Park Hill flats. The problem is finding the match funding to put against any possible Lottery funding, since the HLF can only be expected to part-fund what they describe as the 'conservation deficit' – the additional cost of refurbishing the flats because they are grade II* listed. In the current climate, and taking into account all the other pressing demands for housing capital finance, the Council cannot itself find the level of funds required.

The Council remains committed to retaining Park Hill in the longer term. The next step, therefore, is likely to be the selection of a consultant to advise on the potential for a private–public partnership to carry out the scheme. It is expected that invitations for proposals from consultants will be invited shortly. Even if match funding can be identified, it remains unclear whether the trustees of the Heritage Lottery Fund will be prepared to support a bid on this scale, in view of the precedent it could set for supporting public housing repairs.

References

1   Lynn, J. (1962), 'Park Hill Redevelopment, Sheffield', *RIBA Journal*, (December), 447–463.

CHAPTER 14

FALLINGWATER: SOLVING STRUCTURAL PROBLEMS

Robert Silman

Introduction

Fallingwater is, indeed, a building that might be called a rarity. That is, it is clearly an exceptional structure and one worth saving. In fact, the American Institute of Architects recently voted it the most outstanding work of American architecture in the last 125 years. The house is located in Pennsylvania, some 72 miles southeast of Pittsburgh and is at present owned by the Western Pennsylvania Land Conservancy. Although built in 1936, and therefore not truly a post-World War II structure, it is nevertheless included in this conference.

This paper is a case study in the methodology of how a structural engineer goes about analyzing and designing repairs. It must be noted, and without apology, that in addressing serious structural problems such as this one, we have a great deal of difficulty following the strict letter of the Venice Charter or our own Secretary of Interior's Standards for Historic Preservation: we cannot avoid serious interventions and cannot avoid irreversible actions.

Our office began working on repairs to Frank Lloyd Wright houses some five or six years ago, first with the Darwin D. Martin House in Buffalo, New York, and later at Wingspread in Racine, Wisconsin. As a result of a lecture presenting our solution to the difficult problems at Wingspread, the Executive Director of Fallingwater retained our firm to investigate structural problems at the house. We started in 1995 and issued the report of our initial findings to the Board in May 1996. This paper will summarize those findings and the proposed solution to the inherent problems.

About the house

Edgar Kaufmann Sr owned a successful department store in Pittsburgh. His son, Edgar Kaufmann Jr, spent a short time as an apprentice in Frank Lloyd Wright's studio at Taliesin in Spring Green, Wisconsin. Edgar Jr convinced his father to retain Mr Wright to do some work at the store and later to design a weekend house for the family on a site that had formerly been used during the summers as a recreation camp for employees of the store. Bear Run is a small, swiftly running stream that runs through the property, with a waterfall. The Kaufmanns had always assumed that a house would be located down-stream from the falls, looking back up at it. Of course it was Mr Wright's genius that sited the house above the falls, hanging out over the stream (Figure 14.1).

The house was designed in 1935 and construction started in 1936. Design was conducted at Taliesin with apprentices Bob Mosher and Edgar Tafel participating significantly. Edgar currently lives in New York City, on the same block as our office, and we are fortunate to be able to tap his fantastic memory for details of that period. The structural engineering for the house was done in the same studio by Mendel Glickman and William Wesley Peters; Wes Peters was later to marry the Wrights' daughter.

Early construction problems

Prior to the start of construction, Metzger-Richardson (M-R), the subcontractor who supplied the steel reinforcing bars, raised serious questions about the adequacy of the original design. M-R wrote to Mr Kaufmann informing him of their findings and Mr Kaufmann forwarded the letter to Mr Wright. The letter from M-R insisted that there was insufficient reinforcing in the cantilever beams of the living room and they proposed doubling the number of the one-inch square bars, from eight to sixteen. Mr Wright wrote a reply, now a classic, claiming that such an action would increase

Figure 14.1   Overall view of Fallingwater looking up at house. (Robert Silman Associates)

the weight of the beams too much and would not be safe. M-R appealed to Mr Kaufmann who referred the matter back to his architect. Mr Wright said to Mr Kaufmann, 'Whom do you choose to believe?' Mr Kaufmann appeased his architect by asserting his confidence in him; however, M-R slipped in the extra eight bars in each beam anyway, happily for the history of the house.

As soon as the formwork for the master bedroom terrace was removed, the edge beams deflected downward by 1³/₄ inches (45 mm). Bob Mosher, the apprentice on site, telephoned back to Mendel Glickman at the studio in Taliesin. After a quick check of his calculations Glickman is reported to have exclaimed, 'Oh my God, I forgot the negative reinforcement!' Throughout 1937, Mr Wright defended his design in the face of continuing criticism from M-R,

Figure 14.2   Fallingwater: the cantilevered terrace. (Robert Silman Associates)

who had made load tests and then calculations to show that the stresses in the concrete and reinforcing steel were near, or even exceeded, the total factor of safety against failure. M-R recommended placing permanent props out in the stream to reduce the length of the cantilevers. Once again Mr Wright forced Mr Kaufmann, his client, to choose and Kaufmann chose to go ahead with the house as designed. It turns out that M-R was essentially correct, as we have discovered.

Our commission

Our office was initially asked to investigate the structural adequacy of the master bedroom terrace, that portion of the house with the most severe visible cracks. Work was ongoing to repair the facade, including cracks at the master bedroom terrace, and the client wished to know whether it was wise to continue repairing these cracks cosmetically without first performing structural repairs. We subsequently had to broaden our investigation to include the living room below, because these two floors are structurally interdependent.

The structural system of the house

The cantilever portion of the house that overhangs the stream is essentially supported on four large reinforced concrete piers (Figure 14.2). On top of these are the four main living room reinforced concrete floor beams cantilevering some 15 feet (4.57 metres) beyond the piers, the very beams to which M-R added the eight bars. The floor of the living room is made up of 4-inch wide (102 mm) concrete joists spaced about 4 feet (1.22 metres) centres. A concrete slab on the bottom side of the joists serves as a finished soffit from the underside. On top of the joists are light wood beams with wood sheathing, all covered with local paving stones with carefully mortared joints.

The master bedroom terrace directly above the living room cantilevers an additional 5 feet (1.52 metres) beyond the living room below. However, its outboard (south) edge is supported on the living room floor below by four delicate steel tee window mullions in the south wall of the living room. All of this is beautifully drawn in a book called *Fallingwater* by Edgar Kaufmann Jr.[1]

Monitoring and verification of the existing structure

Our first question was, 'Have the deflections stopped or are they still continuing?' Mr Kaufmann had been concerned about these movements and had commissioned a surveyor to measure the deflections on a regular basis, almost annually, by recording the elevations of the tops of the parapet walls. This was done systematically from 1941 until 1955. Between 1955 and the time we arrived on the scene in 1995, nothing more than one or two random measurements had been recorded. We immediately took extensive water level readings at more than 30 locations, attempting to relate these to the survey readings done earlier. Our measurements indicated maximum deflections of as much as 5 1/2 to 7 inches (140 to 178 mm) on the east and west living room outdoor terraces (Figure 14.3). We then installed two electronic crack monitors and two tiltmeters, all capable of being accessed and read remotely from our office in New York via computer and modem. The results of these readings over more than two years, corrected for temperature variations, indicated that indeed the cracks were still growing and the structure still tilting.

How could we be sure of the as-built conditions? For instance, in the well-documented argument between M-R and Mr Wright about the eight extra reinforcing bars, what was done

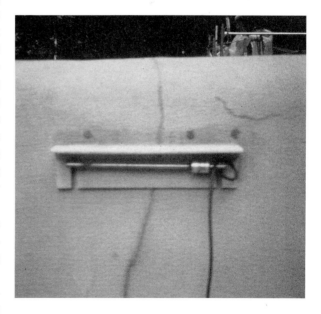

Figure 14.3   Crack in concrete with crackmeter mounted over the crack. (Robert Silman Associates)

in the end? What were the number, size and location of reinforcing bars in other locations such as parapets? We organized a programme of non-destructive evaluation, including techniques such as impulse radar, ultrasonic pulse velocity and high-resolution magnetic detection. The work was performed by GB Geotechnics Ltd of Cambridge, England. These tests located reinforcement in critical areas as well as construction joints, and they gave measurements of concrete quality. In one instance, it was necessary to remove several paving stones from the living room floor to gain access to the hollow space below in order to investigate the main cantilever beams.

Structural analysis

The next step was for our personnel to perform an independent structural analysis. We knew about the M-R analysis in 1936–7, and we had seen a very comprehensive study by a student at the University of Virginia from the early 1990s. Since many readers of this paper will not be engineers or architects, it might be as well to describe some of the pertinent behavioural properties of reinforced concrete. Concrete is essentially strong in compression and weak in tension. When beams bend, one surface compresses while the opposite side stretches. Areas that have stretched are subject to tensile stress and need to be reinforced with steel bars. These bars bond to the concrete; the bond is enhanced by deformations or little ribs rolled into the sides of the bars when they are manufactured. It is possible to have such a high state of bond stress that the bars actually will slip. Concrete is not a perfectly rigid material. It tends to continue to compress or deform under a constant compressive load. We call this property 'creep' or 'plastic flow'. Normally this stops after about twenty years, but in this case it is still continuing.

There are two properties that we are concerned with in the beams at Fallingwater: strength and stiffness. The former has to do with the capacity of the material to carry load before it fails or breaks; the latter has to do with the amount of movement that a structure undergoes by virtue of the loads on it and the materials of which it is constructed. Both depend on the dimensions of the beams, as well as the strength of the concrete and the reinforcing steel of which they are made. However, the effective depth of the concrete beams diminishes at high levels of stress because cracks develop from the tension surface and permeate down into the beam. The so-called cracked beam has a much lower effective depth than a lightly stressed uncracked beam.

We performed a number of variations of analysis, making computer models of all of them. For each variation we came up with a quantity for a force called bending moment, from which we could calculate the stress in the steel and the concrete. We also got deflection calculations. Results of the computer analyses were compared with the actual observed conditions. If the stresses were so high that either the concrete or the steel would have had to fail, we knew that some of our assumptions were incorrect because they had not yet failed, and we tried another set of assumptions. Similarly, if the calculated deflections did not match the observed deflections, then our assumptions were probably incorrect. Iterations continued until reasonable levels of stress were obtained and the calculated deflections matched those that were observed. Three major variations were tested: the master bedroom terrace as a self-supporting cantilever, the living room as a self-supporting cantilever and the combined master bedroom terrace/living room linked by the window mullions.

For the first scenario of the master bedroom terrace serving as a self-supporting cantilever, calculations for the parapet edge beam as a cracked section revealed that the stress in the reinforcing bars would have been 173,000 psi, more than four times the rupture strength. These are the beams that caused Mendel Glickman to bemoan his omission of the negative (top) reinforcing. This scenario was obviously not possible because the structure would have failed.

The second investigation was for the living room as a stand-alone, self-supporting cantilever. Indeed, the four living room beams work just fine on their own. The levels of stress are well within the allowable and, if that is how M-R calculated them, then they were correct. However, the living room floor beams do not stand alone. They must support the master bedroom terrace above through the window mullions because, as we learned in scenario one, the upper floor cannot support itself.

When the two floors are combined and all other physical constraints are entered into the calculations, a final set of numbers comes out that gives extremely high levels of stress, approaching the levels of failure, in both steel reinforcement and concrete, and the observed deflections match the calculated ones very closely. For this condition, we are able to draw a bending moment diagram (Figure 14.4) that shows a maximum moment of some 987 ft-k (1338.37 kNm),[2] result-

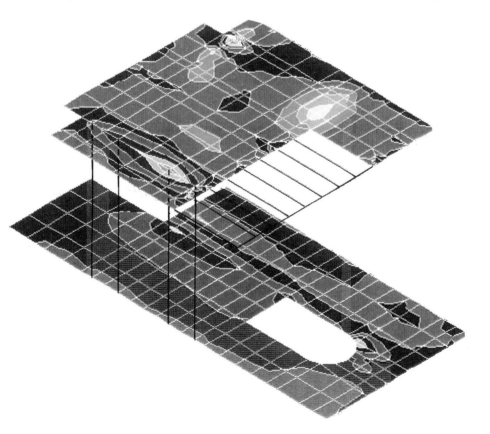

Figure 14.4   Moment diagram of Case 3e. (Robert Silman Associates)

ing in stress in the concrete of 4,380 psi and in the steel of 41,720 psi. These stresses, as stated before, are approaching the failure levels. These bending moments are obtained from a sophisticated three-dimensional finite element computer analysis whose results are plotted as stress contours (Figure 14.5). As part of the three-dimensional analysis, participation of the concrete cross-joists and the concrete slabs is considered.

Temporary shoring

When the trustees received the results of our analysis in May 1996, they were of course concerned. They questioned the safety of the house, both as a place where many people congregate as visitors and as a cherished historic artefact. We could only advise them of the results of

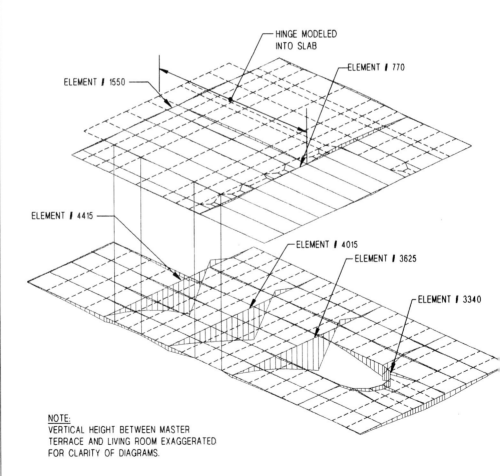

Figure 14.5   Finite element analysis results of Case 3e. (Robert Silman Associates)

our calculations, the observed ongoing deflections and the sixty-year history of the house, during which it had performed reasonably well. When the trustees decided that it was prudent to commence the design of permanent repairs, we advised them that during the construction phase it would be necessary to shore the ends of the living room cantilever beams while repairs were under way. Since they would ultimately have to shore, they wisely decided to shore the house immediately and eliminate the fear that it might collapse or otherwise fail locally before repairs could be made. Thus, in 1997, a relatively unobtrusive line of steel columns and girders was installed, coming up out of the stream. Not only the structure was shored, but also the overhanging rock ledge on which the temporary shoring columns rest. This ledge was shored with pipe struts in a cave behind the waterfall. The temporary shoring will remain in place until permanent repairs are completed, probably in the winter of 1999–2000.

Permanent repairs

Design of permanent repairs began in the late spring of 1998. It has been determined that three out of the four living room concrete cantilever beams will require reinforcing. The fourth (easternmost) beam is unique in that it has a delicate steel strut under it as part of the stair railing for the steps going down to the plunge pool. These remaining three beams are inverted T-beams with slabs on their bottom sides and concrete joists framing into their sides every four feet (1.22 metres). Practically the only method that will develop sufficient strength as a reinforcing system is to post-tension the beams with new, high-strength steel cables. Post-tensioning takes advantage of concrete's ability to resist compressive forces competently: a high-strength steel tendon is anchored at one end of the beam, and a hydraulic jack is used to apply a very large force (hundreds of thousands of pounds) to the other end of the tendon, which is anchored against the concrete before the jack is released. This large induced compressive force overcomes the tensile stresses in the concrete that were being inadequately resisted by the original reinforcing bars.

There are two methods for installing the prestressing cables or strands. One is to cut grooves or slots into the top of the beams, lay the cables in, anchor the far (north) ends, jack the cables and then grout up the whole thing. The other is to apply the prestressing tendons to the beams along their sides externally; this scheme requires very complicated hardware and, in this case, must overcome the interference of the concrete joists that frame into the sides of the beams in the same locations where the tendons would want to be. In either scheme, it appears as though the living room stone floor will have to be removed to gain access to beams. It might be possible to work from underneath by breaking out the concrete soffit slab and then repairing it, but there seem to be other reasons to lift the paving stones so that the tops of the beams may be thoroughly examined for existing cracks before they are prestressed; if the existing cracking is significant, it may have to be repaired before any jacking forces are introduced.

No matter what scheme is selected, the level of intervention will be monumental. However if this is what is required to save the structure and to enable it to remain as a daring and dramatic cantilever, then the work will go forward.

Conclusion

When Alan Powers spoke of the difference between substance and essence, I was reminded of the the 1939 essay by Walter Benjamin, 'Art in the Age of Mechanical Reproduction', in which he comments about our ability in the twentieth century to be familiar with works of art and architecture because they are so beautifully reproduced in accurate photography and movie film. Every student of architecture has 'seen' Fallingwater in those terms. However, Benjamin goes on to say that in a reproduced work of art what is lost is the original aura. It is this aura that we seek to preserve for future generations. That is the 'heritage' that we talk about, not the photographs in some archive.

References

1   Kaufmann, E., Jr (1986), *Fallingwater: A Frank Lloyd Wright Country House*, New York: Abbeville, and London: Architectural Press.

2   The units are feet-kips, where a kip is 1000 lbs; 1 kip-force foot (ft-k) = 1.356 kilonewton metres (kNm); more often used with concrete than with steel structures. A bending moment is the means by which a load on a beam is converted into a meaningful form so that the beam or slab can be structurally sized to perform its duty. In the case of a concrete structure, as here, the bending moment would provide both the depth of the beam and the rod reinforcement in it.

CHAPTER 15
THE CLERICAL MEDICAL AND GENERAL BUILDING, BRISTOL: PRESERVING THE CONCRETE AESTHETIC

Kevin Davies

The Clerical Medical and General Building in Narrow Plain, Bristol, was found to be suffering from corrosion problems affecting the reinforcement steel of the precast panel wall units. The building is a large, post-war, multi-block construction, comprising two tower blocks, one of eight storeys and one of five storeys, with a four-storey interleading block. It is bounded by Temple Way on one side, a car park on the other and a canal on one end (Figure 15.1). It is not a listed building but has a distinctive architectural appearance, which the client wished to retain.

Figure 15.1   The Clerical Medical and General Building, Narrow Plain, Bristol. Building Partnership (Bristol), 1974. (Kevin Davies)

This case study illustrates an approach that is likely to be appropriate for dealing with similar problems when the building is listed.

Site investigation carried out during 1991 revealed substantial cracking of the precast panel walls, particularly along the lower edges of the darker portions. The cause of the problem was traced to corrosion of the steel reinforcement within the panels.

Investigation of the problem

Examination of the concrete revealed carbonation to steel reinforcement depth at a number of locations, and high chloride ion contents above the threshold value deemed to cause corrosion of the steel reinforcement. Laboratory analysis of the cement matrix showed that the probable cause of chloride contamination was calcium chloride-based additives cast into the mix at the time of construction. The carbonation occurred as a result of carbon dioxide in the air reacting with the alkaline pore water to reduce the pH value. This combined effect resulted in loss of the concrete's ability to protect against corrosion.

Figure 15.2   Close-up view of the top of the panel showing the primary anode and the cables run within the void behind the sealant. (Kevin Davies)

Choices of repair

The choices for repair were narrowed down to two practical propositions: either remove and replace all of the chloride-contaminated and carbonated concrete, or remove the physically damaged concrete only and apply an electrochemical protection system.

Other options were considered, including application of anti-carbonation coatings; but these were discounted as ineffective against already contaminated concrete.

The building remained fully occupied and operational during the investigation and the installation/repair stages, so it was appropriate to limit the amount of concrete breakout, noise and dust pollution to allow the offices to function normally. The precast panel walls were fitted in such a way that they actually formed the outer skin of the building, so complete removal/replacement of the panel units was not feasible.

It was determined that the most appropriate repair strategy was:

- breakout, removal and replacement of physically damaged concrete;
- application of an impressed current cathodic protection (ICCP) system;
- coating of the darker portions of the panels;
- abrasive cleaning of the lighter portion of the panels, followed by the application of a clear protective coating.

The repair contract was awarded and carried out during 1994.

Feasibility study

To ensure the selection of the correct repair strategy, on-site trials were carried out to determine the practicality, and the correct coating materials, colour and texture, of the repair materials.

The trial installation of the ICCP system was carried out during May 1994 and involved making electrical connections to two precast panels at the front of the building. The panels, which have an exposed aggregate finish, were abrasively blast cleaned to remove surface contamination. An epoxy layer was applied to the top inclined surface, and a carbon fibre ribbon primary anode was fixed in place. The entire trial area was then coated with a conductive coating anode system.

To monitor the effect of the trial ICCP system, a silver/silver chloride/potassium chloride (Ag/AgCl/KCl) was installed within the concrete alongside a steel re-bar. The steel potential was recorded prior to, and after, energization of the ICCP current. The results were highly satisfactory and showed that the cathodic protection current could be made to flow, providing the necessary level of corrosion protection to the steel.

Aesthetic considerations were of paramount importance to this building, which has a distinctive architectural style. The conductive coating anode system is, unfortunately, available in only one colour: black. Trials were carried out on suitable top coats to provide the required appearance. The client selected a dark green (BS 4800).

Cathodic protection system

The cathodic protection system was designed to provide the corrosion protection, but great importance was placed on the way that it would be installed. The overall intention of the design was to ensure that the outside appearance of the building was not changed to any appreciable extent.

In any cathodic protection installation, a number of cables have to be installed to transfer the small DC electrical current to the steel reinforcement and to the anode system. It was fortunate that in this building there was a gap of some 15 mm between the panels, which was sealed with a mastic sealant. Part of the repair package was to replace this sealant, so the void behind the sealant was used to run the ICCP cabling (Figure 15.2).

The building's elevations were subdivided into fourteen cathodic protection zones, each of surface area between 115 and 200 square metres, but along geometric boundaries. The cabling within each zone was terminated within a non-metallic junction box located on the soffit behind the columns at lower walkway level. Multicore cables connected these zone junction boxes to the DC power supply units located in the basement car park.

To monitor the performance of the ICCP system, two reference electrodes were permanently installed within selected panels on each floor level, 168 in total. The performance of the system can be monitored from within the DC power supply cabinets in the basement.

On completion of the repairs and installation of the ICCP system, the appearance of the building has changed very little. On careful scrutiny, the cable conduits can be seen running along the beams on the walkways, but with careful colour matching these are not obvious. The cathodic protection system cannot be noticed by the casual observer.

Early cathodic protection performance

The cathodic protection system has now been operating for over five years and there are no signs of corrosion on any of the panels. The output currents have been reduced to very low output levels. One of the benefits of applying ICCP is that the steel is charged negatively, which repels negatively charged chloride ions and prevents corrosion. The system is now operating at a total power output of some 200 watts (the same as three domestic light bulbs).

Repair contract details

Client:	Clerical Medical and General Life Assurance Society
Engineer:	Chesterton International
Test consultants:	Oscar Faber Consulting Engineers
Main contractor:	Concrete Repairs Ltd
Material supplier:	PermaRock Products Ltd
Cathodic protection engineer:	Kevin G Davies, corrosion engineer
Cathodic protection electricians:	KBS Electrical Services Ltd
Repair mortar:	Renderoc GP
Panel cleaning:	Cleaning Technology Ltd, Liquibrade system
Fixing adhesive:	PermaRock NM50
Conductive coating:	PermaRock PermaGard water-based conductive coating
Top coat:	Sandtex Smooth
Clear sealant:	PermaRock Disbocrete 535 anti-carbonating coating system

PART FOUR

CONFERENCE
SUMMARY,
SOURCES
AND
BIBLIOGRAPHY

CHAPTER 16

PRESERVING HERITAGE OR REVALUING RESOURCES?

John Allan

The conference *Preserving Post-war Heritage* in June 1998 left me trying to clarify in my own mind how it differed, or was intended to differ, from the first such meeting – *Modern Matters* – held two years previously. The explicit reference to 'post-war' seemed to be the most illuminating clue, and the conference leaflet specifically informed us that *Preserving Post-war Heritage* would take up the debate where the earlier discussion had left off. The poster for the first conference had featured the Penguin Pool – arguably the definitive symbol of British Modernism in its innocent, prelapsarian, listable (and, in this case, listed grade I) state. The poster for the second showed an illustration of the foyer window at Alexander Fleming House, Goldfinger's defiantly Brutalist *chef-d'oeuvre*, and for many years a symbol of the troublesome nature of much post-war urban development.

This contrast could have signified a valid difference in focus, from the rare, the small, the socially peripheral to the generic, the large, the socially engaged. Our attention would turn from the undergraduate pioneering heroic period of modern architecture to the age of the Welfare State, in which Modernism became an official instrument of national reconstruction.

But while these differing poster images superficially suggested the debate would be developmental, a more systematic comparison of the two sets of proceedings shows pre-war and post-war case studies featuring in both meetings and a variety of technical presentation, notably concerning concrete, that would have been equally pertinent in either. I came away feeling less certain than I expected to be of the distinctions to be drawn between the two eras in relation to the conservation issues involved.

Having participated in the second event only as chairman, and having been given the perhaps unfair advantage of an invitation to contribute a paper after the event, I may derive any benefits that hindsight might offer and reflect on the discourse as a whole. So it seems to me that a fruitful area for exploration is this question of what might constitute a distinction between conservation of pre-war and post-war buildings.

As is often the case with specialist gatherings of this sort, one gradually becomes aware of the presence of a 'predisposing mindset' or set of assumptions that tends to determine the way the subject matter is approached even before the discussion begins. I trust it is unnecessary to say that no criticism is intended when I suggest that the 'set of assumptions' in this case may have originated in the organization that hosted both conferences.

English Heritage, as its name implies, is a conservation authority with powers and a remit that necessarily and justifiably ensure that conservation and conservation values are the primary and predisposing criteria in the consideration of its portfolio. One need only examine the *Buildings at Risk Register*[1] to see how a vast number of otherwise unrelated buildings of unimaginable diversity are 'synthesized' through the conservation agenda. To be included in the Register, a building must have listed (or scheduled monument) status; and the question of listing sooner or later surfaces in most English Heritage discussions as the 'trigger issue' in considering each case and formulating the terms of evaluation.

In one of the discussion sessions at the conference, I compared English Heritage and listing to the boxer with a horseshoe in his glove, to draw attention to the pre-emptive bias towards conservation that listing tends to introduce in determining the future of a building at moments of change or uncertainty.

In his philosophical introduction to the first conference, *Modern Matters*, Andrew Saint identified six ways in which modern buildings might differ from older ones in terms of formulating an appropriate conservation response.[2] These yardsticks of number, technique, intention, performance, viability and appeal effectively narrowed the mesh through which that prerequisite of listability, architectural significance, could be filtered in relation to modern buildings.

Notwithstanding such a discriminating approach to selection, the focus was still on the instrument of listing. Indeed, with some judicious retooling – the development of its typological categories, for example – English Heritage has found nothing exceptionable in extending the principle of listing when considering the 'icons' of the inter-war years or the rarer buildings of the post-war period, even the big controversial ones like Alexandra Road and Park Hill. The latter were, after all, the acknowledged flagship schemes of their day, even if some observers at the time and since – including certain Secretaries of State – may have thought they were flagships steaming in the wrong direction.

But what about the rest, the vast mass of work undertaken between, say 1940 and 1980 in what Lionel Esher described as nothing less than 'The Rebuilding of England'?[3] I am thinking of the huge tracts of local authority housing in every major city, the hundreds of schools, health buildings, libraries, office blocks, shopping centres, that collectively constitute a substantial part of the built fabric of modern Britain. This may not quite have been what was intended by the 'Post-war Heritage' in the conference title, but – with or without a capital 'H' – it has assuredly been *inherited* by an oncoming generation of owners and users and is now of an age where important decisions about its value, upkeep or survival will have to be made. Even to refer to this inheritance in the singular is really but a verbal convenience, for its range and heterogeneity render it beyond simple classification.

Does the fact that much of this output, whose sheer volume is perhaps its most incontrovertible post-war characteristic, will never be considered worthy of listing mean that it may be ignored in discussions on conservation such as this one? Surely not. After all, in other areas of its work English Heritage seeks to advance public understanding and good practice in matters of maintenance and repair without necessarily resorting to the coercive pressures of listing; the widely recognized *Framing Opinions* campaign on windows is one such example.

To acknowledge that the very ordinariness of most post-war 'heritage' liberates it from the conservation protocols of listing, is not the same as saying that conservation criteria may play no part at all. The spectacle of an unpopular tower block being blown sky high by jubilant tenants may encapsulate an extreme response to the difficulties posed by post-war heritage, but it can hardly be extended to cover the larger picture indicated above. How and where does the conservation impulse find a place among all the other factors that affect this inheritance, the cumulative product of half a century of capital investment? If most of it is not good enough to list, neither is it bad enough to demolish, or even disguise. It simply has to continue working for its living, upgraded, modified or otherwise 're-engineered' as necessary.

Such issues as urban location, change of use, transport linkages, capacity for spatial reconfiguration, infrastructure longevity, ratio of patent to latent value, tenure revision and commercial remarketability, are likely to play at least as significant a part in determining the future of much post-war heritage – that is 'heritage' spelt with a decidedly small 'h'.

Perhaps concentrating on 'heritage' to be 'preserved' is an inappropriate approach to a period chiefly characterized by its volume of output. Instead, might it not be better to consider its residue as 'resources' to be 'revalued'? This is not an argument for a less rigorous approach to conservation. On the contrary, it is a call for conservation to be explored more holistically in the real arena of active urban renewal. In this context, it might offer a liberating solution in one instance and an impossible constraint in another. For what it's worth, I myself am on record as suggesting that half of Park Hill should be listed and the other half demolished.[4]

One of the interesting points to emerge in conference discussion was the sharp contrast between current inner-city regeneration projects, with their transparent social objectives and considerable budgets, and the typical conservation project with its heavy art-history agenda and invariable shortage of funds. Large amounts of capital are injected into London's East End in the effort to improve standards of living, while conservation projects like that for Lasdun's Keeling House languish for lack of funds. This seemed to resonate with the rather 'unsecular' character of the conference delegate list, in which conservation professionals of various types predominated and building owners and users, or their representatives, were virtually non-existent.

In my paper to the previous conference,[5] I tried to draw attention to the diversity of motives among building owners even in projects where one might have supposed conservation objectives would be paramount. After a decade of dealing with 1930s Modernist 'icons' of grade I listed and lesser status (including the Penguin Pool), I have come to the appreciate that however self-evident the 'art-history' agenda may seem to the professional team, and particularly the architect, the wider operational or commercial aspirations of the client cannot be ignored, but must be understood and addressed if a viable outcome is to be achieved. This is why I am disinclined to regard conservation practice as a self-contained, exclusive branch of architecture, despite the need for special historical or technical knowledge or the application of ethical or procedural protocols. Ultimately it calls for the same quantum of informed judgement as any other sort of building design.

Figure 16.1 Marathon House, London. A redundant office block becomes a marketable apartment complex. (Avanti Architects Ltd)

How much more must this apply to the sort of development embraced by the category 'post-war heritage', which was nominally the subject of the second conference? It may, of course, be argued that English Heritage has no particular business in immersing itself in the welter of ordinary modern buildings that make up the fabric and background of much of present-day Britain. No doubt its resources are sufficiently stretched in the effort to cover even its primary portfolio of significant works. But this surely does not prevent such questions being raised by a conference of this kind, and in any case the dividing line between the 'significant' and the 'ordinary' is not always so easy to draw. I dare say there is even a case for defining a new listing category, to comprise buildings that have been proposed but rejected for listing.

As it is in housing that these problems have tended to appear in their most acute form, it is with a few housing examples – including a case study in which my own practice is involved – that I should like to illustrate the issues raised in this essay.

Marathon House (formerly Castrol House) is, or rather was, a tolerably representative Modern Movement office complex in Central London, designed by the British 'Miesians' Gollins Melvin Ward and completed in 1960 (Figure 16.1). No longer used as offices, it is now a block of flats. Why? Because its previous commercial value as an office building could not compete with its potential value as residential apartments. A conservation agenda would certainly have favoured retention of the original use, even if there had to be modifications to conform to current operational requirements. But this would have ignored the building's capacity as recycled investment. It is the latter reality that has determined the outcome.

Is this a tragedy for conservation? I would not say so, though as a practising architect I would have little difficulty in criticizing details of the conversion (Figure 10.3, *page 142*). But the question is, has the modern conservation fraternity anything to learn from this episode?

Take a second example: Alexander Fleming House, the office complex designed by Ernö Goldfinger (1963), was a modern conservation *cause célèbre* in Britain for over a decade. At various moments within this period, it was threatened with either imminent demolition, or a full post-modern makeover – the latter regarded by some of its defenders as an even worse fate than outright loss. But Alexander Fleming House has been neither demolished nor disguised. In the event, the denouement has been more subtle. The building has been repaired, upgraded and converted into a major new apartment complex.

Once again, any card-carrying conservationist could criticize certain aspects of the conversion – the spandrel replacements, the overcoating of the concrete, the 'taming' of the authentic Brutalism of the building. But set against the fact that Goldfinger's *chef-d'œuvre* after a decade of uncertainty has now acquired a viable future, these misgivings are surely secondary. The form of the complex, its massing, its urban presence and its essential identity have been preserved and, what is more, it now once again supports a social reality – it resumes a useful function as an element of live urban tissue. It is even conceivable that some of the alterations can be reconciled with the conservation principle of reversibility (Figure 16.2).

Now it is relevant to note that both these buildings had been proposed for listing and rejected. And one cannot but ponder whether it was their very failure to achieve listed status that actually enabled these buildings to be recycled, in the sense that it 'liberated' their commercial potential to offer a route out of pure obsolescence. What does this tell us about how

Figure 16.2   Alexander Fleming House, London. Given a new economic future as desirable urban apartments, 1997. (Avanti Architects Ltd)

the life of modern developments of this scale and type is actually extended? Surely, that there may well be viable futures for such buildings if a wider agenda than that of 'straight' conservation is brought to bear.

I suggest that modern conservationists should not shrink from confronting these realities. The location of an existing housing estate relative to an urban centre or sub-centre, its transport links with that centre, its spatial configuration and suitability for major upgrading, and the environmental impact and infrastructure renewal costs of demolition, are arguments likely to be at least as cogent in settling its future as any art-historical lecture to a sceptical owner about recognizing its cultural significance.

I conclude with the example of Wynford House, an inner urban apartment regeneration project currently being undertaken by Avanti Architects in the London Borough of Islington.

Wynford House is part of a large early post-war housing estate, Priory Green, designed by the Russian architect Berthold Lubetkin and his partnership Tecton for the Metropolitan Borough of Finsbury in Inner London (Figure 16.3). Although the project originated in the 1930s, building of the eventual scheme did not start until 1947 and it was completed ten years later in 1957.

It is the largest and the least successful of Lubetkin's three housing projects for Finsbury. Significantly, it is also the only one of the three to have been definitely rejected for listing. It is not, however, without architectural interest and urban design significance as the first substantial post-war attempt to reinterpret the traditional London square in the modern idiom.

Figure 16.3   Wynford House, London, 1957. Robust social housing at an appropriate density for its central location. (John Maltby)

Though popular with its original tenants, the estate had long suffered from neglect and poor management, and had reached the point where a major strategic decision on the part of its owners, Islington Council, could no longer be avoided. In 1996, the Council launched 'The Wynford House Challenge', an open development and design contest to settle its future. After a three-stage competition stretching over a year, in which 35 alternative sets of proposals, including several for total demolition and redevelopment were considered, the Challenge was won by Avanti Architects working with Community Housing Association, one of London's leading social landlords in the housing association sector.

The Avanti design is based on retention and rehabilitation of the Lubetkin buildings, with adaptation of some flats to maisonettes and the addition of four duplex penthouse units in place of redundant rooftop tank rooms. A comprehensive programme of tailored concrete remediation will be undertaken, with fully upgraded fabric and reservicing measures to meet and exceed current energy standards. The estate landscape will be fully reconfigured to provide improved amenities and security. The new scheme will provide a total of 84 units in a mix of fully managed social and private housing.

Why has this scheme beaten off the other 34 contenders? Not, I have to admit, because its original designer is the most venerated pioneer modern architect in England, with more listed buildings to his credit than any other architect of his generation (as a Lubetkin devotee, I would have been glad to think such a justification would be sufficient); but because, by taking a whole range of factors into account, it offered the best balance of mutual advantages to its vendors and its purchasers. In short, Wynford House will be saved by being changed, by being made relevant and responsive to today's social and private housing market. Let me list just a few of the factors involved:

- the financial benefits – a major capital receipt for the Council, and an important property acquisition for the Housing Association;
- the development scale – retention of density greater than current planning policy would favour for redevelopment, and the capacity thereby to generate sufficient return for the incoming purchaser;
- the management proposals – nomination rights for the Council for the social housing component and a customer-friendly, non-paternalistic management service for both social and market elements by an experienced inner-city landlord;
- the technical strategy – a considered response balancing fabric and services upgrade requirements with legitimate conservation concerns;
- the social fit – provision of a range of unit types, meeting precisely the kind of inner-urban apartment demand predicted by recent research;[6]
- the capacity for added value – potential to access a private market through the incorporation of penthouses and high-quality apartments, the installation of a concierge and the provision of social amenities;
- a marketable location – within yards of the forthcoming European railway terminal at St Pancras.

It is clear that a more realistic and diverse set of factors than purely considerations of conservation will have been the key to saving and recycling this estate. But I am equally convinced that there is a vital conservation ingredient in the project that will prevent it from being either a mere repair job or a cynical makeover.

To sum up, I suggest that the meaning and application of modern conservation should be explored beyond the picket fence of statutory listing. Conservationists should not avoid grappling with the more difficult, less glamorous elements of post-war heritage, but in so doing will need to secularize their stance, moving away from revering buildings as vessels of culture towards revaluing buildings as a social resource, thereby acquiring more, and firmer, handholds on the realities of urban renewal. We might then get beyond fighting a constant damage-limitation rearguard action and begin to exploit the range of economic, social and technical tools available for intelligent conservation, with a small 'c'.

Looking back now, it seems clearer to me than it did at the time that *Preserving Post-war Heritage*, though stimulating and informative, in effect contained its conclusion within its premise. The fare was rich and varied; technical presentations on services, concrete, plastic and curtain walling were magisterial; case studies like Fallingwater were enthralling; but we remained within the safe harbour of preservation and heritage. If there were ever to be a third conference in the series, it might be interesting to venture out to sea and explore the application of modern conservation in the harsher dynamics of regeneration, development and urban renewal. The limits of the subject would be difficult to define. There would be a different range of speakers and probably a somewhat different type of audience. The discussion would become untidy. However, it might illuminate the conservation debate from a different angle.

But then, perhaps such a conference would not be organized by English Heritage.

References

1   English Heritage (1998), *English Heritage Register of Buildings at Risk*, London: English Heritage.

2   Saint, A., 'Philosophical Principles of Modern Conservation', in Macdonald, S. (ed) (1996), *Modern Matters: Principles and Practice in Conserving Recent Architecture*, Shaftesbury: Donhead.

3   Esher, L. (1981), *A Broken Wave: The Rebuilding of England, 1940–1980*, London: Allen Lane.

4   Allan, J., 'Park Hill Revisited' in Saint, A. (1996), *Park Hill: What Next?*, London: Architectural Association.

5   Allan, J., 'Conservation of Modern Buildings: A Practitioner's View' in Macdonald, S. (ed) (1996), *op. cit.*

6   The Joseph Rowntree Foundation (1997), 'The Market for a New Private Rented Sector', *JRF Findings*, **214**, (June).

CHAPTER 17
CONSERVATION RESOURCES FOR POST-WAR STRUCTURES

Michael Stratton

This chapter considers some of the key sources for studying post-war architecture and, in particular, different forms of construction and building materials, in order to identify appropriate repair strategies. One might expect that in considering such recent history – when many materials were standardized and made in factories – the task would be an easy one; however, there are some problems that have to be recognized and overcome:

- there is far more variety and variation than might be expected in terms of the materials used and construction methods applied, even in 'pure' Modern Movement buildings. Manufacturers have seen choice rather than absolute standardization as the key to commercial success;
- many suppliers held to craft traditions of varying their products and keeping secret the raw materials and the processes used;
- the construction technology and precise choice of materials often changed during the design, and even during the construction, of the building;
- the move towards larger buildings, rapid erection and higher standards has prompted near-continual change in products and the way in which they have been used;
- much key literature has been lost. Books and journals have been deaccessioned by libraries; planning files have been destroyed by local authorities; trade catalogues and industrial records have too often been treated as worthless ephemera.

There is no published overview of the use of building materials in twentieth-century British architecture.

Materials and modern construction in the post-war period

It is, perhaps, inevitable that most accounts of post-war building focus on what was new and revolutionary, such as prefabrication and rapid building systems. But the reality is that innovation was always balanced with tradition. There have been relatively few revolutions in building materials, and they have typically taken decades to reach maturity and be widely adopted. The key innovations in brickmaking – steam pressing and extrusion and continuous kilns – were devised in the middle of the nineteenth century, but took until the end of the Victorian era to become the norm. Thus, although concrete and steel are often described as the characteristic modern materials, brick and stone have never lost their importance in building and cladding.

Similarly, it has been assumed that this century has seen the death of regional traditions in building construction, the vernacular relationship between the use of stone, clay and timber being supplanted by mass-produced and mass-dispatched Fletton brickwork, blockwork and precast concrete.[1] In fact, regional differentiation survived in many areas until at least the end of the inter-war period. More recently the conservation movement has promoted the use of locally sourced materials and skills, especially in conservation areas and national parks.

It took many decades for steel and concrete construction to reach maturity and be widely adopted. Many, if not most, Modern Movement buildings of the inter-war period were built of bricks and mortar and faced with white render; brick and stone slabwork was much used in the 1950s and returned to favour in the 1980s. Changes in the use of materials have been influenced by fashion, economics – and war, which often caused shortages of steel and skilled labour. The emphasis on housing construction after each World War was a major spur to the development of cost-cutting materials.[2] It is important to note that the materials industry remained under government control until 1954.

Historians researching the story of post-war materials and methods should visit building sites as well as libraries, if only to remind themselves that, for all the new methods and materials at the disposal of the construction industry, the building process continues to take place in apparently chaotic mudbaths of scaffolding, stockpiles of materials, timberwork and cement mixing.

Framed construction: steel and concrete

Framed construction, progressively adopted during the inter-war period, was accepted as the norm after 1945, partly due to the need for rapid, economical erection but also because of a shortage of skilled masons and bricklayers. The tower crane, first used in Britain around 1950, permitted the easy and safe handling of prefabricated sections.

With the government reserving available steel for exportable products such as cars and ships, simplified forms of concrete framing offered particular potential in the late 1940s. Advances in mass production during the war offered a model, and spare capacity in the aviation industry, with its skills in aluminium, an ideal opportunity to develop new systems that depended on pre-cast components to permit rapid on-site work. More than a hundred systems of prefabricated building had been proposed by 1948, employing various combinations of steel, aluminium, concrete, timber and asbestos. By the end of 1948, no fewer than 125,000 aluminium prefab bungalows had been supplied. While the demand for prefabricated housing tailed off in the early 1950s, when brick was once more available, a stronger continuity can be seen in school design. Early experiments in the 1930s and the use of huts during the war had left school authorities and architects open to the advantages of standardized, lightweight systems of steel frames clad in glass and concrete panels.

West Bromwich in the West Midlands was to be the industrial focus for this brave initiative. Hertfordshire County Council was a pioneer, working with Hills and Company of West Bromwich. Ernest Hinchcliffe had founded this patent glazing company and developed it to make light structural steelwork. During the war, it supplied sections for Bailey bridges; with the prospect of peace, it developed a steel-framed and concrete-clad house, the 'Hills Presweld', and then a similar system for system-built schools.[3] J. Brockhouse and Company, also based in West Bromwich, developed the widely adopted CLASP (Consortium of Local Authorities' Special Programme) system. F.W. Lister Heathcote, who had great experience in mechanical engineering with Sunbeam, Ford and Vulcan, was asked by Brockhouse to explore the potential for using cold-rolled steel in building construction. After a couple of experiments with houses, including a group in Coventry, Brockhouse and Heathcote found a market in the city's primary schools, with other examples built on the Hills system. Heathcote went on to develop and supply frames for the CLASP system used in Nottinghamshire (where they were spring loaded to overcome the problem of mining subsidence), and for the University of York campus, developed from the early 1960s.[4]

Steel frames involved manufacture in a large rolling mill and incurred major delivery costs. Concrete, on the other hand, could be obtained more locally. By the 1950s, concrete was dropping in price relative to steel, and could be worked in lighter sections and with simplified forms of shuttering. Pre-stressing provided extra strength, particularly for floors and beams. The use of box-frame or egg-crate construction, whereby the internal walls, floors and ceilings took on a key structural role, was ideal for flats, with their standardized layout and need for separation rather than connection between each unit. Tecton Group architects and the engineers Ove Arup collaborated in developing this approach, which was widely applied by the London County Council in the 1950s, using a variety of cladding systems for the main elevation. The next logical step in industrialized concrete architecture was to use precast concrete panels for the cladding, drawing upon the early example of Quarry Hill flats, Leeds, built in 1936. The most widely adopted concrete building and cladding system was the 'Bison' wall-frame. The producers of 'Bison' blocks, Concrete Ltd, established a series of factories in England and Scotland, in contrast to other firms such as Wates, who continued the tradition of precasting as close as possible to, if not directly on, the actual building site.

Problems with water penetration, condensation, spalling and even collapse brought such concrete construction systems into disfavour. In contrast, the use of steel frames in industrial building was far more consistent in its growth, once post-war shortages were overcome. The steel-framed office block and factory evolved from the late Victorian period, key issues being protection from fire and the choice of cladding. Steel frames with lightweight roof trusses, which could be quickly bolted or rivetted together, became the norm for single-storey factories by the First World War. Since then, there has been a series of innovations to create the 'crinkly tin' shed – with its flat top, rooflights and profiled metal cladding – that marks the perimeter of most western urban conurbations.

The Heinz factory at Kitt Green, near Wigan (1955–9), introduced this now ubiquitous type of development. The industrial designer E.D. Jefferiss Mathews worked with the progressive American practice Skidmore, Owings and Merrill to create a works, clad in aluminium and glass and with 24-hour electric rather than natural lighting, to give flexibility of planning and to improve food hygiene. During their brief partnership, Norman Foster and Richard Rogers developed the aesthetic potential of profiled metal cladding in the minimalist exterior of their Reliance Controls Factory, built in Swindon 1964–5.

Traditional construction and cladding materials

Modern patterns of building have not led to the extinction of traditional brick and stone. It may even be argued that framed and cavity construction have revitalized the use of these materials, allowing them to be used in new ways and more economically than in the traditional masonry wall.

Brick

The most notable feature of brickwork in the twentieth century is that Modernism in design and the imposition of British Standards have conspicuously failed to produce a standard brick, or even a standard range of bricks. The introduction of pressing and extruding machines in the Victorian period enabled some firms to produce harder and more even bricks, while continuous Hoffmann kilns resulted in a more consistent output. But the types of clay used and the techniques of pressing still varied markedly across the country in the 1930s. The industry has subsequently become more rationalized, and major manufacturers often mix clays from different parts of the country; but at the same time conservation interests have encouraged the revival of smaller yards working their adjacent clay bank.

During the inter-war period, the triassic and carboniferous clays of the Midlands and the North of England were still worked by the stiff-plastic and wire-cut methods, while Fletton bricks were made from Oxford clays by the semi-dry process. In a further regional contrast, most of the large number of yards in the South East (there were 298 in 1937) held to hand-made and full plastic pressing to produce the distinctive but expensive and structurally weak London stock brick. This distinction helps to explain why Flettons could supplant traditional bricks closer to London, but not the high-quality mass-produced brickwork of the North of England and North Wales. The market for London stocks was bolstered largely by aesthetic distaste for Flettons and the suspicion that they were not resistant to sulphurous pollution.[5] Further regional variations can be noted, such as the use, from around 1951, of perforated bricks made by Whitaker and Sons of Leeds across West Yorkshire, and of white sand–lime bricks in the South East made with locally available sand, crushed flint and hydrated lime.[6]

Stone

The 'age of steel', the first two decades of the twentieth century, was also the 'age of stone'. Portland stone gained widespread use as a cladding material in the Edwardian and inter-war periods. Bath Stone Firms Ltd dominated this market. Having bought out the key quarries in Dorset in 1899, the firm took over further workings in Devon, Somerset and Rutland in the inter-war period.[7] Locally quarried stone continued to be used for traditional masonry across the North of England at least until the Second World War, while flint remained in demand in East Anglia and slate in Wales and the Lake District.[8] By the 1960s, stone was more likely to be used as a crushed aggregate to face panels of concrete. Then, as architects and their clients became disillusioned with exposed concrete, so they turned to facings of stone, cut as thin as ³/₈ inch (9.5 mm) and mounted in frames at the stoneyard to withstand the strains of delivery, installation and wind pressure.

Artificial stone was widely adopted as a cheap substitute in the 1920s, drawing upon advances in the use of moulds for concrete. Several large firms were based in the East Midlands; Empire Stone of Narborough supplied a range of cinemas and many facades for the Burton chain of stores. Most of these firms passed out of business in the lean, brutalist years of the 1960s and 1970s. Artificial stone is now widely produced again as a cut-price alternative to quarried stone, in particular for housing in conservation areas. Haddonstone of Brixworth, Northampton, is one of the leading firms in this market.

Tiling, terracotta and faience

The new century marked a shift in the use of terracotta to face urban buildings. While bright red or buff terracotta blockwork passed out of fashion, architects found that its glazed counterpart, faience, was ideal for wrapping round steel girders to protect them against fire and to create elevations that were decorative, colourful and soot-resistant. The firms that led and gained from this transition – Doulton, Leeds Fireclay, Shaws and Hathern – invested in new glazing equipment and tunnel kilns. In the 1930s, they introduced non-structural slabs, typically 2 x 1 feet (609 x 304 mm) in surface dimensions, which were used widely on Odeon and other cinema chains. However, the potential for standardization was reduced by the call for special detailing and particular choices of colour. During the Second World War, manufacturers turned to producing sanitary and chemical ware, but in the 1950s there was a renewed demand for slabwork, typically moulded into abstract patterns and glazed in bright colours. The terracotta industry suffered from the 1960s fashion for stark walls of exposed concrete. It has seen a modest revival with the demand for re-manufacture in conserving listed structures and the taste for polychromatic decoration for some new buildings.

Tiles continued to be used to line building interiors throughout the century, though demand has decreased since the Edwardian and inter-war periods, when hospitals and public houses were likely to be fully lined with tiling, and many homes were completed with slabbed-tile fireplaces. During the late 1960s and early 1970s, several architectural practices, in particular Yorke, Rosenberg and Mardall, adopted white tiling for building exteriors, most notably the Arndale Centre in Manchester and the campus of the University of Warwick. Shaws of Darwen received a series of massive orders for their extruded 'Twintiles'. Problems with bonding the tiles straight onto structural concrete resulted in a series of failures and a reluctance to use tile cladding.

Aluminium

Aluminium has had a fascinating role in British building in the post-war years, its development led as much by the growth of the aviation industry as by demand from architects or builders. In 1945, the government, anxious to avoid mass unemployment within aviation firms as the demand for aircraft slumped, sought to direct their energies into mass-producing prefabricated bungalows. Five companies formed AIROH (Aircraft Industry Research on Housing) and worked with the Aluminium Development Association to specify appropriate alloys and to test whether scrap Messerschmitts could be recycled into temporary homes.

The prefabs combined extruded frames and trusses clad with fluted aluminium sheets. The key obstacle was the cost of tooling up; the Bristol Aeroplane Company withdrew from the venture after producing a prototype at their works, though they did go on to develop a system for schools in their home city. Hawkers and Blackburn were among the firms that decided to invest in production lines with a total of 17,000 aluminium prefabs being produced before the renewed supply of brick and demand for aircraft from 1951 dissolved interest among both local councils and industrialists.[9]

Appropriately, the aircraft industry itself made the most dramatic use of aluminium for its own erecting halls. Three pairs of aluminium doors created openings 330 feet (100.5 metres) wide for the Brabazon Hangar at Filton, Bristol, and aluminium trusses permitted the 200-foot (61-metre) spans for the Comet Hangar and De Havilland, Hatfield.[10]

Aluminium and stainless steel were widely used to clad and decorate the elevations of skyscrapers in North America.[11] In Britain, aluminium was more likely to be used, at any rate during the 1950s, for window and door frames, and as a corrugated cladding such as the 'Kynalok' system marketed by ICI.[12]

Glass

Le Corbusier famously summarized the history of architecture as the struggle between the window and the wall and welcomed the victory of the former in the twentieth century.[13] The glass industry had become highly concentrated in the Victorian period, reflecting the capital investment and skilled workforce needed and the relatively low cost of delivery over long distance. Chance, Harley and Pilkington emerged as the key firms producing sheet glass, responding to new demands for train sheds and market halls and the need to optimize natural lighting in offices and factories. Patent glazing systems and wired, patterned and coloured glass were widely advertised in architectural journals.

Pilkington became the dominant force in the new century, having invested in tank furnaces in 1873 and lears (annealing ovens) for plate glass in 1904–5.[14] Both these innovations were imported, from Germany and the United States respectively, and are typical of the glass industry which has been characterized by the transfer of innovations and intense international competition. Production remained an intermittent process until 1921, when Henry Ford succeeded in making plate glass on a production line – as with the Model T car. Just two years later, Pilkington were able to introduce into Britain the technology of running a continuous ribbon of plate glass from a tank furnace.[15] Pilkington also latched on to the popularity of coloured glass in America, establishing the British Vitrolite Company in 1932. Though Vitrolite remained expensive and used mainly in small quantities for store fronts, plate glass was used in the 1930s for complete building elevations, most notably the Boots Wet Processes Building in Manchester and the Daily Express Building in London, and then more widely for schools in many parts of Britain.

In 1959, Pilkington pioneered the production of glass by the float method, which involves floating large sheets of glass on molten tin and heating it from both sides, resulting in perfectly flat surfaces with a consistent thickness. Production quickly spread to other countries. There have been other, though less fundamental, innovations such as double glazing and tinted glass, with firms offering competing systems for glass curtain walls. Early examples of the 1950s included 'Wallspan' (Williams and Williams, Chester), 'Windogrid' (Henry Hope and Sons) and 'Hilsulate' (Hills, West Bromwich).[16]

Partitions

A critical area of innovation largely unsung by historians, has been the substitution of new lining materials for wooden partitions faced with lath and plaster. Plasterboard, fibreboard and asbestos cement sheet were all invented before the First World War. The shortage of craftsmen after 1918 was a major impetus towards their use in building. Manufacture of plasterboard – enclosing a core of plaster between two sheets of paper – was pioneered in the United States and commenced in Britain in 1917 at Wallasey, when the Liverpool builder's merchants, Ferguson and Harvey, established British Plaster Board Ltd. The company grew solidly and during the 1930s gained its own sources of gypsum – the Gotham Company and Gypsum Mines, Robertsbridge – and also bought some paper mills. Through a series of mergers and buy-outs British Plaster Board was left with only one major competitor in the 1950s, ICI.[17]

Another form of lining material, fibreboard, had been invented by D.M. Sutherland around 1882 at a firm of papermill engineers in Edinburgh. He applied the principles of cardboard making to produce a board from wood waste. In 1898, he established the Patent Millboard Company at Sunbury-on-Thames. Subsequent innovations, designed to make a stronger fibreboard through a continuous process, came from countries with extensive forestry, such as the United States and Sweden, resulting in much of Britain's supplies being imported. Production expanded after the Second World War, despite some concern over fire risk.

Timber

The use of timber, in particular for domestic floors and roof trusses, has been one of the more enduring features of building construction. By the turn of the century, heavy king and queen post roofs had been supplemented by the lightweight lattice of the Belfast truss. Softwoods joined by metal connectors were increasingly used.

Both World Wars resulted in shortages of timber due to the lack of imports. At the same time the need to build temporary structures increased demand for timber. Boulton & Paul of Norwich, who built aeroplanes during both wars, offered the most upmarket range of houses in the inter-war period, some featuring thatched roofs. The London County Council was responsible for 689 timber houses on its estates in Watling and Becontree.[18] Experiments with laminated structures for boats and aircraft in the Second World War led to the use of plywood for proprietary structures and to the development of several housing systems, including a group of timber-framed houses in Hull erected by the Yorkshire Development Group.

Glued laminated timber had been used in West Yorkshire in the nineteenth century. Interest was renewed after the Second World War due to expertise with aircraft and boats, and laminated timber was employed extensively for the Festival of Britain buildings and inside the Royal Festival Hall. The high point of this enthusiasm for large laminated surfaces was the use of the Swedish

HB system for hangars at Gatwick, built in 1960, with portal frames of timber I-sections which provided spans of 150 feet (approx. 27 metres).[19]

By far the most significant development of the second half of the century has been the adoption of new designs in roofing, in particular the triangular trussed rafter, launched at the Building Exhibition of 1947. It has formed the basis of the widely used wooden rafters (marketed from 1963), connected by metal plates, delivered on a flatbed lorry and rapidly erected without the need for large, heavy purlins.[20]

There are many other important, though apparently more mundane, innovations in twentieth-century construction that could be mentioned – the adoption of asbestos sheet for factory roofing in the inter-war period,[21] the use of bituminous felt for flat roofs and the introduction of portable buildings, now characterized by the building site Portakabin.

References

1   Yeomans, D. (1997), *Construction Since 1900: Materials*, London: Batsford, 10.

2   Bowley, M. (1960), *Innovations in Building Materials*, London: Duckworth, 132.

3   Saint, A. (1987), *Towards a Social Architecture: The Role of School-Building in Post-War England.* New Haven and London: Yale University Press, 65.

4   *Ibid.*, 214–220.

5   Bowley, M. (1960), *op. cit.*, 173–182.

6   Handisyde, C.C. (1967), *Building Materials: Science and Practice*, London: Architectural Press, 187.

7   Clifton-Taylor, A., and Ireson, A.S. (1994), *English Stone Building*, London: Gollancz, 245.

8   Yeomans, D. (1997), *op. cit.*, 34.

9   Bowley, M. (1960), *op. cit.*, 314–5.

10   De Maré, E. (1948), *New Ways of Building*, London: Architectural Press, 205, 209.

11   Jester, Thomas C. (ed) (1995), *Twentieth-Century Building Materials*, New York: McGraw-Hill, 47–71.

12   De Maré, E. (1948), *op. cit.*, 220.

13   McGrath, R., and Frost, A.C. 1937, 1961), *Glass in Architecture and Design*, London: Architectural Press, 93.

14   Bowley, M. (1960), *op. cit.*, 94–101.

15   *Ibid.*, 280.

16   De Maré, E. (1948), *op. cit.*, 157.

17   Bowley, M. (1960), *op. cit.*, 337.

18   Yeomans, D. (1997), *op. cit.*, 128, 136–7.

19   *Ibid.*, 148.

20   *Ibid.*, 142.

21   Bowley, M. (1960), *op. cit.*, 296.

APPENDIX
SOURCES OF INFORMATION

As previously mentioned, there are few texts that deal specifically with the conservation of more recent materials. However, the opportunity to access primary source material is made possible by the large number of trade organizations, specialist libraries and databases that are dedicated to materials of this period. As many of the materials that came into widespread use in the 1950s and 1960s are still in use, there is considerable research that has already been and continues to be carried out by the various trade and professional bodies.

The sources cited in this chapter cover key international organizations and journals. The list of trade and professional organizations has been restricted to those within the United Kingdom. Similar organizations exist in North America, Australia and other European Countries.

Databases

There has been a proliferation of databases with the new technology of CD-ROMs and the Internet, key amongst those being:

- British Library and university catalogues

- American university library catalogues. Call up 'Library catalogues across the world – the Americas – The United States'.

- The Conservation Information Network, Client Services Canadian Heritage Information Network (CHIN) 365 Laurier Avenue West Ottawa, Ontario CANADA K1A OCE Internet: CAN_SERVICE@immedia.ca

None of the electronic architectural indexes provides information on references earlier than the 1970s. Researchers need to work through such bi-annual or annual indexes as:

- Architectural Publications Index from 1978 (now on CD-ROM)

- Card indexes held in the British Library

- Avery Index to Architectural Periodicals (now on CD-ROM) at Columbia University

- BIDS (Bath Information and Data Services). Database Services need to register. Access under 'Science and Engineering'.

Libraries and Resource Centres

Avery Architectural and Fine Arts Library
Columbia University
1172 Amsterdam Ave.
Mail Code 0301
New York, NY 10027
Tel: +1 212 854-3501
Fax: +1 212 854-8904
www.cc.columbia.edu/cu/libraries/indiv/avery

British Library Document Supply Centre
Boston Spa
Wetherby, West Yorkshire LS23 7BQ
Tel: 01937 546060
Fax: 01973 546333
E-mail: dsc-customer-services@bl.uk
www.bl.uk

Building Centre
26 Store Street
London WC1E 7BT
Tel: 020 7692 4000
Fax: 020 7580 9641
Product Information and Reference Library:
0 906 516 1116
E-mail: information@buildingcentre.co.uk
www.buildingcentre.co.uk

Includes the Technical Library and the Information Exchange Databank of product information.

Institution of Civil Engineers Library
1 Great George Street
London SW1P 3AA
Tel: 020 7665 2251
Fax: 020 7976 7610
www.ice.org.uk

Institution of Structural Engineers Library
11 Belgrave Street
London SW1 8BH
Tel: 020 7235 4535
Fax: 020 7235 4294
E-mail: library@istructe.org.uk
www.istructe.org.uk/library/libintro.html

RIBA British Architectural Library
Royal Institute of British Architects
66 Portland Place
London W1N 4AD
Tel: 020 7580 5533
Fax: 020 7631 1802
E-mail: bal@inst.riba.org
www.viaweb.com/riba-library/oncat.html

Archives

Public Record Office Archive
Public Record Office
Kew, Richmond
Surrey TW9 4DU
Tel: 020 8392 5200
Fax: 020 8878 8905
E-mail: enquiry@pro.gov.uk
www.pro.gov.uk/archives

Building Regulations

Model by-laws were still applied after the Second World War, though they soon became seen as irrelevant to the new world of high-rise and glass-walled construction. From 1952 the regulations came to draw more on British Standards and Codes of Practice. National Building Regulations were introduced in 1966. Since then they have become more tightly focused on aspects relating to health and safety, no longer prescribing the form of the building.

British Standards

Since 1903 British Standards have sought to regularize the sizes of factory-made components and to give some quality assurance in the performance of particular materials. Study of Standards can assist an understanding of why a particular structure was designed in a certain way and with specific dimensions in its steelwork or reinforced concrete.

British Standards Institution
389 Chiswick High Road
London W4 4AL
Tel: 020 8996 9001
Fax: 020 8996 7001
E-mail: info@bsi.org.uk
www.bsi.org.uk

Local authority planning files

Different authorities take different approaches to holding planning application records. For example, Coventry and Leicester have excellent sets; Sheffield's have been heavily pruned; York recently destroyed a large number. Contact the local authority for the current status of their records and access arrangements.

Trade Literature

Information from these sources will usually be specific and up-to-date, but they may be biased and are rarely properly archived. Various catalogues and indexes contain information on products and the key resources are listed below.

Architect's Standard Catalogue – compendium of trade products

Barbour Index
New Lodge
Drift Road
Windsor, Berkshire SL4 4RQ
Tel: 01344 899205
Fax: 01344 899369
E-mail: msc@barbour-index.co.uk
www.barbour-index.co.uk

Barbour have an archive service and some libraries retain old fiches.

The British Library Science Technology and Business (STB)
96 Euston Road
London NW1 2DB
Tel: 020 7412 7288 or 020 7412 7494
Fax: 020 7412 7217 or 020 7412 7495
E-mail: scitech@bl.uk
www.bl.uk
Online catalogue: www.OPAC97.bl.uk

Building Products Index
Acorn Centre
30 Gorst Road
London NW10 6LE.
Tel: 020 8838 1904
Fax: 020 8838 1905
E-mail: admin@bpindex.co.uk
www.bpindex.co.uk

Construction Industry Research and Information Association
6 Storey's Gate
London SW1P 3AU
Tel: 020 7222 8891
Fax: 020 7222 1708
E-mail: switchboard@ciria.org.uk
www.ciria.org.uk/ciria/

Journals – architectural

Contemporary architectural magazines are a valuable resource and it is often possible to find detailed coverage of many of the buildings that have been listed. The key British journals include:

- Architects' Journal

- The Architect and Building News (from 1948 for example included the weekly publication of architects' detail sheets and photographs of what were seen as interesting examples of current architecture).

Trade and professional journals

Contemporary journals showcased new technology and products as well as examples of where products have been used. More recent versions often include historical reviews of the industry and past case studies. Key British trade and professional journals include:

- Brick and Pottery Trades Journal

- British Clayworker (continued as Clayworker), London, British Clayworkers Office

- Concrete and Construction Engineering, (continued as Concrete), London, Concrete Publications

- Concrete Quarterly, British Cement Association, Century House, Telford Avenue, Crowthorne, Berkshire RG45 6YS

- New Civil Engineer, London, Thomas Telford, 1 Heron Quay, London E14 4JA

- Proceedings of the Institution of Civil Engineers, esp. (1996), 'Historic Concrete' 116, 255-480, London, Thomas Telford, 1 Heron Quay, London E14 4JA

- Reinforced Concrete Review, London, Reinforced Concrete Association

- Structural Engineer, London, Batiste Publications, Pembroke House, Campsbourne Rd., London N8 7PE

Conservation journals

Many conservation journals have included articles about the conservation of post-war structures over the last few years, sometimes devoting special issues to the subject. There are also some journals – such as those published by DOCOMOMO – that deal exclusively with twentieth-century issues. The following list includes those that have regular articles on the subject.

APT Bulletin
Association for Preservation Technology International
PO Box 8178, Fredericksburg,
Virginia 22404 USA

See particularly: Special Issue: Mending the Modern, **28**, (4), 1997

ASTM Standardization News
American Society for Testing and Materials
1916 Race Street
Philadelphia, Pennsylvania 19103
USA

Construction Repair
Palladian Publications Ltd
The Old Forge
Elstead
Surrey GU8 6DD

Context
The Journal of the Institute of Historic Building Conservation
3 Stafford Terrace
Tunbridge Wells
Kent TN2 4QZ
www.ihbc.org.uk

DOCOMOMO Journal
DOCOMOMO International
Delft University of Technology, Faculty of
Architecture
Berlageweg 1
2628 CR Delft
The Netherlands
Tel: +31 15-2788755
Fax: +31 15-2788750
E-mail: docomomo@bk.tudelft.nl
www.ooo.nl/docomomo

See also national newsletters

English Heritage Conservation Bulletin
English Heritage
23 Savile Row
London W1X 1AB

Historic Preservation
National Trust for Historic Preservation
1785 Massachusetts Avenue NW
Washington, DC 20036
USA

Twentieth Century Society Journal
Twentieth Century Society
70 Cowcross Street
London EC1H 6PP

Professional, amenity and trade organizations

There is a plethora of organizations, their aims and facilities fluctuating with the state of the market. Some have produced advisory documents and a number have very helpful librarians or archivists. The following is a list of UK based organizations. See Jester, T. (ed), (1995) *Twentieth-Century Building Materials*, New York: McGraw Hill, for a list of similar organizations in North America.

Aluminium Federation
Broadway House
Calthorpe Road
Five Ways, Birmingham B15 1TN
Tel: 0121 456 1103
Fax: 0121 456 2274
E-mail: alfed@compuserve.com
www.metalnet.co.uk

Architectural Cladding Association
60 Charles Street
Leicester LE1 1FB
Tel: 0116 253 6161
Fax: 0116 251 4568
E-mail: info@britishprecast.org
www.britishprecast.org

Association of British Roofing Felt Manufacturers Ltd
Fields House
Gower Road
Haywards Heath, West Sussex RH 16 4PL
Tel: 01444 440027
Fax: 01444 415616

Association of Interior Specialists
Olton Bridge
245 Warwick Road
Solihull, West Midlands B92 7AH
Tel: 0121 707 0077
Fax: 0121 706 1949
E-mail: jane-cook@AIS-interiors.demon.co.uk
www.AIS-interiors.demon.co.uk

Brick Development Association
Woodside House
Winkfield
Windsor, Berkshire SL4 2DX
Tel: 01344 885651
Fax: 01344 890129
www.brick.org.uk

British Cement Association
Century House
Telford Avenue
Crowthorne, Berkshire RG45 6YS
Tel: 01344 762676
Fax: 01344 761214
E-mail: library@bca.org.uk
www.bca.org.uk

The British Cement Association offers expert advice in response to enquiries on concrete and cement. It has a comprehensive library, including a historical section. The library also holds two databases on products and services and on literature. Membership of the BCA includes free literature searches and free access to product and technical information, as well as access to the library.

British Ceramic Federation
Federation House
Station Road
Stoke-on-Trent ST4 2SA
Tel: 01782 744631
Fax: 01782 744102
E-mail: bcc@ceramfed.co.uk
www.ceramfed.co.uk

British Constructional Steelwork Association
4 Whitehall Court
Westminster
London SW1A 2ES
Tel: 020 7839 8566
Fax: 020 7976 1634
E-mail: postroom@bcsa.org.uk
www.bcsa.org.uk

British Gypsum
Technical Services Dept
East Leake
Loughborough LE12 6JT
Tel: 0115 945 6123
Fax: 08705 456 356
E-mail: bgtechnical.enquiries@bpb.com
www.british-gypsum.bpb.com

British Plastics Federation
6 Bath Place, Rivington Street
London EC2A 3JE
Tel: 020 7457 5000
Fax: 020 7457 5045
www.bpf.co.uk

British Precast Concrete Federation
60 Charles Street
Leicester LE1 1FB
Tel: 0116 2536161
Fax: 0116 2514568
E-mail: info@britishprecast.org
www.britishprecast.org

For information on manufacturers of precast units, including historical information.

British Stainless Steel Association
McLaren Building
35 Dale End
Birmingham B4 7LN
Tel: 0121 200 2100
Fax: 0121 200 1306
E-mail: enquiry@bssa.org.uk
www.bssa.org.uk

Building Research Establishment
Garston
Watford WD2 7JR
Tel: 01923 664000
Fax: 01923 664010
E-mail: enquiries@bre.co.uk
www.bre.co.uk

Key source of information on building construction and performance. BRE undertook commercially sponsored research into materials such as concrete and bricks, and their studies of industrialized building methods highlighted its limitations. Following privatization the library is now held in store, and enquiries might be passed on to the BRIX database, for which one must register and pay. The alternative is to find the experts in individual sections, such as the Centre for Heritage Buildings or the Refurbishment and Remediation Section. Digests were produced from 1948 and Information Papers from 1979.

Centre for Window and Cladding Technology
University of Bath
Claverton Down
Bath BA2 7AY
Tel: 01225 826541
Fax: 01225 823556
www.bath.ac.uk/centres/CWCT

Chartered Institute of Building
Englemere
Kings Ride
Ascot, Berkshire SL5 8BJ
Tel: 01344 623355
Fax: 01344 630777
E-mail: reception@ciob.org.uk
www.ciob.org.uk

Chartered Institution of Building Services Engineers (CIBSE)
Delta House
222 Balham High Road
Balham, London SW12 9BS
Tel: 020 8675 5211
Fax: 020 8675 5449
E-mail: secretary@cibse.org
www.cibse.org

CIBSE has a heritage division.

Clay Roofing Tile Council
Federation House
Station Road
Stoke-on-Trent ST4 2SA
Tel: 01782 744 631
Fax: 01782 744102
E-mail: bcc@ceramfed.co.uk
www.claytileroof.com

Concrete Advisory Service
Concrete Society
37 Cowbridge Road
Pontyclun
Glamorgan CF72 9EB
Tel: 01443 237210
Fax: 01443 237271
E-mail: enoch@concrete.org.uk
www.concrete.org.uk

Concrete Repair Association
Association House
235 Ash Road
Aldershot, Hampshire GU12 4DD
Tel: 01252 321302
Fax: 01252 333901
E- mail: john.fairley@associationhouse.org.uk
www.concreterepair.org.uk

An association for contractors in repair of concrete with aims of promoting and developing best practice. They hold regular CITB Courses, and produce publications on concrete repair.

Concrete Society
Century House
Telford Avenue
Crowthorne, Berkshire RG45 6YS
Tel: 01344 466007
Fax: 01344 466008
E-mail: concsoc@concrete.org.uk
www.concrete.org.uk

Copper Development Association
Verulam Industrial Estate
224 London Road
St. Albans, Hertfordshire AL1 1AQ
Tel: 01727 731200
Fax: 01727 731216
E-mail: copperdev@compuserve.com
www.cda.org.uk
www.brass.org

Corrosion & Protection Centre
UMIST
P.O. Box 88
Manchester M60 1QD
Tel: 0161 200 4848
Fax: 0161 200 4865
E-mail: corrosion@umist.ac.uk
www.cp.umist.ac.uk/CPC

Council for Aluminium in Building
191 Sirencester Road
Charlton Kings
Cheltenham, Gloucestershire GL53 8DF
Tel: 01242 578278
Fax: 01242 578283
E-mail: cab@c-a-b.org.uk
www.c-a-b.org.uk

DOCOMOMO International
Delft University of Technology, Faculty of
Architecture
Berlageweg 1
2628 CR Delft
The Netherlands
Tel: +31 15-2788755
Fax: +31 15-2788750
E-mail: docomomo@bk.tudelft.nl

DOCOMOMO International (the international
working party for the Documentation and Conservation of building sites and neighbourhoods
of the Modern Movement) aims to promote
recognition of the Modern Movement and is
actively involved in the identification and
promotion of distinctive Modern Movement
architecture nationally and internationally, acting as advisers to ICOMOS International on
World Heritage listing of modern buildings.
Through specialist committees, including a
technical committee, it is actively involved in
development of appropriate conservation measures including protection, technical development and dissemination of knowledge. It also
attempts to identify and attract funding for documentation and conservation to ensure continued exploration and development of Modern
Movement architecture. There are currently
some 30 member countries. A quarterly journal
and biennial international conferences are some
of the benefits to members. There is also a
database of current technical research into the
conservation of Modern Movement buildings.

DOCOMOMO UK
77 Cowcross Street
London ED1M 6EJ
Tel: 020 7490 7243
Fax: 020 7250 3022
easyweb.easynet.co.uk/~asuka/home/
docomomo.html

DOCOMOMO UK is the British group of the
international organization and is open to all
that are sympathetic to the aims of the organization. Members include architects, engineers,
art and architecture historians and administra-
tors. Annual lecture, quarterly newsletter, exhibitions and biennial symposia. Through the
casework programme the organization assists
statutory bodies in the protection and listing of
modern architecture. Holds a national register
of significant Modern Movement buildings.

DOCOMOMO Scottish National Group

39 Patrick Hill Road
Glasgow G11 7BY
Tel: 0141 242 5520
Fax: 0141 242 5404

Modernist architecture in Scotland – largely a post-war affair – is being assessed, researched and documented by DOCOMOMO Scottish National Group. As well as a regular newsletter, the group has produced detailed research documents such as that on the steel buildings of the Moredun Housing Scheme in Edinburgh and Gillespie Kidd and Coia's St Peter's Seminary at Cardross. They hold a register of fifty modern buildings as part of the drive for comprehensive coverage from all the affiliated groups of DOCOMOMO International.

English Heritage

23 Savile Row
London W1X 1AB
Tel: 020 7973 3000
Fax: 020 7973 3001
www.english-heritage.org.uk

English Heritage is an independent body sponsored by the Department of Culture, Media and Sport. Its aim is to protect England's architectural and archaeological heritage for the benefit of present and future generation. It is the country's principal adviser on the historic environment and is responsible for advising on the listing and scheduling of buildings and monuments to ensure legal protection. Historic Scotland, CADW and Historic Buildings and Monuments (Northern Ireland) are the equivalent organizations for other parts of the UK.

Flat Roofing Alliance

Fields House
Gower Road
Haywards Heath, West Sussex RH 16 4PL
Tel: 01444 440027
Fax: 01444 415616

The Glass and Glazing Federation

44-48 Borough High Street
London SE1 1XB
Tel: 020 7403 7177
Fax: 020 7357 7458
E-mail: info@ggf.org.uk
www.ggf.org.uk

Glued Laminated Timber Association

Chiltern House
Stocking Lane
Hughenden Valley
High Wycombe, Buckinghamshire HP14 4ND
Tel: 01494 565180
Fax: 01494 565487
www.glulam.co.uk

ICOM Modern Materials Working Group

The National Museum of Denmark
Department of Conservation
P.O. Box 260, Brede
DK-2800 Lyngby
Denmark
Fax: +45 33 473 327
E-mail: yvonne.shashoua@natmus.dk
palimpsest.stanford.edu/icom

Institute of Materials

1 Carlton House Terrace
London SW1Y 5DB
Tel: 020 7451 7300
Fax: 020 7839 1702
E-mail: Admin@materials.org.uk
www.materials.org.uk

International links and has extensive library facilities and technical information.

The Institution of Structural Engineers
11 Upper Belgrave Street
London SW1X 8BH
Tel: 020 7235 4535
Fax: 020 7235 4294
E-mail: mail@istructe.org.uk
www.istructe.org.uk

The Institution of Structural Engineers is recognized internationally as the professional body for structural engineering. Founded in 1908, and granted a royal charter in 1934, the Institution now has a total membership of over 22,000. It is an authorized and nominated body of the Engineering Council and a founder member of the Construction Industry Council. The Institute publishes a yearbook of members and a directory of firms for the UK. Courses, including concrete repair, are offered on a regular basis.

Metal Cladding and Roofing Manufacturers Association
18 Mere Farm Road
Prenton
Wirral, Cheshire CH43 9TT
Tel: 0151 652 3846
Fax: 0151 653 4080

National Federation of Terrazzo, Marble and Mosaic Specialists
PO Box 2843
London W1A 5PG
Tel: 0845 6090050
Fax: 0845 6078610
E-mail: dslade@nftmms.demon.co.uk

Natural Slate Quarries Association (merged with Stone Federation Great Britain)
Construction House
56-64 Leonard Street
London EC2A 4JX
Tel: 020 7608 5094
Fax: 020 7680 5081
E-mail: jane.buxey@nscc.org.uk
www.stone-federationgb.org.uk

Rubber and Plastics Research Association
Shawbury
Shrewsbury, Shropshire SY4 4NR
Tel: 01939 250383
Fax: 01939 25118
E-mail: info@rapra.net
www.rapra.net

Steel Construction Institute
Silwood Park
Ascot, Berkshire SL5 7QN
Tel: 01344 623345
Fax: 01344 622944
E-mail: sci@cityscape.co.uk
www.steel-sci.org

Steel Window Association
The Building Centre
26 Store Street
London WC1E 7BT
Tel: 020 7637 3571
Fax: 020 7637 3572
E-mail: info@steel-window-association.co.uk
www.steel-window-association.co.uk

An association for contractors involved in the repair and maintenance of steel windows. Gives advice and produces guidelines for the specification of repair and replacement of steel windows.

Stone Federation, Great Britain
Construction House
56–64 Leonard Street
London EC2A 4JX
Tel: 020 7608 5094
Fax: 020 7680 5081
E-mail: jane.buxey@nscc.org.uk
www.stone-federationgb.org.uk

Twentieth Century Society
70 Cowcross Street
London EC1M 6EJ
Tel: 020 7250 3857
Fax: 020 7251 8985
E-mail: administrator@c20society.demon.co.uk
www.c20society.demon.co.uk

Originally the Thirties Society, the Twentieth Century Society was founded with the aim of promoting and protecting British architecture and design after 1914. It offers an annual lecture programme, visits, newsletter and journals on twentieth-century design and architecture. Through casework the Society assists statutory bodies in protection of twentieth-century architecture.

Wallcovering Manufacturers Association
James House
Bridge House
Leatherhead, Surrey KT22 7EP
Tel: 01372 360660
Fax: 01372 376069
E-mail: enquiry@bcf.co.uk
www.coatings.org.uk

Wood Panel Industries Federation
28 Market Place
Grantham, Lincolnshire NG31 6LR
Tel: 01476 563707
Fax: 01476 579314
E-mail: wpif.panelboards@virgin.net

Currently working on producing a technical information CD-Rom on wood based panels.

BIBLIOGRAPHY

Since *Modern Matters: Principles and Practice in Conserving Recent Architecture* was published in 1996, there have been a number of more specific conferences and a few texts have been published on the subject of the conservation of post-war heritage. The bibliography of *Modern Matters* included a number of individual articles that appeared in journals on the subject of the conservation of twentieth-century architecture, as this was where most of the discourse on the subject was to be found at that time.

English Heritage's post-war listing programme and a general revival of interest in post-war architecture have prompted a number of historical, architectural and conservation texts. This bibliography seeks to build on those provided in *Modern Matters* and is specific to the post-war period.

Texts have been included that are accessible to English speakers; many of them published in the UK. Key international conservation texts have also been included.

Conservation theory and methodology
(including general charters, legislation and twentieth-century conservation theory)

Brereton, C. (1994), *The Repair of Historic Buildings: Advice on Principles and Methods*, London: English Heritage.

Burns, J.A. (ed) (1989), *Recording Historic Structures: Historic American Buildings Survey/Historic American Engineering Record*, Washington, DC: The American Institute of Architects Press.

Council of Europe (1994), *Twentieth-Century Architectural Heritage: Strategies for Conservation and Promotion, Cultural Heritage Series No. 29*, Strasbourg: Council of Europe Press.

DOCOMOMO (1990), *The Eindhoven Statement*, Eindhoven, The Netherlands: DOCOMOMO International.

Department of the Environment (1994), *Planning Policy Guidance Note 15: Historic Buildings and Conservation Areas*, London: HMSO.

English Heritage (1993), *Repair Grants*, leaflet, London: English Heritage.

English Heritage (1995), *Agreements for the Management of Listed Buildings*, London: English Heritage.

Firoini, L., and Conti, A. (1993), *La conservazione del moderno: Teoria e practica. Bibliografia di architecttura e urbanistica*, Florence: Alinea Editrice.

ICOMOS Australia (1999), *Charter for the Conservation of Places of Cultural Significance (The Burra Charter)*, Sydney: Australia ICOMOS.

ICOMOS (1966), *International Charter for the Conservation and Restoration of Monuments and Sites (The Venice Charter)*, Venice: ICOMOS.

Kerr, J.S. (1990), *The Conservation Plan*, (3rd edn), Sydney: National Trust of Australia (NSW).

Le Corbusier (1941), *Recommandations de l'Assemblée de la Société des Nations Adoptées le Octobre 1932, (The Athens Charter)*, Athens: Société des Nations.

Ministry of Housing and Local Government (1944), *Instructions to Investigators*, London: unpublished document.

Morton, W. Brown, III, Hume, G.L., Weeks, K.D., and Jandl, H.W. (1992), *The Secretary of the Interior's Standards for Rehabilitation and Illustrated Guidelines for Rehabilitating Historic Buildings*, Washington, DC: US Department of the Interior.

National Park Service (1991), *National Register Bulletin 15: How to apply the national register criteria for evaluation*, Washington, DC: US Department of the Interior.

Planning (Listed Buildings and Conservation Areas) Act 1990, London: HMSO.

Sherfy, M., and Luce, W.R. (1989), *National Register Bulletin 22: Guidelines for evaluating and nominating properties that have achieved significance within the last fifty years* (rev edn), Washington, DC: US Department of the Interior.

Contemporary studies

Banham, R. (1966), *The New Brutalism*, London: The Architectural Press.

Banham, R. (1975), *The Age of the Masters*, London: The Architectural Press.

Bertram, A. (1938), *Design*, Harmondsworth: Penguin.

Bowley, M. (1960), *Innovations in Building Materials*, London: Duckworth.

Brown, Hiram (1948), *Aluminum and Its Applications*, New York: Pitman Publishing Corporation.

Building Research Institute (1955), 'Metal Curtain Walls,' *Proceedings of the Building Research Institute*, Washington, DC: National Academy of Sciences, National Research Council.

Dannatt, T. (1959), *Modern Architecture in Britain*, London: Batsford.

De Maré, E. (1948), *New Ways of Building*, London: Architectural Press.

Department of Scientific and Industrial Research, BRS (1939), *Principles of Modern Building,* (1st edn), Watford: BRS.

Department of Scientific and Industrial Research, BRS (1959), *Principles of Modern Building*, (3rd edn), Watford: BRS.

Dowswell, H.R. (1931), 'Walls, Floors, and Partitions in the Tall Building', *Engineering News-Record*, (19 February), 319–321.

Fistere, J. C. (1931), 'Use of White Metals', *Architectural Forum*, **55**, (August), 232–240.

Faber, O., and Kell, J.R. (1936, 1943, 1957, 1966, 1971, 1979 and subsequently revised), *Heating and Air Conditioning of Buildings*, London: Architectural Press.

Giedion, S. (1948), *Mechanization takes Command: A Contribution to an Anonymous History*, New York: Oxford University Press.

Handisyde, C.C. (1967), *Building Materials: Science and Practice*, London: Architectural Press.

Hitchcock, H.R., and Drexler, A. (1952), *Built in the USA: Post-War Architecture*, New York: Simon and Schuster.

Le Corbusier (1946), *Towards a Modern Architecture*, London: Architectural Press.

Maxwell, R. (1972), *New British Architecture*, London: Thames and Hudson.

Mills, E. (ed) (1952), *Architects' Detail Sheets*, London: Architect and Building News.

Mills, E. (ed) (1954), *Architects' Detail Sheets: Second Series*, London: Architect and Building News.

Quarmby, A. (1974), *The Plastic Architect*, London: Pall Mall Press.

Rostron, R.M. (1964), *Light Cladding of Buildings*, London: Architectural Press.

Smithson, A., and Smithson, P. (1967), *Urban Structuring,* London: Studio Vista.

Stirling, J. (1975), *Buildings and Projects 1950–1974*, London: Thames and Hudson.

Upjohn, E.M. (1935), 'Buffington and the Skyscraper', *The Art Bulletin*, **XVII**, (1), (March), 53.

Yorke, F.R.S. (ed) (various dates), *Specifications*, (3 vols), London: Architectural Press.

Yorke, F.R.S. (1932), 'Details', *Architectural Review*, **72**, (429), (August), 65.

Warland, E.G. (1929, 2nd edn 1953), *Modern Practical Masonry*, London: Batsford.

Historical/critical studies on post-war architecture

Banham, R. (1986), *A Concrete Atlantis*, Cambridge, Massachusetts: MIT Press.

Brett, L., and Esher, V. (1981), *A Broken Wave: The Rebuilding of England, 1940–1980*, London: Allen Lane.

Burchard, John, and Bush Brown, Albert (1966), *The Architecture of America. A Social and Cultural History*, Boston, Massachusetts: Little, Brown and Company.

Carter, Peter (1974), *Mies van der Rohe at Work*, New York: Praeger Publishers.

Chartered Institution of Building Services Engineers (1996), *The Quest for Comfort*, London: CIBSE.

Dormer, P. (1993), *Design Since 1945*, London: Thames and Hudson.

Fitch, James Marston (1966), *American Building and the Historical Forces that Shaped It*, Boston, Massachusetts: Houghton Mifflin Company.

Ford, E.R. (1990), *The Details of Modern Architecture*, Cambridge, Massachusetts: MIT Press.

Glendinning, M., and Muthesius, S. (1994), *Tower Block*, London: Yale University Press.

Goldberger, Paul (1989), *The Skyscraper*, New York: Alfred A. Knopf.

Griffiths, Howard (1987), 'Colors of the City', *The Construction Specifier*, (August), 105–107.

Hamlin, Talbot (ed) (1952), *Forms and Functions of Twentieth-Century Architecture*, New York: Columbia University Press.

Hitchcock, Henry-Russell (1977), *Architecture: Nineteenth and Twentieth Centuries*, New York: Penguin Books.

Jackson, L. (1994), *'Contemporary': Architecture and Interiors of the 1950s*, London: Phaidon.

Pawley, M. (1992), *Design Heroes: Buckminster Fuller*, London: Grafton.

Pawley, M. (1998), *Terminal Architecture*, London: Reaktion Books.

Pevsner, Nikolaus (1964), *Pioneers of Modern Design*, Harmondsworth, Middlesex and Baltimore, Maryland: Penguin.

Pevsner, Nikolaus (1986), *The Sources of Modern Architecture and Design*, London: Thames and Hudson.

Richards, J.M. (1962), *An Introduction to Modern Architecture*, Baltimore, Maryland: Penguin.

Saint, A. (1987), *Towards a Social Architecture: The Role of School-Building in Post-War England*, London: Yale University Press.

Schulze, F. (1985), *Mies van der Rohe: A Critical Biography*, London and Chicago: Chicago University Press.

Williams, T.I. (1978), *A History of Technology*, Oxford: Clarendon Press.

Conservation of post-war heritage – general including conference proceedings

Allen, J., (1994) 'The Conservation of Modern Buildings' in Mills, E. (ed), *Building Maintenance and preservation: A Guide to Design and Management* (rev edn), London: Butterworth-Heinemann.

Bronson, S., and Jester, T. (eds) (1997), *Special Issue: Mending the Modern, APT Bulletin*, **28**, (4), Albany, NY: Mount IDA Press.

Burman, P., Garner, K., and Schmidt, L. (eds) (1996), *The Conservation of Twentieth Century Historic Buildings*, York: The Institute of Advanced Architectural Studies.

Callender, John Hancock (1955), 'The Design of Metal Curtain Walls,' *Proceedings of the Building Research Institute*, Washington, DC: National Academy of Sciences, National Research Council, 79–97.

DOCOMOMO International Conference proceedings: *First International Conference, September 1990, Eindhoven, The Netherlands; Second International Conference, September 1992, Dessau, Germany; Third International Conference, September 1994, Barcelona, Spain; Fourth International Conference, September 1996, Bratislava, Slovakia; Fifth International Conference, September 1998, Stockholm, Sweden.*

Grattan, D.W. (ed) (1993), *Saving the Twentieth Century: The Conservation of Modern Materials*, Ottawa: Canadian Conservation Institute.

International Council on Monuments and Sites (ICOMOS) (1995), *Seminar on Twentieth Century Heritage, Helsinki, June 18–19, 1995, working papers*, Helsinki: ICOMOS. (Recommendations and Council of Europe Principles developed from the conference are available through the ICOMOS website: www.icomos.org).

Institute of Historic Building Conservation (2000), Special issue on twentieth-century heritage, *Context*, (65), (March), London: IHBC.

Jackson, M. (ed) (1991), Special Issue: Preserving What's New, *APT Bulletin*, **23**, (2), Albany, NY: Mount IDA Press.

Johnson, D.L. (1980), *Assessment of Twentieth Century Architecture: Notes for Conservationists*, Adelaide, Australia: Flinders University of South Australia.

Macdonald, S. (ed) (1996), *Modern Matters: Principles and Practice in Conserving Recent Architecture*, Shaftesbury: Donhead.

Saint, A. (1994), *A Change of Heart*, London: RCHME.

Saint, A. (1995), *The Age of Optimism: Postwar Architecture in England 1945–70*, London: English Heritage.

Schiffer, R., and Park, S. (eds) (1993), Special Issue: Cultural Resources from the Recent Past, *Cultural Resource Management*, **16**, (6), Washington, DC: National Park Service.

Schiffer, R., and Park, S. (eds) (1995), Special Issue: Cultural Resources from the Recent Past, *Cultural Resource Management*, **18**, (8), Washington, DC: National Park Service.

Slaton, D., and Shiffer, R.A. (ed) (1995), *Preserving the Recent Past*, Washington: Historic Preservation Education Foundation.

Stratton, M. (ed) (1997), *Structure and Style: Conserving Twentieth Century Buildings*, London: E. & F.N. Spon.

Materials, construction techniques and their conservation

General

Allen, N.S., Edge, M., and Horie, C.V. (eds) (1992), *Polymers in Conservation*, Cambridge: Royal Society of Chemistry.

Ashurst, N. (1994), *Cleaning Historic Buildings*, Shaftesbury: Donhead.

Brantley, L.R., and Brantley, R.T. (1996), *Building Materials Technology*, New York: McGraw-Hill.

British Standards Institution (2000), *BS 8221-1:2000, Code of Practice for Cleaning and Surface Repair of Buildings, Part 1: Cleaning of Natural Stones, Brick, Terracotta and Concrete*, London: British Standards Institution.

Brookes, A. J. (1990), *Cladding of Buildings*, London: Longman Scientific and Technical.

Chandler, I. (1991), *The Repair and Refurbishment of Modern Buildings*, London: Batsford.

Cowan, H., and Smith, P.J. (1998), *The Science and Technology of Building Materials*, New York: Van Nostrand Reinhold Company.

Curwell, S.R., and March, C.G. (1986), *Hazardous Materials*, London: E. & F.N. Spon.

Deeson, A.F.L. (ed) (1964), *The Comprehensive Industrialised Building Systems Annual 1965*, London: House Publications.

Jester, T.C. (ed) (1995), *Twentieth-Century Building Materials*, New York: McGraw-Hill.

Lea, F.M. (1971), *Science and Building*, London: HMSO.

Mostafavi, M., and Leatherbarrow, D. (1993) On *Weathering: the Life of Buildings in Time*, Cambridge, Massachusetts: MIT Press.

National Park Service (1993), *Twentieth Century Building Materials: 1900–1950, an annotated bibliography*, Washington, DC: US Department of the Interior, National Park Service, Preservation Assistance Division.

Russell, B. (1981), *Building Systems, Industrialisation and Architecture*, London: Wiley.

Simpson, J., and Horrobin, P. (1971), *The Weathering and Performance of Building Materials*, Aylesbury, Buckinghamshire: Medical and Technical Publishing.

Strike, J. (1991), *Construction into Design: The Influence of New Methods of Construction on Architectural Design 1690–1990*, Oxford: Butterworth-Heinemann.

Taylor, G.D. (1991), *Construction Materials*, London: Longman.

Weaver, M., with Matero, F., (1993) *Conserving Buildings: A Guide to Techniques and Materials*, New York: John Wiley.

Whitford, M.J. (1992), *Getting Rid of Graffiti*, London: E. & F.N. Spon.

Yeomans, D. (1997), *Construction Since 1900: Materials*, London: Batsford.

Concrete

Building Research Establishment Digests 263–5 (1982), *The Durability of Steel in Concrete*, Watford: BRE.

Building Research Establishment Digest 366 (1991), *Structural Appraisal of Existing Buildings for Change of Use*, Watford: BRE.

Building Research Establishment Digest 405 (1995), *Carbonation of Concrete and its Effect on Durability*, Watford: BRE.

Broomfield, J.P. (1997), *Corrosion of Steel in Concrete: Understanding, Investigation and Repair*, London: E. & F.N. Spon.

Bussell, M. N. (1996), 'The development of reinforced concrete: design theory and practice', *Proceedings of the Institution of Civil Engineers: Structures and Buildings*, **116**, 317–334.

Concrete Society (1984), *Technical Report No. 26: Repair of Concrete Damaged by Reinforcement Corrosion*, London: Concrete Society.

Concrete Society (1992), *Technical Report No. 22: Non-structural cracks in concrete*, (3rd edn), Slough: Concrete Society.

Concrete Society (1989), *Technical Report No. 36: Cathodic protection of reinforced concrete*, London: Concrete Society.

Coney, W. (1996), *Preservation Brief No. 15: Preservation of Historic Concrete: Problems and General Approaches*, Washington, DC: The US Department of the Interior, National Park Service.

Currie, R., and Robery, P. (1994), *Repair and Maintenance of Reinforced Concrete*, Watford: BRE.

De Jonge, W., and Doolaar, A. (1997), *The Fair Face of Concrete: Conservation and Repair of Exposed Concrete, Preservation Dossier No. 2*, Eindhoven, The Netherlands: DOCOMOMO International.

Institution of Civil Engineers (1996), 'Historic Concrete', *Proceedings of the Institution of Civil Engineers: Structures and Buildings*, **116**, (August/November).

Kay, T. (1992), *Assessment and Renovation of Concrete Structures*, London: Longman.

Macdonald, S. (1997) 'Authenticity is more than skin deep: conserving Britain's post-war concrete architecture', *Mending the Modern: Special issue, APT Bulletin*, **28**, (4), 37–44.

Morris, A.E.J. (1966), *Precast-concrete Cladding*, London: Fountain Press.

Neville, A.M. (1981), *Properties of Concrete*, (3rd edn), London: Pitman.

Pullar-Strecker, P. (1987), *Corrosion-Damaged Concrete: Assessment and Repair*, London: Butterworth.

Standards Australia, Standards of New Zealand, ACRA & CSIRO (1996), *Guide to Concrete Repair and Protection*, Sydney.

Stanley, C. (1979), *Highlights in the History of Concrete*, London: Cement and Concrete Association.

Glass
McGrath, R., and Frost, A.C. (1937, 1961), *Glass in Architecture and Design*, London: Architectural Press.

National Park Service (1984), *Preservation Brief No. 12: The Preservation of Historic Pigmented Structural Glass (Vitrolite and Carrara Glass)*, Washington, DC: US Department of the Interior, National Park Service.

Persson, Rune (1969), *Flat Glass Technology*, New York: Plenum Press.

Pulker, H.K (1984), *Coatings on Glass*, New York: Elsevier Science Publishing Company.

Masonry
Ashurst, J., and Dimes, F.G. (1977), *Stone Building: Its Use and Potential Today*, London: Architectural Press.

Brunskill, R.W. (1990), *Brick Building in Britain*, London: Gollancz.

Clifton-Taylor, A., and Ireson, A.S. (1994), *English Stone Building*, London: Gollancz.

Herbert, T., and Huggins, K. (1995) *The Decorative Tile*, London: Phaidon.

Stratton, M. (1993), *The Terracotta Revival*, London: Gollancz.

Metals and curtain walling
American Architectural Manufacturers Association (1979), *Aluminum Curtain Walls, Volume 5*, Chicago: AAMA.

Addis, B. (1997), 'Concrete and Steel in Twentieth Century Construction', in M.J. Stratton (ed), *Structure and Style*, London: E. & F.N. Spon, 103–142.

Blanc, A., et al. (1993), *Architecture and Construction in Steel*, London: E. & F.N. Spon.

De Jonge, W., and Doolaar, A. (1997), *Curtain Wall Refurbishment: A Challenge to Manage*, Eindhoven, The Netherlands, DOCOMOMO International.

English Heritage (1994), *Metal Windows: Framing Opinions Leaflet No. 3*, London: English Heritage.

Hunt, W.D. (1958), *The Contemporary Curtain Wall: Its Design, Fabrication and Erection*, New York: F.W. Dodge Corporation.

Johnson, P. (1993), *The Restoration of Bronze and Aluminium Windows*, London: R. Fox and Sons.

Park, S. (1984), *Preservation Brief No. 13: The Repair and Upgrading of Historic Steel Windows*, Washington, DC: US Department of the Interior, National Park Service.

Rostron, R.M. (1964), *Light Cladding*, London: Architectural Press.

Van Horn, Kent R. (ed) (1967), *Aluminum, Volume III: Fabrication and Finishing*, Metals Park, Ohio: American Society for Metals.

Weidlinger, P. (1956), *Aluminum in Modern Architecture*, Louisville, Kentucky: Reynolds Metal Co.

Plastics

Davidson, J.G., and McClure, H.B. (1933), 'Applications of vinyl resins', *Industrial and Engineering Chemistry*, **25**, (6), 645–652.

DiNoto, A. (1984), *Art Plastic*, New York: Abbeville Press.

Fielding, T.J. (1940s), *The History of Bakelite Limited*, London: Bakelite.

Katz, S. (1985), *Classic Plastics*, London: Thames and Hudson.

Morgan, J. (1991), *Conservation of Plastics*, London: Plastics Historical Society and The Conservation Unit of the Museums Galleries Commission.

Meikle, J. (1995), *American Plastic*, New Jersey: Routledge.

Mossman, S.T.I. and Morris, P.T.J. (1994), *The Development of Plastics*, Cambridge: Royal Society of Chemistry.

Panek, J.R., and Cook, J.P. (1984), *Construction Sealants and Adhesives*, (2nd edn), New York: John Wiley and Sons.

Van Tulleken, Kit (1982), *Working with Plastics*, Amsterdam: Time Life Books.

Walker, A. (1995), 'Fiber Reinforced Plastic' in Jester, Thomas (ed), *Twentieth-Century Building Materials*, New York: McGraw-Hill.

Walker, A. (1996), 'Plastics and the Modern House', *The Modern House Revisited*, London: Twentieth Century Society.

Yarsley, V.E. and Couzens, E.G. (1941), *Plastics*, London: Pelican.